TALEEMUL HAQ

VOLUME ONE

Sunnats of Istinjaa, Wudhu, Ghusl, Miswaak, Azaan, Iqaamah, Musjid and Salaah according to the Hanafi Mazhab

DETAILED VERSION

Volume 1 of 3

Written By

MUFTI ZAKARIYYA MAKADA

PUBLISHED BY ISLAMIC BOOK STORE

Taleemul Haq
THE BLESSED SUNNAH OF RASULULLAH ﷺ

~ VOLUME ONE ~

Sunnats of Istinjaa, Wudhu, Ghusl, Miswaak, Azaan, Iqaamah, Musjid and Salaah according to the Hanafi Mazhab

DETAILED VERSION

PUBLISHED BY

Islamic Book Store

Gujarat, India 394601

Written by: Mufti Zakariyya Makada

Madrasah Ta'leemuddeen
4 Third Avenue
P.O. Box 26393
Isipingo Beach
4115
South Africa

Tel: (+27) 31 902 9818
Fax: (+27) 31 902 5681
E-mail: info@ihyaauddeen.co.za
First Edition: Safar 1441 / October 2019

CONTENTS

بسم الله الرحمن الرحيم الحمد لله رب العالمين والصلاة والسلام على أشرف الأنبياء والمرسلين
سيدنا ومولانا محمد وآله وصحبه أجمعين وبعد

INTRODUCTION

All praise is due to Allah تَبَارَكَوَتَعَالَى and may the choicest durood (salutations) and salaam (peace) descend upon the noblest of Ambiyaa and Rasuls, our master and leader, Hazrat Muhammad صَلَّى ٱللَّهُ عَلَيْهِ وَسَلَّمَ, as well as upon his blessed household and all his illustrious companions رَضِىَ ٱللَّهُ عَنْهُمْ.

It is the belief of every Muslim that those who enjoy the highest rank from the creation of Allah تَبَارَكَوَتَعَالَى are the Ambiyaa عَلَيْهِمُ ٱلسَّلَامُ. From the galaxy of Ambiyaa عَلَيْهِمُ ٱلسَّلَامُ, the highest in rank and status is Hazrat Rasulullah صَلَّى ٱللَّهُ عَلَيْهِ وَسَلَّمَ. Hence, not only is Hazrat Rasulullah صَلَّى ٱللَّهُ عَلَيْهِ وَسَلَّمَ the final messenger of Allah تَبَارَكَوَتَعَالَى and the seal of prophethood, but he is also the leader of all the Ambiyaa and Rasuls عَلَيْهِمُ ٱلسَّلَامُ.

The esteemed position which Hazrat Rasulullah صَلَّى ٱللَّهُ عَلَيْهِ وَسَلَّمَ enjoys in the sight of Allah تَبَارَكَوَتَعَالَى can be gauged from the fact that Allah تَبَارَكَوَتَعَالَى has declared in the Quraan Majeed that the only way to gain His love is to emulate the mubaarak sunnah of His beloved Rasul ﷺ in all aspects of life.[1]

Likewise, in another verse of the Quraan Majeed, Allah تَبَارَكَ وَتَعَالَى declares, "They shall never be believers until they make you the judge in all their affairs in which they dispute among themselves, and they find no resistance in their hearts against your decision, but accept your decision with full submission."[2]

In this verse of the Quraan Majeed, Allah تَبَارَكَ وَتَعَالَى informs the Ummah that in order for one to be a believer, he has to wholeheartedly accept Hazrat Rasulullah ﷺ and make him the deciding factor in all aspects of life.

When Hazrat Rasulullah ﷺ is the greatest of Allah's تَبَارَكَ وَتَعَالَى creation, it is undoubtedly the greatest honour for every ummati of Hazrat Rasulullah ﷺ to be linked to him. Furthermore, Allah تَبَارَكَ وَتَعَالَى has made Hazrat Rasulullah ﷺ the source of hidaayat (guidance) for humanity at large, for it was none other than Hazrat Rasulullah ﷺ who had shown us the path of guidance and conveyed the entire Deen of Islam to us, through which we can earn success in this world and eternal bliss and salvation in the Hereafter.

---

[1] سورة آل عمران: ٣١

[2] سورة النساء: ٦٥

When one studies the mubaarak life of Hazrat Rasulullah ﷺ, he will realize the deep and intense love which Hazrat Rasulullah ﷺ had for not only his family and the Sahaabah رَضِيَ اللّٰهُ عَنْهُمْ, but for each and every ummati. The perpetual concern and overwhelming anxiety that Hazrat Rasulullah ﷺ had for the hidaayat of every ummati is inconceivable.

Generally, a person will honour and show importance to people according to their positions and the favours that he enjoys from them. Hence, one will show utmost respect and honour to his parents on account of their love for him and the favours which he enjoys through them. However, the ultimate favour and bounty that every ummati enjoys is that of Deen, as Deen is the basis of eternal success and salvation, and it is only through Hazrat Rasulullah ﷺ that we have gained this bounty. Therefore, when Hazrat Rasulullah ﷺ had the greatest love for us, and he is our greatest benefactor, then the greatest love, obedience and submission ought to be shown to him.

Among the rights that we owe to Hazrat Rasulullah ﷺ is that we love him the most, believe and accept everything that he has brought to us, and we lead our lives in total obedience and conformity to his mubaarak sunnah.

Through his mubaarak sunnah, Hazrat Rasulullah ﷺ taught us how to transform our worldly affairs and activities into acts of ibaadah which will be a means of pleasing Allah تَبَارَكَ وَتَعَالَى

and a source of mercy to mankind. Every person needs to eat, drink, sleep, conduct business, socialize and fulfil other needs in order to exist in the world. However, through carrying out these mundane activities in accordance to the sunnah, one will gain reward and the proximity of Allah تَبَارَكَ وَتَعَالَى and His beloved Rasul صَلَّى ٱللَّهُ عَلَيْهِ وَسَلَّمَ.

In these times of fitnah, where Deen is under constant attack, through holding onto the mubaarak sunnah, one will safeguard one's Deen and receive the reward of one hundred martyrs. Hazrat Rasulullah صَلَّى ٱللَّهُ عَلَيْهِ وَسَلَّمَ said, "The one who holds onto my sunnah, at the time of fitnah and fasaad, will receive the reward of one hundred martyrs."[3]

Alhamdulillah, with the grace and fadhl of Allah تَبَارَكَ وَتَعَالَى, we have prepared this kitaab on the mubaarak sunnah of Hazrat Rasulullah صَلَّى ٱللَّهُ عَلَيْهِ وَسَلَّمَ. The first volume of this kitaab is complete and deals with the chapters of relieving oneself and istinjaa, wudhu, miswaak, ghusl, azaan, iqaamah, the musjid, and males' and females' salaah.

Many of the sunnats and aadaab (etiquettes) mentioned in this kitaab have been acquired from my beloved and respected Shaikh, Hazrat Mufti Ebrahim Salejee (daamat barakaatuhu) who dictated them to Moulana Yusuf Mulla to teach the students of the Madrasah (Ta'leemuddeen). These sunnats were thereafter

---

[3] الترغيب والترهيب، الرقم: ٦٥

periodically posted onto the Ihyaauddeen website during the last eight years.

An effort was also undertaken to gather the relevant Ahaadith from which these sunnats and aadaab were sourced. Together with sourcing the Ahaadith, the hukm (status and reliability) of the Ahaadith has also been explained for the benefit of the Ulama and for the benefit of proving that all these sunnats and aadaab are worthy of practice. Together with the Ahaadith, a quotation from the kitaabs of Hanafi Fiqh has also been provided. In certain places where a Hadith could not be located, the statements of the Fuqahaa have been relied upon.

Two versions have been prepared of this kitaab. The first version is a concise version that only explains the sunnats and aadaab, without the Ahaadith and quotations of the Fuqahaa. This version has been prepared for those who wish to learn the sunnats and aadaab without referring to their proofs.

The second version is a detailed version which also explains the relevant Ahaadith and quotations of the Fuqahaa. This version has been prepared for those who wish to learn the sunnats and aadaab together with viewing their proofs. This is the detailed version.

As far as the section on the sunnah method of males' salaah and females' salaah is concerned, we did not present the Ahaadith but sufficed on presenting the quotations of the Fuqahaa under each point. The reason is that including all these Ahaadith would have resulted in this kitaab becoming too lengthy. Apart from this, a separate women's salaah kitaab has already been prepared, and a men's salaah kitaab is under preparation, and these two kitaabs contain all the relevant Ahaadith for the men's and women's salaah.

During the eight years in which this effort was undertaken, I was assisted by my close friend, Moulana Irfaan Joosab. I was also assisted in the completion of this kitaab by Moulana Yusuf Mitha, Moulana Abdul Hamid Nana, Moulana Hasan Salejee, Moulana Ebrahim Karodia, Moulana Ebrahim Makada and Moulana Hamza Hassim. May Allah تَبَارَكَ وَتَعَالَى reward all these Ulama abundantly in this world and the next for their valuable contribution and effort.

May Allah تَبَارَكَ وَتَعَالَى bless our Hazrat Mufti Saheb, who was the actual means of passing on the knowledge of the sunnah to us, with the best of rewards, and may Allah تَبَارَكَ وَتَعَالَى bless him with long life and make him the means of the mubaarak sunnah of Hazrat Rasulullah صَلَّى اللَّهُ عَلَيْهِ وَسَلَّمَ reaching the four corners of the globe.

We make dua to Allah تَبَارَكَ وَتَعَالَى to accept this kitaab and make it a means for the sunnah of Hazrat Rasulullah صَلَّى اللَّهُ عَلَيْهِ وَسَلَّمَ being revived in the Ummah, and a means for us all being blessed with the intercession of Hazrat Rasulullah صَلَّى اللَّهُ عَلَيْهِ وَسَلَّمَ and his mubaarak company in the Hereafter.

(Mufti) Zakariyya Makada

CHAPTER ONE

RELIEVING ONESELF AND ISTINJAA

IMPORTANCE OF CLEANLINESS

Islam is a religion of complete purity and cleanliness. Islam advocates adopting purity and cleanliness in all departments of human living. Hazrat Rasulullah ﷺ said:

الطهور شطر الإيمان

"Purity is half of imaan." [4]

In fact, Islam has adequately guided us and shown us the way to remain pure internally and externally. Just as we are commanded to remain physically pure by adopting physical and oral hygiene, we are also commanded to remain spiritually pure by protecting our hearts and minds from sins e.g. jealousy, pride, greed, etc. Allah تَبَارَكَ وَتَعَالَى mentions in the Quraan Majeed:

---

[4] عن أبي مالك الأشعري قال قال رسول الله صلى الله عليه وسلم الطهور شطر الإيمان (صحيح مسلم، الرقم: ٢٢٣)

قَدْ اَفْلَحَ مَنْ تَزَكّٰى

Indeed he who has attained inner purity is successful.[5]

If one has to view the various injunctions of Shari'ah e.g. making istinjaa after relieving oneself, making wudhu for performing salaah, cleansing the mouth with the miswaak upon awakening, before performing salaah, when the mouth emits an unpleasant odour, before sleeping, etc., performing ghusl when entering into ihraam or joining the gatherings of Eid or Jumuah, one will realise that Islam is second to none in emphasizing the highest levels of purity and cleanliness in all facets of a person's life.

Hazrat Rasulullah ﷺ said, "Four actions are from the sunnats of all the Ambiyaa عَلَيْهِمُ السَّلَام; adopting hayaa (modesty in all spheres of human living), applying itr, using the miswaak, and making nikaah (getting married)."[6]

When we examine the actions mentioned in the above Hadith, we find that they all relate to acquiring internal and external purity.

On the other hand, there are severe admonishments and punishments recorded in the Ahaadith for neglecting cleanliness. Through remaining negligent in cleansing oneself, one will remain impure, thereby causing one's salaah and other

---

[5] سورة الأعلى: ١٤

[6] عن أبي أيوب رضي الله عنه قال قال رسول الله صلى الله عليه وسلم أربع من سنن المرسلين الحياء والتعطر والسواك والنكاح (سنن الترمذي، الرقم: ١٠٨٠) قال أبو عيسى: حديث أبي أيوب حديث حسن غريب

ibaadaat for which cleanliness is a prerequisite to be invalid. Similarly, through neglecting oral and physical hygiene, one will be a cause of inconvenience to others.

ADMONISHMENTS FOR NEGLECTING CLEANLINESS DURING ISTINJAA

First Hadith:

عن أبي هريرة رضي الله عنه قال قال رسول الله صلى الله عليه وسلم أكثر عذاب القبر من البول (المستدرك على الصحيحين للحاكم، الرقم: ٦٥٣)[7]

Hazrat Abu Hurairah رَضِيَٱللَّهُعَنْهُ *reports that Hazrat Rasulullah* صَلَّىٱللَّهُعَلَيْهِوَسَلَّمَ *said, "Most of the punishment (meted out to most people) in the grave will be on account of urine (i.e. being unmindful regarding urine splashes and impurities. Therefore, their wudhu, salaah and other ibaadaat will not gain acceptance due to remaining impure)."*

Second Hadith:

عن أنس رضي الله عنه قال قال رسول الله صلى الله عليه وسلم تنزهوا من البول فإن عامة عذاب القبر من البول (الترغيب والترهيب، الرقم: ٢٥٨)[8]

Hazrat Anas رَضِيَٱللَّهُعَنْهُ *reports that Hazrat Rasulullah* صَلَّىٱللَّهُعَلَيْهِوَسَلَّمَ *said, "Refrain from urine (i.e. being soiled with urine splashes), for indeed most of the punishment (meted out to most people) in the grave will be on account of urine (i.e. being unmindful regarding urine splashes and impurities)."*

---

[7] هذا حديث صحيح على شرط الشيخين ولا أعرف له علة ولم يخرجاه وله شاهد من حديث أبي يحيى القتات

قال الذهبي في التلخيص: على شرطهما ولا أعلم له علة وله شاهد

[8] قال المنذري: رواه الدارقطني وقال المحفوظ مرسل

Third Hadith:

عن أبي أمامة رضي الله عنه عن النبي صلى الله عليه وسلم قال اتقوا البول فإنه أول ما يحاسب به العبد في القبر (الترغيب والترهيب، الرقم: ٢٦٥)[9]

Hazrat Abu Umaamah رضي الله عنه *reports that Hazrat Rasulullah* صلى الله عليه وسلم *said, "Refrain from urine splashes (when relieving yourself), for indeed this will be the first thing the servant will be taken to account for in the grave."*

Fourth Hadith:

عن ابن عباس رضي الله عنهما قال مر النبي صلى الله عليه وسلم بقبرين فقال إنهما ليعذبان وما يعذبان في كبير أما أحدهما فكان لا يستتر من البول وأما الآخر فكان يمشي بالنميمة (صحيح البخاري، الرقم: ٢١٨)

Hazrat Ibnu Abbaas رضي الله عنهما *reports that Hazrat Rasulullah* صلى الله عليه وسلم *once passed by two graves, and then (in reference to these two graves,) he said, "The inmates of these two graves are being punished, and they are not being punished for something that was major (difficult for them to refrain from). As for one of them, he would not refrain from urine splashes. As for the other, he used to carry tales (thereby causing mischief and corruption among people)."*

---

[9] قال المنذري: رواه الطبراني في الكبير أيضا بإسناد لا بأس به

SUNNAH METHOD OF ISTINJAA

1. Relieve yourself in a secluded place which is protected from the gazes of people.[10]

عن جابر بن عبد الله رضي الله عنهما قال إن النبي صلى الله عليه وسلم كان إذا أراد البراز انطلق حتى لا يراه أحد (سنن أبي داود، الرقم: ٢)[11]

Hazrat Jaabir رَضِیَ اللّٰہُ عَنْہُ *reports, "When Rasulullah* صَلَّی اللّٰہُ عَلَیْہِ وَسَلَّمَ *intended to relieve himself, he would go to a place which was protected from the gazes of people."*

2. Do not relieve yourself in such a place where you will cause inconvenience to others e.g. on a pathway or a place where people sit.[12]

---

[10] عن عبد الله بن جعفر قال أردفني رسول الله صلى الله عليه وسلم ذات يوم خلفه فأسر إلي حديثا لا أحدث به أحدا من الناس وكان أحب ما استتر به رسول الله صلى الله عليه وسلم لحاجته هدف أو حائش نخل قال ابن أسماء في حديثه يعني حائط نخل (صحيح مسلم ، الرقم: ٣٤٢)

المستنجي لا يكشف عورته عند أحد للإستنجاء فإن كشفها صار فاسقا لأن كشف العورة حرام ومرتكب الحرام فاسق (حاشية الطحطاوي على مراقي الفلاح ص ٤٩)

[11] سكت الحافظ عن هذا الحديث في الفصل الثاني من هداية الرواة (٢٠٠/١) فالحديث حسن عنده

عن المغيرة بن شعبة رضي الله عنه قال كنت مع النبي صلى الله عليه وسلم في سفر فأتى النبي صلى الله عليه وسلم حاجته فأبعد في المذهب قال وفي الباب عن عبد الرحمن بن أبي قراد وأبي قتادة وجابر ويحيى بن عبيد عن أبيه وأبي موسى وابن عباس وبلال بن الحارث قال أبو عيسى هذا حديث حسن صحيح (سنن الترمذي، الرقم: ٢٠)

[12] ويكره البول والغائط في الماء جاريا كان أو راكدا ويكره على طرف نهر أو بئر أو حوض أو عين أو تحت شجرة مثمرة أو في زرع أو في ظل ينتفع بالجلوس فيه ويكره بجنب المساجد ومصلى العيد وفي المقابر وبين الدواب وفي طرق المسلمين (الفتاوى الهندية ٥٠/١)

عن معاذ بن جبل قال قال رسول الله صلى الله عليه وسلم اتقوا الملاعن الثلاثة البراز في الموارد وقارعة الطريق والظل (سنن أبي داود، الرقم: ٢٦)

عن أبي هريرة رضي الله عنه أن رسول الله صلى الله عليه وسلم قال اتقوا اللعانين قالوا وما اللعانان يا رسول الله صلى الله عليه وسلم قال الذي يتخلى فى طريق الناس أو في ظلهم (صحيح مسلم، الرقم: ٢٦٩)

Hazrat Abu Hurairah ﷺ *mentions that Hazrat Rasulullah* ﷺ *said, "Refrain from the two great causes of earning curses of people." The Sahaabah* ﷺ *asked, "What are the two great causes of earning curses, O Rasulullah* ﷺ*?" Hazrat Rasulullah* ﷺ *replied, "Relieving oneself on the pathways or in places where people take shade."*

3. If you are forced to relieve yourself in an open field or place, then look for a suitable place where you will not be seen and the ground is soft so that the urine does not splash onto you.[13]

عن أبي موسى رضي الله عنه قال إني كنت مع رسول الله صلى الله عليه وسلم ... ثم قال إذا أراد أحدكم أن يبول فليرتد لبوله موضعا (سنن أبي داود، الرقم: ٣)[14]

Hazrat Abu Moosa ﷺ *reports, "I was with Rasulullah* ﷺ *... then Rasulullah* ﷺ *said, 'When you intend relieving yourself, search for a suitable place to do so (i.e. when urinating in the open, then look for such a place where you will be concealed from the gazes of people, and the ground is such that it*

---

[13] فإذا أراد أن يبول وكانت الأرض صلبة دقها بحجر أو حفر حفيرة حتى لا يترشرش عليه البول (الفتاوى الهندية ٥٠/١)

[14] وقد روى الحاكم مثل هذا فى المستدرك (٥٢٨/٣) وقال هذا حديث صحيح الإسناد ولم يخرجاه وأقره الذهبي فى التلخيص

will absorb the urine and it will not cause the urine to splash onto you).'"

4.   Cover your head and feet before entering the toilet.[15]

عن حبيب بن صالح رحمه الله قال كان رسول الله صلى الله عليه وسلم إذا دخل الخلاء لبس حذاءه وغطى رأسه (السنن الكبرى للبيهقي، الرقم: ٤٦٥)[16]

Hazrat Habeeb bin Saalih رَحِمَهُٱللَّه reports that Hazrat Rasulullah صَلَّىٱللَّهُعَلَيْهِوَسَلَّم would wear his shoes and cover his mubaarak head when entering the toilet.

---

[15] (ويدخل الخلاء) ... (برجله اليسرى) ابتداء مستور الرأس استحبابا تكرمة لليمنى لأنه مستقذر يحضره الشيطان (مراقي الفلاح ص ٥١)

[16] وفي إعلاء السنن (عن حبيب بن صالح الخ) قلت فيه دلالة على ندب لبس الحذاء عند دخول المرفق أي الخلاء صونا للرجل عما عسى أن يصيبها وعلى استحباب تغطية الرأس حياء من الله تعالى لأن هذا المحل معد لكشف العورة كذا في العزيزي وشرح الحفني (١٢٥/١) قلت فالمراد تغطية الرأس بنحو رداء أو منديل لأنه هو المتعارف عند الحياء لا بنحو القلنسوة فحسب فليتأمل (إعلاء السنن ٣٢٣/١)

عن ابن المبارك عن يونس عن الزهري عن عروة أخبرني عن أبيه أن أبا بكر الصديق قال وهو يخطب الناس يا معشر المسلمين استحيوا من الله فوالذي نفسي بيده إني لأظل حين أذهب إلى الخلاء في الفضاء مغطيا رأسي استحياء من ربي (المصنف لابن أبي شيبة، الرقم: ١١٣٣)

قال الشيخ محمد عوامة: روى البخاري في كتاب المغازي باب قتل أبي رافع بن أبي الحقيق وفيه قول عبد الله بن عَتِيك رضي الله عنه يحكي عن نفسه فأقبل حتى دنا من الباب ثم تقنع بثوبه كأنه يقضي حاجة ومعنى تقنع بثوبه ما جاء في الرواية الثانية قال فغطيت رأسي كأني أقضي حاجة وهذا يفيد أن صنيع معلوم عندهم هو الأصل في هذه الحال (أثر الحديث الشريف ص ١٨٨)

عن سعيد بن عبد الله بن ضرار قال رأيت أنس بن مالك أتى الخلاء ثم خرج وعليه قلنسوة بيضاء مزرورة (مصنف عبد الرزاق، الرقم: ٧٤٥)

عن أشعث عن أبيه أن أبا موسى خرج من الخلاء وعليه قلنسوة (المصنف لابن أبي شيبة، الرقم: ٢٤٨٥٩)

وقال السيوطي في الجامع الصغير: ابن سعد عن حبيب بن صالح مرسلا وقال شارحه المناوي في فيض القدير (١٥٦/٥) ظاهر صنيعه أنه لا علة له غير الإرسال والأمر بخلافه فقد قال الذهبي أبو بكر ضعيف وقال العزيزي في شرحه السراج المنير (١٣٤/٣) قال الشيخ حديث حسن لغيره

قال إمام الحرمين والبغوي والغزالي وآخرون يستحب أن لايدخل الخلاء مكشوف الرأس قال بعض أصحابنا فإن لم يجد شيئا وضع كمه على رأسه ويستحب أن لايدخل الخلاء حافيا ذكره جماعة منهم أبو العباس بن سريج في كتاب الأقسام وروى البيهقي بإسناده حديثا مرسلا أن النبي صلى الله عليه وسلم (كان إذا دخل الخلاء لبس حذاءه وغطى رأسه) وروى البيهقي أيضا عن عائشة كان النبي صلى الله عليه وسلم إذا دخل الخلاء غطى رأسه وإذا أتى أهله غطى رأسه قال البيهقي لكنه ضعيف وروي في تغطية الرأس عند دخول الخلاء عن أبي بكر الصديق رضي الله عنه وهو صحيح عنه: (قلت) وقد اتفق العلماء على أن الحديث المرسل والضعيف والموقوف يتسامح به في فضائل الأعمال ويعمل بمقتضاه (المجموع شرح المهذب ٧٨/٢)

5. Before entering the toilet, recite bismillah and the following dua:[17]

بِسْمِ اللهِ اَللّٰهُمَّ إِنِّي أَعُوذُ بِكَ مِنَ الْخُبُثِ وَالْخَبَائِثْ[18]

In the name of Allah تَبَارَكَ وَتَعَالَى. O Allah, I seek your protection from the male and female jinn (shayaateen).

Through reciting bismillah, one's private parts will be veiled from the shayaateen and one will be saved from the harm of the shayaateen.

عن علي رضي الله عنه أن رسول الله صلى الله عليه وسلم قال ستر ما بين أعين الجن وعورات بني آدم إذا دخل أحدهم الخلاء أن يقول بسم الله (سنن الترمذي، الرقم: ٦٠٦)[19]

---

[17] قال العلامة ابن عابدين رحمه الله فإذا وصل إلى الباب يبدأ بالتسمية قبل الدعاء هو الصحيح فيقول بسم الله اللهم إني أعوذ بك من الخبث والخبائث (رد المحتار ١/٣٤٥)

(و) لهذا (يستعيذ) أي يعتصم (بالله من الشيطان الرجيم قبل دخوله) وقبل كشف عورته ويقدم تسمية الله تعالى على الاستعاذة لقوله عليه الصلاة والسلام ستر ما بين أعين الجن وعورات بني آدم إذا دخل أحدكم الخلاء أن يقول بسم الله ولقوله عليه السلام إن الحشوش محتضرة فإذا أتى فليقل أعوذ بالله من الخبث والخبائث (مراقي الفلاح ص ٥١)

[18] عن أنس رضي الله عنه قال كان النبي صلى الله عليه وسلم إذا دخل الخلاء قال اللهم إني أعوذ بك من الخبث والخبائث تابعه ابن عرعرة عن شعبة وعن غندر عن شعبة إذا أتى الخلاء وقال موسى عن حماد إذا دخل وقال سعيد بن زيد حدثنا عبد العزيز إذا أراد أن يدخل (صحيح البخاري، الرقم: ١٤٢)

عن أنس أن النبي صلى الله عليه وسلم كان إذا دخل الكنيف قال بسم الله اللهم إني أعوذ بك من الخبث والخبائث (المصنف لابن أبي شيبة، الرقم: ٥)

[19] قال الترمذي: حديث غريب لا نعرفه الا من هذا الوجه وإسناده ليس بذاك القوي

قال المغلطاي (١/٩٤) بعد نقل كلام الترمذي: ولا أدري ما الموجب لذلك لأن جميع من في إسناده غير مطعون عليه بوجه من الوجوه فيما رأيت بل لو قال فيه قائل إن إسناده صحيح لكان مصيبا وبيان ذلك أن محمد بن حميد قال فيه يحيى ليس به بأس كيس وقال جعفر بن أبي عثمان الطيالسي ثقة وسئل عنه الذهلي فقال ألا ترى أني هو ذا أحدث عنه وقيل للصنعاني تحدث عن ابن حميد فقال: وما لي لا أحدث عنه وقد حدث عنه الإمام أحمد وابن معين انتهى ونقل المناوي كلامه في فيض القدير (٤/١٢٥) وأقره

Hazrat Ali رَضِيَ ٱللَّهُ عَنْهُ reports that Hazrat Rasulullah صَلَّى ٱللَّهُ عَلَيْهِ وَسَلَّمَ said, "The veil between the eyes of the jinn and the private parts of a person is the recitation of bismillah when entering the toilet (bismillah prevents the jinn from staring at one's private parts or causing harm)."

One may also recite the following dua:

اَللّٰهُمَّ إِنِّيْ أَعُوْذُ بِكَ مِنَ الرِّجْسِ النَّجِسِ الْخَبِيْثِ الْمُخْبِثِ الشَّيْطَانِ الرَّجِيْمْ [20]

O Allah تَبَارَكَ وَتَعَالَىٰ, I seek refuge in You from the filthy and impure, the one who is evil and leads people towards evil, the accursed Shaitaan.

قال العيني في عمدة القاري (٢٧٢/٢): وكذا جاء لفظ الكنيف ولفظ المرفق فالأول في حديث علي رضي الله تعالى عنه بسند صحيح وإن كان أبو عيسى: قال إسناده ليس بالقوي قال ستر ما بين الجن وعورات بني آدم إذا دخل الكنيف أن يقول بسم الله

قال العزيزي في السراج المنير (٣٤٢/٢): إسناد صحيح

وقال الحافظ في نتائج الأفكار (١٩٧/١): قلت رواته موثقون وفي كل من محمد بن حميد وشيخه وشيخ شيخه وكذا الحكم الثاني مقال وأشدهم ضعفا محمد بن حميد لكنه لم ينفرد به فقد أخرجه البزار عن يوسف بن موسى عن عبد الرحمن بن الحكم بن بشير عن أبيه به وقال لا يعرف إلا بهذا الإسناد وقد جاء مثله عن أنس

قال الشيخ عوامة في تعليقه على المصنف لابن أبي شيبة (٣٥١/١٥ الرقم: ٣٠٣٥٤): أما حديث علي فرواه الترمذي (الرقم: ٦٠٦) وقال حديث غريب لا نعرفه إلا من هذا الوجه وإسناده ليس بذاك القوي وابن ماجة (الرقم: ٢٩٧) وشيخهما فيه محمد بن حميد الرازي وهو ضعيف... إلى أن قال (الشيخ عوامة) نعم بمجموع طرقه يقوى

[20] عن ابن عمر رضي الله عنهما أن النبي صلى الله عليه وسلم كان إذا دخل الخلاء قال اللهم إني أعوذ بك من الرجس النجس الخبيث المخبث الشيطان الرجيم وإذا خرج قال الحمد لله الذي أذاقني لذته وأبقى في قوته وأذهب عني أذاه (عمل اليوم والليلة لابن السني ، الرقم: ٢٥)

قال الحافظ في نتائج الأفكار (١٩٨/١): قوله (وروينا عن ابن عمر) أخبرني إمام الأئمة أبو الفضل بن الحسين الحافظ رحمه الله بالسند الماضي غير مرة إلى الطبراني ثنا محمد بن عثمان بن أبي شيبة وأحمد بن بشير الطيالسي قال الأول ثنا عبد الحميد بن صالح والثاني ثنا خالد بن مرداس قالا ثنا حبان بن علي عن إسماعيل بن رافع عن دويد وهو ابن عمر ن نافع عن ابن عمر قال كان رسول الله صلى الله عليه وسلم إذا دخل الخلاء قال اللهم إني أعوذ بك من الرجس النجس الخبيث المخبث الشيطان الرجيم

هذا حديث حسن غريب وحبان بكسر المهملة وتشديد الموحدة فيه ضعف وكذا في شيخه لكن للحديث شواهد

6. Before entering the toilet, remove any item upon which the name of Allah ﺗَﺒَﺎﺭَﻙَﻭَﺗَﻌَﺎﻟَﻰ, Hazrat Rasulullah ﺻَﻠَّﻰﺍﻟﻠَّﻪُﻋَﻠَﻴْﻪِﻭَﺳَﻠَّﻢَ or any aayat of the Quraan Majeed is written e.g. a ring or chain.[21]

عن أنس رضي الله عنه قال كان النبي صلى الله عليه وسلم إذا دخل الخلاء نزع خاتمه

(سنن الترمذي، الرقم: ١٧٤٦)[22]

Hazrat Anas ﺭَﺿِﻲَﺍﻟﻠَّﻪُﻋَﻨْﻪُ *reports that Hazrat Rasulullah* ﺻَﻠَّﻰﺍﻟﻠَّﻪُﻋَﻠَﻴْﻪِﻭَﺳَﻠَّﻢَ *would remove his ring when he entered the toilet.*

7. Enter the toilet with your left foot.[23]

---

[21] ويكره أن يدخل في الخلاء ومعه خاتم عليه اسم الله تعالى أو شيء من القرآن كذا في السراج الوهاج (الفتاوى الهندية ٥٠/١)

قال العلامة ابن عابدين رحمه الله إذا أراد أن يدخل الخلاء ينبغي أن يقوم قبل أن يغلبه الخارج ولا يصحبه شيء عليه اسم معظم (رد المحتار ٣٤٥/١)

[22] قال في إعلاء السنن: رواه الأربعة وصححه الترمذي كذا في النيل (٧٢/١) وفي العزيزي (١٢٥/٣) عزاه إلى صحيح ابن حبان ومستدرك الحاكم أيضا ثم قال قال الشيخ حديث صحيح اه وفي رواية للبخاري كان نقش الخاتم ثلاثة أسطر محمد سطر ورسول سطر والله سطر كما في المشكوة

قال المؤلف دلالة مجموع أحاديث الباب عليه ظاهرة وحديث أنس رضي الله عنه قد تكلم فيه لكن قال المنذري الصواب عندي تصحيحه فإن رواته ثقات أثبات كما في النيل (ومثله في التلخيص الحبير ١٠٨/١، الرقم: ١٤٠) (إعلاء السنن ٣٠٣/١)

[23] عن حفصة زوج النبي صلى الله عليه وسلم أن النبي صلى الله عليه وسلم كان يجعل ليمينه لأكله وشربه ووضوئه وثيابه وأخذه وعطائه وشماله لما سوى ذلك أخرجه أحمد بإسناد صحيح (العزيزي ١٥٤/٣) قلت وابن حبان والحاكم أيضا وعن عائشة رضي الله عنها قالت كانت يد رسول الله صلى الله عليه وسلم اليمنى لطهوره وطعامه وكانت يده اليسرى لخلائه وما كان من أذى رواه أحمد وأبو داود والطبراني من حديث إبراهيم عن عائشة وهو منقطع ورواه أبو داود في رواية أخرى موصولا اه (التلخيص الحبير ٤١/١)

(عن حفصة الخ) قلت معناه أنه صلى الله عليه وسلم كان يجعل يمينه لما لا دناءة فيه من الأعمال وشماله لما سوى ذلك مما لا تكريم فيه قال العيني في العمدة وقال الشيخ محي الدين هذه قاعدة مستمرة في الشرع وهي أن ما كان من باب التكريم والتشريف كلبس الثوب والسراويل والخف ودخول المسجد والسواك والاكتحال وتقليم الأظفار وقص الشارب وترجيل الشعر ونتف الإبط وحلق الرأس والسلام من الصلوة وغسل أعضاء الطهارة والخروج من الخلاء والأكل والشرب والمصافحة واستلام الحجر الأسود وغير ذلك مما هو في معناه يستحب التيامن فيه وأما ما كان بضده كدخول الخلاء والخروج من المسجد والإمتخاط والإستنجاء ووضع الثوب والسراويل والخف وما أشبه ذلك فيستحب التياسر فيه اه فثبت استحباب البداءة باليسرى عند الدخول في الخلاء والبداءة باليمنى وقت الخروج منها فما أخرجه البخاري عن عائشة رضي الله عنها قالت كان النبي صلى الله عليه وسلم يعجبه التيمن في تنعله وترجله وطهوره في شأنه كله وفي رواية أبي الوقت (وفي شأنه كله) بالعاطف كما في العمدة

8. Do not remove your lower garment while standing. Instead, remove your lower garment after you draw close to the ground so that the least amount of time is spent with the satr exposed.[24]

عن ابن عمر رضي الله عنهما قال كان النبي صلى الله عليه وسلم إذا أراد الحاجة لا يرفع ثوبه حتى يدنو من الأرض (سنن أبي داود، الرقم: ١٤)[25]

Hazrat Abdullah bin Umar رَضِيَٱللَّهُعَنْهُمَا *reports that when Hazrat Nabi* صَلَّىٱللَّهُعَلَيْهِوَسَلَّمَ *intended to relieve himself, he would not raise his lower garment until he drew close to the ground.*

9. When relieving yourself, do not face towards the qiblah. Similarly, your back should not be towards the qiblah.[26]

للعيني (٧٧٣/١) عام مخصوص بالأدلة الخارجية منها حديث حفصة هذا وعائشة أيضا عند أحمد والطبراني وأبي داود لما فيه من التصريح بأنه صلى الله عليه وسلم كان يحب التيامن في أعمال والتياسر في الأخرى والله أعلم (إعلاء السنن ٣٢٣/١)

ثم يدخل باليسرى ... ثم يخرج برجله اليمنى (رد المحتار ٣٤٥/١)

[24] قال العلامة ابن عابدين رحمه الله ولا يكشف قبل أن يدنو إلى القعود (رد المحتار ٣٤٥/١)

ولا يكشف عورته وهو قائم (الفتاوى الهندية ٥٠/١)

[25] وحاصل ما قال أبو داود أن ههنا روايتين رواية عن الأعمش عن رجل عن ابن عمر ورواية عبد السلام بن حرب عن الأعمش عن أنس فضعف أبو داود رواية أنس بن مالك لأن هذه الرواية مرسلة فإن الأعمش لم يلق أنس بن مالك ولا أحدا من أصحاب رسول الله صلى الله عليه وسلم ولم يحكم بضعف رواية ابن عمر لأن الأعمش لا يرويها عن ابن عمر بلا واسطة بل يرويها عن رجل عن ابن عمر فالظاهر أن الرجل المبهم عنده ثقة فلهذا لم يحكم بضعفها ولو كان الرجل المبهم عنده مجهولا أو كان غياث بن إبراهيم أحد الكذابين لحكم بضعفه أما الترمذي رحمه الله تعالى فإنه أخرج الروايتين كلتيهما عن أنس وابن عمر مرسلتين فلهذا قال في آخره وكلا الحديثين مرسل فلم تصح عنده الروايتان والله أعلم (بذل المجهود ١٠/١)

قال السيوطي في درجات مرقاة الصعود: قال الضياء المقدسي قد سماه (الرجل المبهم) بعضهم القاسم بن محمد ثم قال السيوطي هو بسنن البيهقي كذلك بطريق أحمد بن محمد بن أبي رجاء المصيصي عن وكيع عن الأعمش عن القاسم عن ابن عمر رضي الله عنهما اه وكذلك قال الحافظ في التقريب وتهذيب التهذيب في باب المبهمات: سليمان الأعمش عن رجل عن ابن عمر في قضاء الحاجة لا يرفع ثوبه حتى يدنو من الأرض قيل هو قاسم بن محمد اه

جاء في السنن الكبرى للبيهقي (٩٦/١) أحمد بن محمد بن أبي رجاء المصيصي شيخ جليل حدثنا وكيع حدثنا الأعمش عن القاسم بن محمد عن ابن عمر قال كان رسول الله صلى الله عليه وسلم إذا أراد الحاجة تنحى ولا يرفع ثيابه حتى يدنو من الأرض

عن أبي أيوب الأنصاري رضي الله عنه قال قال رسول الله صلى الله عليه وسلم إذا أتى أحدكم الغائط فلا يستقبل القبلة ولا يولها ظهره (صحيح البخاري، الرقم: ١٤٤)

Hazrat Abu Ayyoob Ansaari رَضِيَ ٱللَّهُ عَنْهُ *reports that Hazrat Rasulullah* صَلَّى ٱللَّهُ عَلَيْهِ وَسَلَّمَ *said, "When any of you wishes to relieve himself, he should not do so while facing the qiblah nor should he turn his back towards the qiblah."*

10. Do not talk while relieving yourself, unless there is a need to speak.[27]

عن أبي هريرة رضي الله عنه قال قال رسول الله صلى الله عليه وسلم لا يخرج اثنان إلى الغائط فيجلسان يتحدثان كاشفين عورتهما فإن الله عز وجل يمقت على ذلك (مجمع الزوائد، الرقم: ١٠٢١)[28]

Hazrat Abu Hurairah رَضِيَ ٱللَّهُ عَنْهُ *reports that Hazrat Rasulullah* صَلَّى ٱللَّهُ عَلَيْهِ وَسَلَّمَ *said, "Two people should not go to relieve themselves at a place where both sit together while relieving themselves and speak to each other with their satr (private parts) exposed, for certainly Allah* تَبَارَكَ وَتَعَالَى *greatly dislikes this."*

---

[26] (كره) تحريما (استقبال قبلة واستدبارها ل) لأجل (بول أو غائط) فلو للاستنجاء لم يكره (ولو في بنيان) لإطلاق النهي (فإن جلس مستقبلا لها) غافلا (ثم ذكره انحرف) ندبا لحديث الطبري من جلس يبول قبالة القبلة فذكرها فانحرف عنها إجلالا لها لم يقم من مجلسه حتى يغفر له (إن أمكنه وإلا فلا) بأس (الدر المختار ٣٤١/١)

[27] عن ابن عمر رضي الله عنهما أن رجلا مر ورسول الله صلى الله عليه وسلم يبول فسلم فلم يرد عليه (صحيح مسلم، الرقم: ٣٧٠)

(ولا يتكلم إلا لضرورة) لأنه يمقت به (مراقي الفلاح صـ ٥٢)

[28] رواه الطبراني في الأوسط ورجاله موثقون (مجمع الزوائد، الرقم: ١٠٢١)

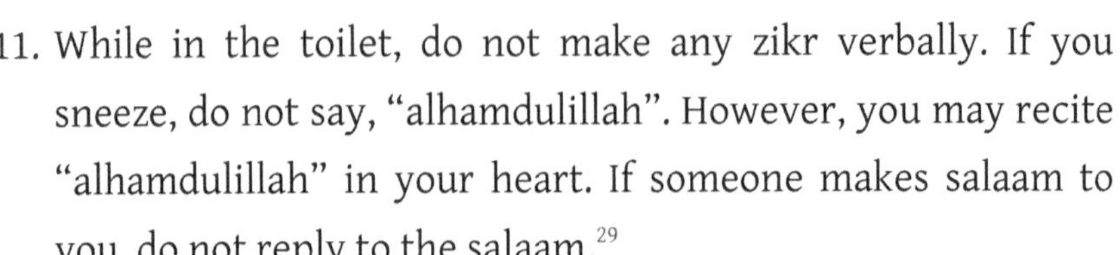

11. While in the toilet, do not make any zikr verbally. If you sneeze, do not say, "alhamdulillah". However, you may recite "alhamdulillah" in your heart. If someone makes salaam to you, do not reply to the salaam.[29]

12. Do not eat or drink in the toilet.[30]

13. Do not look at the sky, the private part or the stool and urine while relieving yourself.[31]

14. Do not spend more time in the toilet than is necessary. If the toilet is shared between a few people or is a public toilet, then spending more time than necessary may cause inconvenience to others.[See 30]

15. Relieve yourself in the squatting position. It is makrooh for one to relieve himself while standing.[32]

عن عائشة رضي الله عنها قالت من حدثكم أن النبي صلى الله عليه وسلم كان يبول قائما فلا تصدقوه ما كان يبول إلا قاعدا (سنن الترمذي، الرقم: ١٢)[33]

---

[29] ولا يتكلم ولا يذكر الله تعالى ولا يشمت عاطسا ولا يرد السلام ولا يجيب المؤذن فإن عطس يحمد الله بقلبه ولا يحرك لسانه (الفتاوى الهندية ١/٥٠)

عن جابر بن عبد الله أن رجلا مر على النبي صلى الله عليه وسلم وهو يبول فسلم عليه فقال له رسول الله صلى الله عليه وسلم إذا رأيتني على مثل هذه الحالة فلا تسلم علي فإنك إن فعلت ذلك لم أرد عليك (سنن ابن ماجة، الرقم: ٣٥٢)

[30] إن هذه الحشوش محتضرة (سنن أبي داود، الرقم: ٦)

ولا يطيل القعود على البول والغائط (الفتاوى الهندية ١/٥٠)

[31] ولا ينظر لعورته إلا لحاجة ولا ينظر إلى ما يخرج منه ... ولا يرفع بصره إلى السماء (الفتاوى الهندية ١/٥٠)

[32] ويكره أن يبول قائما أو مضطجعا أو متجردا عن ثوبه من غير عذر فإن كان بعذر فلا بأس به (الفتاوى الهندية ١/٥٠)

[33] قال الترمذي: حديث عائشة أحسن شيئ في هذا الباب وأصح

Hazrat Aaishah رَضِىَ ٱللَّهُ عَنْهَا mentions, "Whoever informs you that Rasulullah صَلَّى ٱللَّهُ عَلَيْهِ وَسَلَّمَ would relieve himself standing, then do not believe him. Rasulullah صَلَّى ٱللَّهُ عَلَيْهِ وَسَلَّمَ would only relieve himself while sitting (squatting)."

16. Exercise extreme caution in ensuring that urine does not splash onto your body. Negligence in this regard results in severe punishment in the grave.[34]

عن أبي هريرة رضي الله عنه قال قال رسول الله صلى الله عليه وسلم أكثر عذاب القبر من البول (سنن ابن ماجة، الرقم: ٣٤٨)[35]

Hazrat Abu Hurairah رَضِىَ ٱللَّهُ عَنْهُ reports that Hazrat Rasulullah صَلَّى ٱللَّهُ عَلَيْهِ وَسَلَّمَ said, "Most of the punishment (meted out to most people) in the grave will be on account of urine (i.e. being unmindful regarding urine splashes and impurities. Therefore, their wudhu, salaah and other ibaadaat will not gain acceptance due to remaining impure)."

17. When making istinjaa, use clods of sand (or toilet paper) as well as water to clean yourself. Ensure that you fill the jug

---

قال النووي: رواه أحمد بن حنبل والترمذي والنسائي وآخرون وإسناده جيد والله أعلم وقد روي في النهي عن البول قائما أحاديث لا تثبت ولكن حديث عائشة هذا ثابت (شرح النووي على الصحيح لمسلم ١٣٣/١)

[34] والتطهير إما إثبات الطهارة بالمحل أو إزالة النجاسة عنه ويفترض فيما لا يعفى منها وقد ورد أن أول شيء يسأل عنه العبد في قبره الطهارة وأن عامة عذاب القبر من عدم الاعتناء بشأنها والتحرز عن النجاسة خصوصا البول

قال العلامة الطحطاوي رحمه الله (قوله خصوصا البول) فإنه ورد فيه ورد فيه استنزهوا من البول فإن عامة عذاب القبر منه وورد أن عذاب القبر من أشياء ثلاثة الغيبة والنميمة وعدم الاستنزاه من البول وقوله خصوصا مفعول مطلق والبول مفعول به بأي أخص البول بأن عامة عذاب القبر منه خصوصا (حاشية الطحطاوي على مراقي الفلاح ص ١٥٢)

[35] قال العلامة البوصيري في زوائد ابن ماجة (ص٨١): هذا إسناد صحيح رجاله عن آخرهم محتج بهم في الصحيحين

with water before relieving yourself, as you may put yourself through difficulty if there is no water.[36]

عن أبي هريرة رضي الله عنه عن النبي صلى الله عليه وسلم قال نزلت هذه الآية في أهل قباء فيه رجال يحبون أن يتطهروا قال كانوا يستنجون بالماء فنزلت فيهم هذه الآية (سنن الترمذي، الرقم: ٣١٠٠)[37]

Hazrat Abu Hurairah رَضِيَٱللَّهُعَنْهُ reports that Hazrat Nabi صَلَّىٱللَّهُعَلَيْهِوَسَلَّمَ said, "The aayah فِيهِ رِجَالٌ يُحِبُّونَ أَن يَتَطَهَّرُوا (in it are men who like to observe purity) was revealed regarding the people of Qubaa on account of them making istinjaa with water."

قال علي رضي الله عنه إن من كان قبلكم كانوا يبعرون بعرا وإنكم تثلطون ثلطا فأتبعوا الحجارة بالماء (المصنف لابن أبي شيبة، الرقم: ١٦٤٥)

---

[36] (وأركانه) أربعة شخص (مستنج و) شيء (مستنجى به) كماء وحجر (و) نجس (خارج) من أحد السبيلين وكذا لو أصابه من خارج وإن قام من موضعه على المعتمد (ومخرج) دبر أو قبل (بنحو حجر) مما هو عين طاهرة قالعة لا قيمة لها كمدر (منق) لأن المقصود فيختار الأبلغ والأسلم عن التلويث ولا يتقيد بإقبال وإدبار شتاء وصيفا (وليس العدد) ثلاثا (بمسنون فيه) بل مستحب (والغسل) بالماء إلى أنه يقع في قلبه له طهر ما لم يكن موسوسا فيقدر بثلاث كما مر (بعده) أي الحجر (بلا كشف عورة) عند أحد مر معه فيتركه أما من فلو كشف كما مر فيترك لو صار فاسقا لا لو كشف لاغتسال أو تغوط كما بحثه ابن الشحنة (سنة) مطلقا به يفتي سراج

قال العلامة ابن عابدين رحمه الله (قوله سنة مطلقا) أي في زماننا وزمان الصحابة لقوله تعالى فيه رجال يحبون أن يتطهروا والله يحب المطهرين قيل لما نزلت قال رسول الله يا أهل قباء إن الله أثنى عليكم عند الغائط فماذا تصنعون عند الغائط قالوا نتبع الغائط لأحجار ثم نتبع الأحجار لماء فكان الجمع سنة على الإطلاق في كل زمان وهو الصحيح وعليه الفتوى وقيل ذلك في زماننا لأنهم كانوا يبعرون اه إمداد ثم اعلم أن الجمع بين الماء والحجر أفضل ويليه في الفضل الاقتصار على الماء ويليه الاقتصار على الحجر وتحصل السنة بالكل وإن تفاوت الفضل كما أفاده في الإمداد وغيره (رد المحتار ٣٣٨/١)

فتاوى محمودية ٨٩/٨ ، ٩١

[37] وأما حديث أبي هريرة رضي الله عنه فأخرجه أبو داود والترمذي وابن ماجه مرفوعا قال نزلت هذه الآية في أهل قباء فيه رجال يحبون أن يتطهروا والله يحب المطهرين قال كانوا يستنجون بالماء فنزلت فيهم هذه الآية وسنده ضعيف وفي الباب أحاديث صحيحة أخرى ومن هنا ظهر أن قول من قال من الأئمة إنه لم يصح في الاستنجاء بالماء حديث ليس بصحيح (تحفة الأحوذي ٩٤/١)

Hazrat Ali رَضِىَ اللّٰهُ عَنْهُ *mentioned, "The stool of the people before you was dry and hard and the stool of you people is more soft (i.e. due to the nature of their food being different). Therefore, make istinjaa with clods of sand and thereafter cleanse with water (as soft stool soils the area around the passage)."*

18. Use your left hand to clean yourself. To make istinjaa with the right hand is impermissible (makrooh-e-tahreemi). Similarly, do not touch your private part with your right hand.[38]

عن عبد الله بن أبي قتادة عن أبيه رضي الله عنه عن النبي صلى الله عليه وسلم قال إذا بال أحدكم فلا يأخذن ذكره بيمينه ولايستنجي بيمينه (صحيح البخاري، الرقم: ١٥٤)

Hazrat Abdullah bin Abi Qataadah رَضِىَ اللّٰهُ عَنْهُ *narrates from his father that Hazrat Nabi* صَلَّى اللّٰهُ عَلَيْهِ وَسَلَّمَ *said, "When any of you relieves himself then he should not hold his private part with his right hand nor should he make istinjaa with his right hand."*

19. Exit the toilet with the right foot and thank Allah تَبَارَكَ وَتَعَالَى for allowing the waste to leave your body and for blessing you with good health. The manner of thanking Allah تَبَارَكَ وَتَعَالَى is to

---

[38] قال العلامة ابن عابدين رحمه الله ثم يفيض الماء باليمنى على فرجه ويعلي الإناء ويغسل فرجه باليسرى ... (رد المحتار ١/٣٤٥)

ويكره الاستنجاء بالعظم والروث والرجيع والطعام واللحم والخزف والزجاج وورق الشجر والشعر وكذا باليمين هكذا في التبيين (الفتاوى الهندية ١/٥٠)

(وكره تحريما بعظم وطعام وروث) يابس كعذرة يابسة وحجر استنجي به إلا بحرف آخر (وآجر وخزف وزجاج و) شيء محترم (كخرقة ديباج ويمين) ولا عذر بيسراه (الدر المختار ١/٣٤٠)

recite the following dua upon leaving the toilet after relieving yourself:[39]

غُفْرَانَكَ اَلْحَمْدُ لِلّٰهِ الَّذِيْ أَذْهَبَ عَنِّيْ الْأَذٰى وَعَافَانِيْ[40]

O Allah تَبَارَكَوَتَعَالَى, *I seek Your forgiveness. All praise is due to Allah* تَبَارَكَوَتَعَالَى *who has removed from me impurity and filth (that would have been harmful if it remained in my body) and granted me relief and ease.*

One may also recite the following duas:

اَلْحَمْدُ لِلّٰهِ الَّذِيْ أَذْهَبَ عَنِّيْ مَا يُؤْذِيْنِيْ وَأَمْسَكَ عَلَيَّ مَا يَنْفَعُنِيْ[41]

All praise is due to Allah تَبَارَكَوَتَعَالَى *who has removed from me that which harms me and kept within me that which benefits me.*

---

[39] (ويخرج من الخلاء برجله اليمنى) لأنها أحق بالتقدم لنعمة الانصراف عن الأذى ومحل الشياطين (ثم يقول) بعد الخروج (الحمد لله الذي أذهب عني الأذى) بخروج الفضلات الممرضة بحبسها (وعافاني) بإبقاء خاصية الغذاء الذي لو أمسك كله أو خرج لكان مظنة الهلاك وقال رسول الله صلى الله عليه وسلم عند خروجه غفرانك وهو كناية عن الاعتراف بالقصور عن بلوغ حق شكر نعمة الإطعام وتصريف خاصية الغذاء وتسهيل خروج الأذى لسلامة البدن من الآلام أو عدم الذكر باللسان حال التخلي (مراقي الفلاح ص ٥٥)

[40] عن عائشة رضي الله عنها قالت كان النبي صلى الله عليه وسلم إذا خرج من الخلاء قال غفرانك قال أبو عيسى هذا حديث حسن غريب (سنن الترمذي، الرقم: ٧)

قوله (هذا حديث غريب حسن) قال القاضي الشوكاني في نيل الأوطار هذا الحديث أخرجه الخمسة إلا النسائي وصححه الحاكم وأبو حاتم قال في البدر المنير ورواه الدارمي وصححه ابن خزيمة وابن حبان انتهى (تحفة الأحوذي ٥٠/١)

عن أنس بن مالك رضي الله عنه قال كان النبي صلى الله عليه وسلم إذا خرج من الخلاء قال الحمد لله الذي أذهب عني الأذى وعافاني (سنن ابن ماجة، الرقم: ٣٠١)

قال الشيخ محمد عوامة في تعليقه (٢٢٥/١): رواه ابن السني في عمل اليوم والليلة (٢٥) والطبراني في كتاب الدعاء له (٣٧٠) وقد قال الحافظ فيه في نتائج الأفكار (١٩٨/١): حسن غريب وحبان فيه ضعف وكذا في شيخه لكن للحديث شواهد

[41] قال العلامة ابن عابدين رحمه الله ثم يخرج برجله اليمنى ويقول غفرانك الحمد لله الذي أذهب عني ما يؤذيني وأمسك علي ما ينفعني (رد المحتار ٣٤٥/١)

عن طاوس قال قال رسول الله صلى الله عليه وسلم إذا خرج أحدكم من الخلاء فليقل الحمد لله الذي أذهب عني ما يؤذيني وأمسك علي ما ينفعني (المصنف لابن أبي شيبة، الرقم: ١٢)

اَلْحَمْدُ لِلهِ الَّذِيْ أَذَاقَنِيْ لَذَّتَهُ وَأَبْقَى فِيَّ قُوَّتَهُ وَأَذْهَبَ عَنِّيْ أَذَاهُ[42]

All praise is due to Allah تَبَارَكَوَتَعَالَى *who allowed me to enjoy the taste (of the food), and retained within me its nourishment (and energy), and removed from me its harm (i.e. the harm of the food after it was transformed into waste).*

20. After relieving yourself, wait for the remaining droplets of urine to come out before making wudhu.[43]

21. When using the toilet, do not leave it in a dirty condition e.g. by messing around the pan or on the floor, by not flushing, etc. If you are using a toilet that is shared with other people then you should be extra particular in this regard so that inconvenience is not caused to them.[44]

---

[42] عن ابن عمر رضي الله عنهما أن النبي صلى الله عليه وسلم كان إذا دخل الخلاء قال اللهم إني أعوذ بك من الرجس النجس الخبيث المخبث الشيطان الرجيم وإذا خرج قال الحمد لله الذي أذاقني لذته وأبقى في قوته وأذهب عني أذاه (عمل اليوم والليلة لابن السني، الرقم: ٢٥) انظر أيضا 20

[43] عن ابن عباس رضي الله عنهما قال مر رسول الله صلى الله عليه وسلم بحائط من حيطان مكة أو المدينة سمع صوت إنسانين يعذبان في قبورهما فقال رسول الله صلى الله عليه وسلم وما يعذبان وما يعذبان في كبير ثم قال بلى كان أحدهما لا يستبرئ من بوله وكان الآخر يمشي بالنميمة ثم دعا بجريدة فكسرها كسرتين فوضع على كل قبر منهما كسرة فقيل له يا رسول الله لم فعلت هذا قال لعله أن يخفف عنهما ما لم ييبسا أو إلى أن ييبسا (سنن النسائي، الرقم: ٢٠٦٨)

فروع يجب الاستبراء بمشي أو تنحنح أو نوم على شقه الأيسر ويختلف بطباع الناس

قال العلامة ابن عابدين رحمه الله ومحله إذا أمن خروج شيء بعده فيندب ذلك مبالغة في الاستبراء أو المراد الاستبراء بخصوص هذه الأشياء من نحو المشي والتنحنح أما نفس الاستبراء حتى يطمئن قلبه بزوال الرشح فهو فرض وهو المراد بالوجوب ولذا قال الشرنبلالي يلزم الرجل الاستبراء حتى يزول أثر البول ويطمئن قلبه وقال عبرت باللزوم لكونه أقوى من الواجب لأن هذا يفوت الجواز لفوته فلا يصح له الشروع في الوضوء حتى يطمئن بزوال الرشح اه (رد المحتار ١/٣٤٤)

[44] عن أبي مالك الأشعري رضي الله عنه قال قال رسول الله صلى الله عليه وسلم الطهور شطر الإيمان (صحيح مسلم، الرقم: ٢٢٣)

22. After relieving yourself, clean your hands by rubbing them on sand or through using soap to remove any bad odour.[45]

عن أبي هريرة رضي الله عنه قال كان النبي صلى الله عليه وسلم إذا أتى الخلاء أتيته بماء في تور أو ركوة فاستنجى ثم مسح يده على الأرض ثم أتيته بإناء آخر فتوضأ (سنن أبي داود، الرقم: ٤٥)[46]

Hazrat Abu Hurairah رَضِيَ اللهُ عَنْهُ reports, "When Rasulullah صَلَّى اللهُ عَلَيْهِ وَسَلَّم would go to relieve himself, I would present water in a utensil to him (for making istinjaa). After he made istinjaa, he would rub his mubaarak hand on the ground (though there was no bad odour emanating from the mubaarak hand of Rasulullah صَلَّى اللهُ عَلَيْهِ وَسَلَّم, he did this to teach the Ummah how they should remove the bad odour from their hands after relieving themselves). I would then bring another utensil of water to him from which he would make wudhu."

عن صالح بن أبي حسان قال سمعت سعيد بن المسيب يقول إن الله طيب يحب الطيب نظيف يحب النظافة كريم يحب الكرم جواد يحب الجود فنظفوا أراه قال أفنيتكم ولا تشبهوا باليهود قال فذكرت ذلك لمهاجر بن مسمار فقال حدثنيه عامر بن سعد بن أبي وقاص عن أبيه عن النبي صلى الله عليه وسلم مثله إلا أنه قال نظفوا أفنيتكم قال أبو عيسى هذا حديث غريب وخالد بن إلياس يضعف (سنن الترمذي، الرقم: ٢٧٩٩) لهذا الحديث شاهد ضعيف من حديث عائشة في المعجم الأوسط للطبراني والأفراد للدارقطني: نعيم بن مورع عن هشام بن عروة عن أبيه عن عائشة رضي الله عنها مرفوعا بلفظ الإسلام نظيف فتنظفوا فإنه لا يدخل الجنة إلا نظيف قال السخاوي في المقاصد الحسنة (الرقم: ٣٠٢) ونعيم ضعيف

[45] صحيح البخاري، الرقم: ٢٥٩

باب مسح اليد بالتراب لتكون أنقى ... عن ابن عباس رضي الله عنهما عن ميمونة رضي الله عنها أن النبي صلى الله عليه وسلم اغتسل من الجنابة فغسل فرجه بيده ثم دلك بها الحائط ثم غسلها ثم توضأ وضوءه للصلاة فلما فرغ من غسله غسل رجليه (صحيح البخاري، الرقم: ٢٦٠) قال العلامة ابن عابدين رحمه الله ثم يدلك يده على حائط أو أرض طاهرة ثم يغسلها ثلاثا (رد المحتار ١/٣٤٦)

[46] سكت الحافظ عن هذا الحديث في الفصل الثاني من هداية الرواة (١/٢٠٦) فالحديث حسن عنده

23. If a person is terminally ill or hospitalised and is unable to go to the toilet, it will be permissible for him to pass urine in a bottle. The urine should thereafter be disposed of.

عن حكيمة بنت أميمة بنت رقيقة عن أمها رضي الله عنها أنها قالت كان للنبي صلى الله عليه وسلم قدح من عيدان تحت سريره يبول فيه بالليل (سنن أبي داود، الرقم: ٢٤)[47]

Hazrat Hukaimah bintu Umaimah رَحِمَهَااللّٰه reports that her mother, Hazrat Umaimah bintu Ruqaiqah رَضِيَاللّٰهُعَنْهَا, said, "Rasulullah صَلَّىاللّٰهُعَلَيْهِوَسَلَّم had a wooden utensil kept beneath his bed (while he was ill) in which he would pass water during the night."

<hr>

[47] هذا الحديث سكت عنه أبو داود والمنذري (مختصر سنن أبي داود ٢٧/١)

عن حكيمة بنت أميمة عن أمها قالت كان للنبي صلى الله عليه وسلم قدح من عيدان يبول فيه ويضعه تحت سريره فقام فطلبه فلم يجده فسأل فقال أين القدح قالوا برة خادم أم سلمة التي قدمت معها من أرض الحبشة فقال النبي صلى الله عليه وسلم لقد احتظرت من النار بحظار

رواه الطبراني ورجاله رجال الصحيح غير عبد الله بن أحمد بن حنبل وحكيمة وكلاهما ثقة (مجمع الزوائد، الرقم: ١٤٠١٤)

GENERAL MASAAIL PERTAINING TO RELIEVING ONESELF

1. **Q:** Is it permissible for one to read literature such as newspapers and magazines, or use his phone to chat, browse the net, etc. while in the toilet?

    A: The toilet is a place where one relieves oneself, hence it is undesirable for one to use his phone or read any material or literature in the toilet.[See 30]

2. **Q:** Can one use the urinals available in public toilets to relieve oneself?

    A: One should not use the urinals to relieve oneself. Instead, one should sit and relieve himself in a secluded area.[See 32 and 10]

3. **Q:** Is it permissible for one to suffice on using toilet paper for istinjaa?

    A: In cleaning stool, tissue paper will not be sufficient. One has to use water.[See 36]

4. **Q:** Is it permissible to speak while relieving oneself in the toilet?

    A: It is makrooh to speak while relieving oneself, except if there is a need to speak.[See 27]

5. **Q:** Is it better for one to relieve oneself using the Western toilet (high pan) or Eastern toilet (low pan)?

A: It is sunnah for one to relieve oneself in a squatting posture, and the squatting posture is possible using the Eastern pan. If one is forced to use the high pan then he should ensure that he saves himself from urine splashes.[See 34 and 35]

CHAPTER TWO

WUDHU

VIRTUES OF WUDHU

1. Wudhu is a purification from minor sins.

عن عثمان بن عفان رضي الله عنه قال قال رسول الله صلى الله عليه وسلم من توضأ فأحسن الوضوء خرجت خطاياه من جسده حتى تخرج من تحت أظفاره (صحيح مسلم، الرقم: ٢٤٥)

Hazrat Uthmaan رَضِيَ اللهُ عَنْهُ *reports that Hazrat Rasulullah* صَلَّى اللهُ عَلَيْهِ وَسَلَّمَ *said, "Whoever performs wudhu, and does it in a perfect manner, his (minor) sins are removed (and washed away) from his body to the extent that they fall off from beneath his nails."*

2. Wudhu will cause the limbs of wudhu to be illuminated with a special noor on the Day of Qiyaamah.

عن أبي هريرة رضي الله عنه أن رسول الله صلى الله عليه وسلم أتى المقبرة فقال السلام عليكم دار قوم مؤمنين وإنا إن شاء الله بكم لاحقون وددت أنا قد رأينا إخواننا قالوا

أولسنا إخوانك يا رسول الله قال أنتم أصحابي وإخواننا الذين لم يأتوا بعد قالوا كيف تعرف من لم يأت بعد من أمتك يا رسول الله قال أرأيت لو أن رجلا له خيل غر محجلة بين ظهري خيل دهم بهم ألا يعرف خيله قالوا بلى يا رسول الله قال فإنهم يأتون غرا محجلين من الوضوء وأنا فرطهم على الحوض (صحيح مسلم، الرقم: ٢٤٩)

Hazrat Abu Hurairah ﷺ reports that Hazrat Rasulullah ﷺ once entered the graveyard and recited the following dua:

اَلسَّلَامُ عَلَيْكُمْ دَارَ قَوْمٍ مُّؤْمِنِيْنَ وَإِنَّا إِنْ شَاءَ اللهُ بِكُمْ لَاحِقُوْنَ

"O (inmates of) the resting abode of the believers, may peace descend upon you from the side of Allah تَبَارَكَ وَتَعَالَى, insha Allah we will soon be joining you."

Hazrat Nabi ﷺ then said, "I wish I had met our brothers." The Sahaabah ﷺ enquired, "Are we not your brothers, O Rasulullah ﷺ?" Hazrat Nabi ﷺ replied, "You are my companions (i.e. you have a greater position than the rest of the Ummah. You are my brothers and you are also blessed with my companionship). My brothers are those who have not yet come in the world (i.e. they will still be born and appear in the world after my demise)." The Sahaabah ﷺ further enquired, "O Rasulullah ﷺ, how will you recognize those of your followers who will come after you?" Hazrat Nabi ﷺ replied, "If a person owns black horses with white foreheads and legs and they are mixed with horses that are completely black, will he not recognize his own horses from among them?" The Sahaabah replied, *"He will certainly recognize them, O Rasulullah* رَضِىَٱللَّهُعَنْهُمْ*."* *Hazrat Nabi* صَلَّىٱللَّهُعَلَيْهِوَسَلَّمَ *replied, "They (my followers) will come on the Day of Qiyaamah with their foreheads and limbs illuminated with special noor on account of them performing wudhu for salaah (and it is through this sign that I will recognize them from others) and I will precede them (in reaching the Hereafter) and I will serve them water at the hawdh of Kawthar (when they will meet me on the Day of Qiyaamah)."*

3. Remaining in the state of wudhu is a sign of a true believer.

عن ثوبان قال قال رسول الله صلى الله عليه وسلم استقيموا ولن تحصوا واعلموا أن خير أعمالكم الصلاة ولا يحافظ على الوضوء إلا مؤمن (سنن ابن ماجة، الرقم: ٢٧٧)[48]

Hazrat Thowbaan رَضِىَٱللَّهُعَنْهُ *reports that Hazrat Rasulullah* صَلَّىٱللَّهُعَلَيْهِوَسَلَّمَ *said, "Try your best to adopt istiqaamah (steadfastness) in all matters, even though you will never manage to do so entirely, and remember that the most virtuous of deeds is salaah, and safeguarding the wudhu is a sign of a true believer (i.e. to perform a complete and perfect wudhu and to remain in the state of wudhu at all times is a sign of a true believer)."*

4. The one who passes away in the state of wudhu is blessed with the rank of a martyr.

---

[48] قال البوصيري في الزوائد (١٠٢/١): رجاله إسناده ثقات أثبات إلا أن فيه انقطاعا بين سالم وثوبان ولكن أخرجه الدارمي وابن حبان في صحيحه من طريق ثوبان متصلا

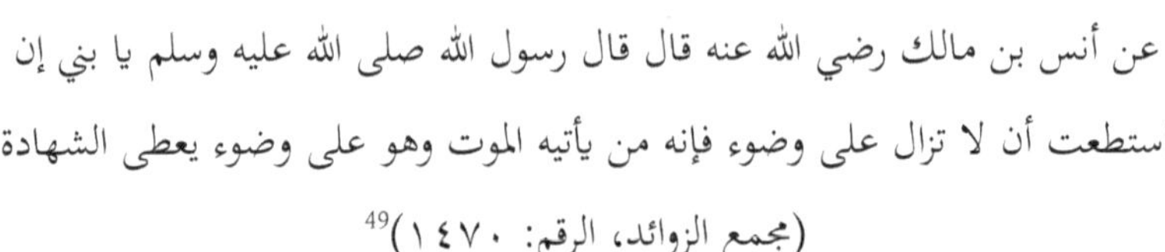

عن أنس بن مالك رضي الله عنه قال قال رسول الله صلى الله عليه وسلم يا بني إن استطعت أن لا تزال على وضوء فإنه من يأتيه الموت وهو على وضوء يعطى الشهادة (مجمع الزوائد، الرقم: ١٤٧٠)[49]

Hazrat Anas bin Maalik رَضِیَٱللَّهُعَنْهُ *reports that Hazrat Rasulullah* صَلَّیٱللَّهُعَلَیْهِوَسَلَّمَ *said, "O my beloved son! If you are able to remain in the state of wudhu (then do so), as the one who passes away in the state of wudhu is blessed with the rank of a martyr."*

5. The one who performs a complete wudhu safeguards himself from Shaitaan, just as those who guard the Islamic frontiers safeguard the Muslims from the enemies of Islam.

عن أبي هريرة رضي الله عنه أن رسول الله صلى الله عليه وسلم قال ألا أدلكم على ما يمحو الله به الخطايا ويرفع به الدرجات قالوا بلى يا رسول الله قال إسباغ الوضوء على المكاره وكثرة الخطا إلى المساجد وانتظار الصلاة بعد الصلاة فذلكم الرباط (صحيح مسلم، الرقم: ٢٥١)

Hazrat Abu Hurairah رَضِیَٱللَّهُعَنْهُ *reports that Hazrat Rasulullah* صَلَّیٱللَّهُعَلَیْهِوَسَلَّمَ *once asked the Sahaabah* رَضِیَٱللَّهُعَنْهُمْ*, "Should I not inform you of such actions through which Allah* تَبَارَكَوَتَعَالَی *will erase your sins and raise your ranks?" The Sahaabah* رَضِیَٱللَّهُعَنْهُمْ *replied, "Certainly inform us, O Rasul of Allah* صَلَّیٱللَّهُعَلَیْهِوَسَلَّمَ*!" Hazrat*

[49] قال الهيثمي: رواه أبو يعلى والطبراني في الصغير وزاد يا بني إذا خرجت من بيتك فلا يقعن بصرك على أحد من أهل القبلة إلا ظننت أنه له الفضل عليك يا بني إن ذلك من سنتي ومن أحيا سنتي فقد أحبني ومن أحبني كان معي في الجنة وفيه محمد بن الحسن بن أبي يزيد وهو ضعيف قال البوصيري في الإتحاف (الرقم: ٥٤٠): علي بن زيد بن جدعان ضعيف لكن لم ينفرد به علي بن زيد فقد رواه أحمد بن منيع ثنا يؤيد أبنا العلاء أبو محمد الثقفي سمعت أنس بن مالك ... فذكره وسيأتي لفظه في آخر كتاب المواعظ إن شاء الله روى الترمذي قطعة منه في الصلاة وأخرى في العلم من طريق أعلى بن زيد

Rasulullah ﷺ said, "Performing a complete wudhu despite difficulties, taking abundant steps in walking towards the masaajid and awaiting the next salaah after one salaah is performed. These actions resemble the action of those who protect the Islamic frontiers against the enemies of Islam (through these actions, one protects himself from the evils of nafs and Shaitaan, just as those guarding the frontiers protect the Muslims against the enemies of Islam)."

SUNNAH METHOD OF MAKING WUDHU

1. When making wudhu, sit on a raised place (e.g. a chair) and face the qiblah. The place where one makes wudhu should be a clean place.[50]

عن عبد خير عن علي رضي الله عنه أنه أتي بكرسي فقعد عليه ثم دعا بتور فيه ماء فكفأ على يديه ثلاثا (سنن النسائي، الرقم: ٩٣)

Hazrat Abd Khair رَحِمَهُ ٱللَّهُ *reports that a chair was brought to Hazrat Ali* رَضِيَ ٱللَّهُ عَنْهُ*. He then sat on the chair (in order to demonstrate the wudhu of Hazrat Rasulullah* صَلَّى ٱللَّهُ عَلَيْهِ وَسَلَّمَ*). Thereafter, he requested that a utensil of water be brought. He then commenced by pouring water on his hands thrice (i.e. he washed his hands thrice till the wrists).*

2. Make the intention for wudhu.[51]

3. Recite the masnoon dua before commencing the wudhu:[52]

بِسْمِ اللهِ وَالْحَمْدُ للهِ

(I commence) in the name of Allah تَبَارَكَ وَتَعَالَى *and all praise belongs to Allah* تَبَارَكَ وَتَعَالَى.

عن أبي هريرة رضي الله عنه قال قال رسول الله صلى الله عليه وسلم يا أبا هريرة إذا توضأت فقل بسم الله والحمد لله فإن حفظتك لا تبرح تكتب لك الحسنات حتى تحدث من ذلك الوضوء (مجمع الزوائد، الرقم: ١١١٢)[53]

Hazrat Abu Hurairah رَضِيَ ٱللّٰهُ عَنْهُ *reports that Hazrat Rasulullah* صَلَّى ٱللّٰهُ عَلَيْهِ وَسَلَّمَ *said, "O Abu Hurairah! When you perform wudhu, then (first) recite the dua* بِسْمِ اللهِ وَالْحَمْدُ لله *. Through reciting this dua, the malaa'ikah (angels) which protect you (are commanded to) continuously record good deeds for you until you break that wudhu."*

4. Wash both the hands up to the wrists thrice.[54]

عن حمران مولى عثمان أن عثمان بن عفان رضي الله عنه دعا بوضوء فتوضأ فغسل كفيه ثلاث مرات (صحيح مسلم، الرقم: ٢٢٦)[55]

Hazrat Humraan رَحِمَهُ ٱللّٰهُ*, the freed slave of Hazrat Uthmaan* رَضِيَ ٱللّٰهُ عَنْهُ*, reports that Hazrat Uthmaan* رَضِيَ ٱللّٰهُ عَنْهُ *requested that water be brought (to demonstrate to the people how to perform wudhu). He then commenced the wudhu by washing his hands (till the wrists) thrice. (In this narration, which appears in Saheeh Bukhaari,*

---

[53] قال الهيثمي: رواه الطبراني في الصغير وإسناده حسن

[54] الفصل الثاني في سنن الوضوء وهي ثلاث عشرة على ما ذكر في المتون ... ومنها غسل اليدين إلى الرسغين ثلاثا ابتداء (الفتاوى الهندية ١/٦)

[55] صحيح البخاري، الرقم: ١٦٤

Hazrat Uthmaan رَضِىَٱللَّهُعَنْهُ *said, "I had seen Rasulullah* صَلَّىٱللَّهُعَلَيْهِوَسَلَّمَ *perform wudhu in this manner."*

5. Cleanse the mouth with a miswaak. When using the miswaak, brush the teeth in a horizontal manner and the tongue in a vertical manner. In the absence of a miswaak, you may use your finger as a substitute.[56]

عن عائشة رضي الله عنها قالت قال رسول الله صلى الله عليه وسلم تفضل الصلوة التي يستاك لها على الصلوة التي لا يستاك لها سبعين ضعفا (المستدرك على الصحيحين للحاكم، الرقم: ٥١٥)[57]

Hazrat Aaishah رَضِىَٱللَّهُعَنْهَا *reports that Hazrat Rasulullah* صَلَّىٱللَّهُعَلَيْهِوَسَلَّمَ *said, "The salaah performed after cleansing the mouth with the miswaak is seventy times superior and more rewarding than the salaah performed without using the miswaak."*

---

[56] (والسواك) سنة مؤكدة كما في الجوهرة عند المضمضة وقيل قبلها وهو للوضوء عندنا إلا إذا نسيه فيندب للصلاة كما يندب لاصفرار سن وتغير رائحة وقراءة قرآن وأقله ثلاث في الأعالي وثلاث في الأسافل (بمياه) ثلاثة (و) ندب إمساكه (بيمناه) وكونه لينا مستويا بلا عقد في غلظ الخنصر وطول شبر ويستاك عرضا لا طولا ولا مضطجعا فإنه يورث كبر الطحال ولا يقبضه فإنه يورث الباسور ولا يمصه فإنه يورث العمى ثم يغسله وإلا فيستاك الشيطان به ولا يزاد على الشبر وإلا فالشيطان يركب عليه ولا يضعه بل ينصبه وإلا فخطر الجنون قهستاني ويكره بمؤذ ويحرم بذي سم ومن منافعه أنه شفاء لما دون الموت ومذكر للشهادة عنده وعند فقده أو فقد أسنانه تقوم الخرقة الخشنة أو الأصبع مقامه

قال العلامة ابن عابدين رحمه الله (قوله ويستاك عرضا لا طولا) أي لأنه يخرج لحم الأسنان وقال الغزنوي طولا وعرضا والأكثر على الأول بحر لكن وفق في الحلية بأنه يستاك عرضا في الأسنان وطولا في اللسان جمعا بين الأحاديث ثم نقل عن الغزنوي أنه يستاك بالمداراة خارج الأسنان وداخلها أعلاها وأسفلها ورؤوس الأضراس وبين كل سنين (رد المختار ١/١١٤)

وعند فقده أو فقد أسنانه تقوم الخرقة الخشنة أو الأصبع مقامه

قال العلامة ابن عابدين رحمه الله (قوله أو الأصبع) قال في الحلية ثم بأي أصبع استاك لا بأس به والأفضل أن يستاك بالسبابتين يبدأ بالسبابة اليسرى ثم باليمنى وإن شاء استاك بإبهامه اليمنى والسبابة اليمنى يبدأ بالإبهام من الجانب الأيمن فوق وتحت ثم بالسبابة من الأيسر كذلك (رد المختار ١/١١٥)

[57] قال الحاكم: هذا حديث صحيح على شرط مسلم ولم يخرجاه وأقره الذهبي وقال على شرط مسلم

عن أنس رضي الله عنه قال قال رسول الله صلى الله عليه وسلم يجزئ من السواك الأصابع (التلخيص الحبير ١/١٠٤)[58]

Hazrat Anas رَضِيَٱللَّهُعَنْهُ *reports that Hazrat Rasulullah* صَلَّىٱللَّهُعَلَيْهِوَسَلَّمَ *said,
"The finger can be used as a substitute in the absence of a miswaak."*

6. Gargle the mouth thrice by taking three handfuls of water with the right hand. Gargle thoroughly, allowing the water to reach all the parts of the mouth.[59]

عن وهيب عن عمرو عن أبيه شهدت عمرو بن أبي حسن سأل عبد الله بن زيد رضي الله عنه عن وضوء النبي صلى الله عليه وسلم فدعا بتور من ماء فتوضأ لهم وضوء النبي

---

[58] ومنها حديث (يجزي من السواك الأصابع) رواه ابن عدي والدارقطني والبيهقي من حديث عبد الله بن المثنى عن النضر بن أنس عن أنس وفي إسناده نظر وقال الضياء المقدسي لا أرى بسنده بأسا وقال البيهقي المحفوظ عن ابن المثنى عن بعض أهل بيته عن أنس نحوه ورواه أيضا من طريق ابن المثنى عن ثمامة عن أنس ورواه أبو نعيم والطبراني وابن عدي من حديث عائشة وفيه المثنى بن الصباح ورواه أبو نعيم من حديث كثير بن عبد الله بن عمرو بن عوف عن جده عن أبيه ضعفوه وكثير من ذلك ما رواه أحمد في مسنده من حديث علي بن أبي طالب أنه دعا بكوز من ماء فغسل وجهه وكفيه ثلاثا وتمضمض فأدخل بعض أصابعه في فيه الحديث وفي آخره هذا وضوء رسول الله صلى الله عليه وسلم وروى أبو عبيد في كتاب الطهور عن عثمان أنه كان إذا توضأ يسوك فاه بإصبعه وروى الطبراني في الأوسط من حديث عائشة قلت يا رسول الله الرجل يذهب فوه أيستاك قال نعم قلت كيف يصنع قال يدخل أصبعه في فيه رواه من طريق الوليد بن مسلم ثنا عيسى بن عبد الله الأنصاري عن عطاء عنها وقال لا يروى إلا بهذا الإسناد قلت عيسى ضعفه ابن حبان وذكر له ابن عدي هذا الحديث من مناكيره (التلخيص الحبير ١/١٠٤)

قوله روى أن النبي صلى الله عليه وسلم كان عند السواك يعالج بالإصبع لم أجده من فعله وإنما جاء من قوله فأخرج البيهقي عن أنس مرفوعا يجزيء من السواك الأصابع وذكره من طرق ووهاها وقد صحح بعض طرقه أيضا وروى الطبراني في الأوسط عن عائشة قلت يا رسول الله الرجل يذهب فوه أيستاك قال نعم قلت فكيف يصنع قال يدخل إصبعه في فيه وإسناده ضعيف (الدراية في تخريج أحاديث الهداية ص ١٨)

[59] (وغسل الفم) أي استيعابه ولذا عبر بالغسل أو للاختصار (بمياه) ثلاثة (والأنف) ببلوغ الماء المارن (بمياه) وهما سنتان مؤكدتان مشتملتان على سنن خمس الترتيب والتثليث وتجديد الماء وفعلهما باليمنى

قال العلامة ابن عابدين رحمه الله (قوله بمياه) إنما قال بمياه ولم يقل ثلاثا ليدل على أن المسنون التثليث بمياه جديدة أفاده في المنح ط قوله (وتجديد الماء) أي أخذه ماء جديدا في كل مرة فيهما قوله (وفعلهما باليمنى) أي ويمخط ويستنثر باليسرى كما في المنية والمعراج (رد المحتار ١/١١٦)

صلى الله عليه وسلم فأكفأ على يده من التور فغسل يديه ثلاثا ثم أدخل يديه في التور

فمضمض واستنشق واستنثر ثلاث غرفات (صحيح البخاري، الرقم: ١٨٦)

Hazrat Abdullah bin Zaid رَضِيَٱللَّهُعَنْهُ *was asked regarding the wudhu of Hazrat Rasulullah* صَلَّىٱللَّهُعَلَيْهِوَسَلَّمَ*. Hence, he requested that a utensil of water be brought. He then demonstrated to them the manner in which Hazrat Rasulullah* صَلَّىٱللَّهُعَلَيْهِوَسَلَّمَ *used to perform wudhu. He poured water onto his hands from the utensil and then washed his hands (till the wrists) thrice. Thereafter, he inserted his hands in the utensil and (took water and) gargled his mouth and rinsed his nose thrice.*

7. Insert water into the nostrils with the right hand thrice, and if there is a need to clean the nose, do so with the left hand.[60]

عن أبي هريرة رضي الله عنه أن رسول الله صلى الله عليه وسلم قال إذا توضأ أحدكم

فليستنشق بمنخريه من الماء ثم لينتثر (صحيح مسلم، الرقم: ٢٣٧)

---

[60] وعن عائشة رضي الله عنها قالت كانت يد رسول الله صلى الله عليه وسلم اليمنى لطهوره وطعامه وكانت يده اليسرى لخلائه وما كان من أذى (سنن أبي داود، الرقم: ٣٣)

عن أبي حية قال رأيت عليا توضأ فغسل كفيه حتى أنقاهما ثم مضمض واستنشق ثلاثا وغسل وجهه ثلاثا وذراعيه ثلاثا ومسح برأسه مرة ثم غسل قدميه إلى الكعبين ثم قام فأخذ فضل طهوره فشربه وهو قائم ثم قال أحببت أن أريكم كيف كان طهور رسول الله صلى الله عليه وسلم (سنن الترمذي، الرقم: ٤٨)

(و) يسن (المبالغة في المضمضة) وهي إيصال الماء لرأس الحلق (و) المبالغة في (الاستنشاق) وهي إيصاله إلى ما فوق المارن (لغير الصائم) والصائم لا يبالغ فيها خشية إفساد الصوم لقوله عليه الصلاة والسلام بالغ في المضمضة والاستنشاق إلا أن تكون صائما

قال العلامة الطحطاوي رحمه الله (قوله وهي إيصال الماء لرأس الحلق الخ) ... وفي الاستنشاق أن يجذب الماء بنفسه إلى ما اشتد من أنفه اه قال في البحر وهو الأولى والاستنثار مطلوب والإجماع على عدم وجوبه والمستحب أن يستنثر بيده اليسرى ويكره بغير يد لأنه يشبه فعل الدابة وقيل لا يكره ذكره البدر العيني والأولى أن يدخل أصبعه في فمه وأنفه قهستاني (حاشية الطحطاوي على مراقي الفلاح صـ ٧٠)

(و) كون (المضمضة والاستنشاق باليد اليمنى) لشرفها (والامتخاط باليسرى) لامتهانها (حاشية الطحطاوي على مراقي الفلاح صـ ٧٦)

(ويستنثر ما فيها) أي في الأنف بقوة النفس بيده اليسرى فإن كان بباطنها شيء من الوسخ استعان بخنصر يده فأزال ما فيها (إتحاف السادة المتقين ٢/٣٥٥)

Hazrat Abu Hurairah رَضِيَٱللّٰهُعَنْهُ *reports that Hazrat Rasulullah* صَلَّىٱللّٰهُعَلَيْهِوَسَلَّمَ *said, "When any one of you performs wudhu then he should insert water into the nostrils and thereafter clean the nose (with the left hand)."*

8. When fasting, exercise caution in gargling the mouth and rinsing the nose. Do not exert yourself in doing so, as water may go down the throat or nasal passage, thus causing the fast to break.[See 60]

عن لقيط بن سمرة رضي الله عنه قلت يا رسول الله صلى الله عليه وسلم أخبرني عن الوضوء قال أسبغ الوضوء وخلل بين الأصابع وبالغ فى الاستنشاق إلا أن تكون صائما

(سنن الترمذي، الرقم: ٧٨٨)[61]

Hazrat Laqeet bin Samurah رَضِيَٱللّٰهُعَنْهُ *reports, "I once asked Rasulullah* صَلَّىٱللّٰهُعَلَيْهِوَسَلَّمَ *regarding wudhu. Hazrat Rasulullah* صَلَّىٱللّٰهُعَلَيْهِوَسَلَّمَ *said, 'Perform a complete and perfect wudhu, ensure that you make khilaal of the fingers and rinse the nose thoroughly, except in the case where you are fasting.'"*

9. Recite the following dua at any time during the wudhu or after the wudhu:[62]

اَللّٰهُمَّ اغْفِرْ لِيْ ذَنْبِيْ وَوَسِّعْ لِيْ فِيْ دَارِيْ وَبَارِكْ لِيْ فِيْ رِزْقِيْ

---

[61] قال أبو عيسى: هذا حديث حسن صحيح

سنن أبي داود، الرقم: ١٤٢

[62] قال النووي في الأذكار (الرقم: ٧٨): ترجم ابن السني لهذا الحديث باب ما يقول بين ظهراني وضوئه وأما النسائي فأدخله في باب ما يقول بعد فراغه من وضوئه وكلاهما محتمل

O Allah تَبَارَكَ وَتَعَالَى, forgive my sins, grant me spaciousness in my home and bless me with barakah in my sustenance.

عن أبي موسى الأشعري رضي الله عنه قال أتيت رسول الله صلى الله عليه وسلم بوَضوء فتوضأ فسمعته يدعو ويقول اللهم اغفر لي ذني ووسع لي في داري وبارك لي في رزقي فقلت يا نبي الله سمعتك تدعو بكذا وكذا قال وهل تركن من شيء (الأذكار للإمام النووي، الرقم: ٧٨)[63]

Hazrat Abu Moosa Ash'ari رَضِيَ اللَّهُ عَنْهُ reports, "I brought water to Rasulullah صَلَّى اللَّهُ عَلَيْهِ وَسَلَّمَ to perform wudhu. He performed wudhu and I heard him recite the dua اَللّٰهُمَّ اغْفِرْ لِيْ ذَنْبِيْ وَوَسِّعْ لِيْ فِيْ دَارِيْ وَبَارِكْ لِيْ فِيْ رِزْقِيْ. *I then asked him, 'O Nabi of Allah صَلَّى اللَّهُ عَلَيْهِ وَسَلَّمَ! While you were making wudhu, I heard you reciting the dua:* اَللّٰهُمَّ اغْفِرْ لِيْ ذَنْبِيْ وَوَسِّعْ لِيْ فِيْ دَارِيْ وَبَارِكْ لِيْ فِيْ رِزْقِيْ.' *Hazrat Rasulullah صَلَّى اللَّهُ عَلَيْهِ وَسَلَّمَ replied, 'Has this dua left out any goodness? (It has encompassed all the bounties and favours of Allah تَبَارَكَ وَتَعَالَى within it)'"*

10. Wash the face thrice. The procedure of washing the face is to take water in both hands and pass it gently over the face. It is makrooh to splash the water on the face. The face has to be washed from the top of the forehead to beneath the chin and from one ear till the other. Ensure that water reaches all

---

[63] وقد روى النسائي وابن السني في كتابيهما عمل اليوم والليلة بإسناد صحيح عن أبي موسى الأشعري رضي الله عنه قال أتيت رسول الله صلى الله عليه وسلم بوضوء فتوضأ فسمعته يدعو يقول اللهم اغفرلي ذني ووسع لي في داري وبارك لي في رزقي فقلت يا نبي الله سمعتك تدعو بكذا وكذا قال وهل تركن من شيئ ترجم ابن السني به باب ما يقول بين ما طهر إلى وضوئه فأدخله في باب ما يقوله أما النسائي بعد فراغه من وضوئه وكلاهما محتمل كذا في الأذكار (غنية المتملي ص ٣٢)

parts of the face, including the corner of the eyes and the skin between the earlobes and sideburns.[64]

عن عبد الله بن زيد بن عاصم المازني ثم الأنصاري رضي الله عنه أنه رأى رسول الله صلى الله عليه وسلم توضأ... ثم غسل وجهه ثلاثا (صحيح مسلم، الرقم: ٢٣٦)

Hazrat Abdullah bin Zaid bin Aasim رَضِيَٱللَّهُعَنْهُ *reports that he saw Hazrat Rasulullah* صَلَّىٱللَّهُعَلَيْهِوَسَلَّمَ *perform wudhu... (while Hazrat Rasulullah* صَلَّىٱللَّهُعَلَيْهِوَسَلَّمَ *was performing wudhu,) he then washed his face thrice.*

11. Make khilaal of the beard. Khilaal of the beard should be made by passing wet fingers through the beard from the

---

bottom (from beneath the chin). Khilaal is sunnah for the one whose beard is thick due to which the skin beneath the hair is not visible. If the beard is thin and the skin beneath the hair is visible, then in this case, khilaal of the beard will not be made. Instead, when washing the face, it will be necessary to make the water reach the skin of the face.[65]

عن أنس بن مالك رضي الله عنه أن رسول الله صلى الله عليه وسلم كان إذا توضأ أخذ كفا من ماء فأدخله تحت حنكه فخلل به لحيته وقال هكذا أمرني ربي (سنن أبي داود، الرقم: ١٤٥)[66]

Hazrat Anas رَضِيَٱللَّهُعَنْهُ *reports that when Hazrat Rasulullah* صَلَّىٱللَّهُعَلَيْهِوَسَلَّمَ *would make wudhu, he would take a handful of water and place it under his chin to make khilaal of his beard, and Hazrat Rasulullah* صَلَّىٱللَّهُعَلَيْهِوَسَلَّمَ *said, "My Rabb has commanded me (to make khilaal of the beard) in this manner."*

12. Take water in both the palms and wash the right arm including the elbow thrice. Thereafter, take water in both the palms and wash the left arm including the elbow thrice. It is

---

[65] (وتخليل اللحية) لغير المحرم بعد التثليث ويجعل ظهر كفه إلى عنقه

قال العلامة ابن عابدين رحمه الله (قوله وتخليل اللحية) هو تفريق شعرها من أسفل إلى فوق بحر وهو سنة عند أبي يوسف وأبو حنيفة ومحمد يفضلانه ورجح في المبسوط قول أبي يوسف كما في البرهان شرنبلالية وفي شرح المنية والأدلة ترجحه وهو الصحيح اه قال في الحلية والظاهر أن هذا كله في الكثة أما الخفيفة فيجب إيصال الماء إلى ما تحتها اه وجزم به الشرنبلالي في متنه بقوله (لغير المحرم) أما المحرم فمكروه نهر قوله (بعد التثليث) أي تثليث غسل الوجه إمداد ... ثم اعلم أن هذا التخليل باليد اليمنى كما صرح به في الحلية وهو ظاهر (رد المحتار ١١٧/١)

[66] سكت عنه ثم المنذري بعده (مختصر سنن أبي داود ٨٥/١)

سكت الحافظ عن هذا الحديث في الفصل الثاني من هداية الرواة (٢٢١/١) فالحديث حسن عنده

عن عثمان بن عفان رضي الله عنه أن النبي صلى الله عليه وسلم كان يخلل لحيته قال أبو عيسى هذا حديث حسن صحيح (سنن الترمذي، الرقم: ٣١)

sunnah to commence the washing of the arms from the fingers going up to the elbows. If one washes the arms from the elbows going down towards the fingers, the washing will be valid, however this is against the sunnah method of washing the arms.[67]

عن عبد الله بن زيد بن عاصم المازني ثم الأنصاري رضي الله عنه أنه رأى رسول الله صلى الله عليه وسلم توضأ ... ثم غسل وجهه ثلاثا ويده اليمنى ثلاثا والأخرى ثلاثا (صحيح مسلم، الرقم: ٢٣٦)

Hazrat Abdullah bin Zaid bin Aasim رضى ٱللَّهُ عَنْهُ reports that he saw Hazrat Rasulullah صَلَّى ٱللَّهُ عَلَيْهِ وَسَلَّمَ perform wudhu ... (While performing wudhu,) Hazrat Rasulullah صَلَّى ٱللَّهُ عَلَيْهِ وَسَلَّمَ then washed his face thrice. Thereafter, he washed his right arm thrice and then his left arm thrice.

13. Make khilaal of the fingers. Khilaal of the right hand will be made before the left hand. Khilaal will be made by placing the left hand above the right hand and passing the fingers of the left hand through the fingers of the right hand, and thereafter placing the right hand above the left hand and passing the fingers of the right hand through the fingers of

---

the left hand. Khilaal can also be made through intertwining the fingers of the right hand with the fingers of the left hand.[68]

عن عاصم بن لقيط بن صبرة عن أبيه رضي الله عنه قال قال النبي صلى الله عليه وسلم إذا توضأت فخلل الأصابع (سنن الترمذي، الرقم: ٣٨)[69]

Hazrat Laqeet bin Sabirah رَضِىَٱللَّهُعَنْهُ *reports that Hazrat Rasulullah* صَلَّىٱللَّهُعَلَيْهِوَسَلَّمَ *said, "When you perform wudhu, ensure that you make khilaal of the fingers."*

14. Make masah of the entire head once. The method of masah is for one to take both his hands and pass them over the entire head, commencing from the front and moving towards the back of the head.[70]

---

[68] الفصل الثاني في سنن الوضوء ... ومنها تخليل الأصابع وهو إدخال بعضها في بعض بماء متقاطر وهذا سنة مؤكدة اتفاقا كذا في النهر الفائق هذا إذا وصل الماء إلى أثنائها وإن لم يصل بأن كانت منضمة فواجب كذا في التبيين ويغني عنه إدخالها في الماء ولو غير جار والأولى في اليدين التشبيك وفي الرجلين أن يخلل بخنصر يده اليسرى خنصر رجله اليمنى ويختم بخنصر رجله اليسرى كذا في النهر الفائق ويدخل الإصبع من أسفل كذا في المضمرات (الفتاوى الهندية ١/ ٧)

الفصل الثالث في المستحبات والمذكور منها في المتون اثنان الأول التيامن وهو أن يبدأ باليد اليمنى قبل اليسرى وبالرجل اليمنى قبل اليسرى وهو فضيلة على الصحيح وليس في أعضاء الطهارة عضوان لا يستحب تقديم الأيمن منهما على الأيسر إلا الأذنان ولو لم يكن له إلا يد واحدة أو بإحدى يديه علة ولا يمكنه مسحهما معا يبدأ بالأذن اليمنى ثم باليسرى كذا في الجوهرة النيرة (الفتاوى الهندية ١/ ٨)

[69] قال أبو عيسى: هذا حديث حسن صحيح

[70] (ومسح كل رأسه مرة) مستوعبة فلو ترك وداوم عليه أثم (وأذنيه) معا ولو (بمائه)

قال العلامة ابن عابدين رحمه الله (قوله مستوعبة) هذا سنة أيضا كما جزم به في الفتح ثم نقل عن القنية أنه إذا داوم على ترك الاستيعاب بلا عذر يأثم قال وكأنه لظهور رغبته عن السنة قال الزيلعي وتكلموا في كيفية المسح والأظهر أن يضع كفيه وأصابعه على مقدم رأسه ويمدهما إلى القفا على وجه يستوعب جميع الرأس ثم يمسح أذنيه بأصبعيه اه وما قيل من أنه يجافي المسبحتين والإبهامين ليمسح بهما الأذنين والكفين ليمسح بهما جانبي الرأس خشية الاستعمال فقال في الفتح لا أصل له في السنة لأن الاستعمال لا يثبت قبل الانفصال والأذنان من الرأس (رد المختار ١/ ١٢١)

عن سلمة بن الأكوع رضي الله عنه قال رأيت رسول الله صلى الله عليه وسلم توضأ فمسح رأسه مرة (سنن ابن ماجة، الرقم: ٤٣٧)[71]

Hazrat Salamah bin Akwa' ﷺ *reports, "I saw Hazrat Rasulullah* ﷺ *performing wudhu. (While performing wudhu, I saw that) he made masah of his head once."*

15. Make masah of the ears. When making masah, use the index finger to make masah of the internal portion of the ear and the thumb to make masah of the external portion of the ear (behind the ear). Thereafter, insert the small finger or index finger into the ears.[72]

---

[71] قال البوصيري في الزوائد (١٥٠/١): إسناد حديث سلمة ضعيف محمد بن الحارث ذكره ابن حبان في الثقات وقال يخطئ ويحيى بن راشد ضعيف

لهذا الحديث شاهد من حديث أبي حية قال رأيت عليا توضأ فغسل كفيه حتى أنقاها ثم مضمض ثلاثا واستنشق ثلاثا وغسل وجهه ثلاثا وذراعيه ثلاثا ومسح برأسه مرة ثم غسل قدميه إلى الكعبين ثم قام فأخذ فضل طهوره وهو قائم فشربه قال أحببت أن أريكم كيف كان طهور رسول الله صلى الله عليه وسلم (سنن الترمذي، الرقم: ٤٨)

[72] (ومسح كل رأسه مرة) مستوعبة فلو تركه وداوم عليه أثم (وأذنيه) معا ولو (بمائه) (الدر المختار ١٢٠/١)

قال العلامة ابن عابدين رحمه الله (قوله وأذنيه) أي باطنهما بباطن السبابتين وظاهرهما بباطن الإبهامين قهستاني قوله (معا) أي فلا تيامن فيهما كما سيذكره (رد المحتار ١٢١/١)

حدثنا محمود بن خالد ويعقوب بن كعب الأنطاكي لفظه قالا حدثنا الوليد بن مسلم عن حريز بن عثمان عن عبد الرحمن بن ميسرة عن المقدام بن معديكرب قال رأيت رسول الله صلى الله عليه وسلم توضأ فلما بلغ مسح رأسه وضع كفيه على مقدم رأسه فأمرهما حتى بلغ القفا ثم ردها إلى المكان الذى بدأ منه قال محمود قال أخبرني حريز

حدثنا محمود بن خالد وهشام بن خالد المعنى قالا حدثنا الوليد بهذا الإسناد قال ومسح بأذنيه ظاهرهما وباطنهما زاد هشام وأدخل أصابعه في صماخ أذنيه (سنن أبي داود، الرقم: ١٢٢-١٢٣)

ومن الأدب ذلك أعضائه وإدخال خنصره صماخي أذنيه (الفتاوى الهندية ٩/١)

(قوله ومسح الأذنين) هو سنة مؤكدة ويمسح باطنهما وظاهرهما وهو أن يدخل سبابتيه في صماخيه وهما ثقبا الأذنين ويديرهما في زوايا أذنيه ويدير إبهاميه على ظاهر أذنيه (الجوهرة النيرة ٦/١)

عن عمرو بن شعيب عن أبيه عن جده (أي عبد الله بن عمرو بن العاص) رضي الله

عنهما قال إن رجلا أتى النبي صلى الله عليه وسلم فقال يا رسول الله كيف الطهور

فدعا بماء في إناء ... ثم مسح برأسه وأدخل إصبعيه في أذنيه ومسح بإبهاميه على

ظاهر أذنيه وبالسباحتين باطن أذنيه (سنن أبي داود، الرقم: ١٣٥)[73]

Hazrat Abdullah bin Amr bin Aas رَضِيَٱللَّهُعَنْهُا *reports that a person
once came to Hazrat Rasulullah* صَلَّىٱللَّهُعَلَيْهِوَسَلَّمَ *and asked, "O
Rasulullah* صَلَّىٱللَّهُعَلَيْهِوَسَلَّمَ*! How should one perform wudhu?" Hazrat
Rasulullah* صَلَّىٱللَّهُعَلَيْهِوَسَلَّمَ *requested for some water to be brought in a
utensil ... (Hazrat Rasulullah* صَلَّىٱللَّهُعَلَيْهِوَسَلَّمَ *then began to demonstrate
the method of performing wudhu until) he thereafter made masah
of his head and placed his fingers in his ears, making masah of the
outer portion of the ears with his thumbs and the inner portion of
the ears with his index fingers.*

16. Make masah of the nape (the back of the neck) using the back
of the fingers. Masah will not be made on the throat.[74]

---

[73] قال الشيخ تقي الدين في الإمام: وهذا الحديث صحيح عند من يصحح حديث عمرو بن شعيب عن أبيه عن جده لصحة الإسناد إلى عمرو انتهى (نصب الراية، الرقم: ١٤٠)

أخرجه الأربعة إلا الترمذي وإسناده قوي (الدراية، الرقم: ١٠)

[74] (و) يسن (مسح الرقبة) لأنه صلى الله عليه وسلم توضأ وأومأ بيديه من مقدم رأسه حتى بلغ بهما أسفل عنقه من قبل قفاه و (لا) يسن مسح (الحلقوم) بل هو بدعة (حاشية الطحطاوي على مراقي الفلاح صـ ٧٤)

الفصل الثالث في المستحبات والمذكور منها في المتون اثنان الأول التيامن وهو أن يبدأ باليد اليمنى قبل اليسرى وبالرجل اليمنى قبل اليسرى وهو فضيلة على الصحيح وليس في أعضاء الطهارة عضو لا يستحب تقديم الأيمن منهما على الأيسر إلا الاذنان ولو لم يكن له إلا يد واحدة أو بإحدى يديه علة ولا يمكنه مسحهما معا يبدأ بالاذن اليمنى ثم باليسرى كذا في الجوهرة النيرة وهو مسح الرقبة والثاني مسح بظهر اليدين (الفتاوى الهندية ١/٨)

(ومستحبه) ويسمى مندوبا وأدبا وفضيلة وهو ما فعله النبي صلى الله عليه وسلم مرة وتركه أخرى وما أحبه السلف (التيامن) ... (ومسح الرقبة) بظهر يديه (لا الحلقوم) لأنه بدعة

عن ابن عمر رضي الله عنهما أن النبي صلى الله عليه وسلم قال من توضأ ومسح

بيديه على عنقه وقي الغل يوم القيامة (التلخيص الحبير ١٣٦/١) ⁷⁵

Hazrat Abdullah bin Umar رَضِيَٱللَّهُعَنْهُ *narrates that Hazrat Rasulullah* صَلَّىٱللَّهُعَلَيْهِوَسَلَّمَ *said, "Whoever performs wudhu and makes masah on his nape, he will be saved from wearing a necklace (of fire) around his neck on the Day of Judgement."*

17. Wash the feet including the ankles thrice. It is mustahab to commence washing the feet from the toes towards the ankles.^{See 67}

عن حمران مولى عثمان أن عثمان بن عفان رضي الله عنه دعا بوضوء فتوضأ ... ثم

غسل رجله اليمنى إلى الكعبين ثلاث مرات ثم غسل اليسرى مثل ذلك ثم قال رأيت

رسول الله صلى الله عليه وسلم توضأ نحو وضوئي هذا (صحيح مسلم، الرقم: ٢٢٦)

Hazrat Humraan رَحِمَهُٱللَّهُ, *the freed slave of Hazrat Uthmaan* رَضِيَٱللَّهُعَنْهُ, *reports that Hazrat Uthmaan* رَضِيَٱللَّهُعَنْهُ *requested for some water to perform wudhu ... (He then commenced performing wudhu until) he washed his right foot until the ankles thrice, followed by the left*

قال العلامة ابن عابدين رحمه الله (قوله ومسح الرقبة) هو الصحيح وقيل إنه سنة كما في البحر وغيره قوله (بظهر يديه) أي لعدم استعمال

بلتهما بحر فقول المنية بماء جديد لا حاجة إليه كما في شرحها الكبير وعبر في المنية بظهر الأصابع ولعله المراد هنا قوله (لأنه بدعة) إذ لم يرد في

السنة (رد المحتار ١٢٤/١)

⁷⁵ حديث ابن عمر أن النبي صلى الله عليه وسلم قال (من توضأ ومسح عنقه وقي الغل يوم القيامة) قال أبو نعيم في تاريخ أصبهان ثنا محمد

بن أحمد ثنا عبد الرحمن بن داود ثنا عثمان بن خرزاد ثنا عمر بن محمد بن الحسن ثنا محمد بن عمرو الأنصاري عن أنس بن سيرين عن ابن

عمر أنه كان إذا توضأ مسح عنقه ويقول قال رسول الله صلى الله عليه وسلم من توضأ ومسح عنقه لم يغل بالأغلال يوم القيامة وفي البحر

للروياني لم يذكر الشافعي مسح العنق وقال أصحابنا هو سنة وأنا قرأت جزءا رواه أبو الحسين بن فارس بإسناده عن فليح بن سليمان عن نافع

عن ابن عمر أن النبي صلى الله عليه وسلم قال من توضأ ومسح بيديه على عنقه وقي الغل يوم القيامة وقال هذا إن شاء الله حديث صحيح

قلت بين ابن فارس وفليح مفازة فينظر فيها (التلخيص الحبير ١٣٦/١)

foot in a similar manner. He then mentioned, "I saw Hazrat Rasulullah ﷺ perform wudhu in the manner I performed wudhu."

18. Make khilaal of the toes using the small finger of the left hand. Commence with the small toe of the right foot and end with the small toe of the left foot.[76]

عن المستورد بن شداد رضي الله عنه قال رأيت النبي صلى الله عليه وسلم إذا توضأ دلك أصابع رجليه بخنصره (سنن الترمذي، الرقم: ٤٠)[77]

---

[76] (و) تخليل (الأصابع) اليدين بالتشبيك والرجلين بخنصر يده اليسرى بادئا بخنصر رجله اليمنى وهذا بعد دخول الماء خلالها فلو منضمة فرض قال العلامة ابن عابدين رحمه الله (قوله والرجلين الخ) ذكر هذه الكيفية في المعراج وغيره وقال بذلك ورد الخبر وكذا ذكرها القدوري مروية مع تقييد التخليل بكونه من أسفل وتعقب في الفتح ورود هذه الكيفية بقوله والله أعلم به ومثله فيما يظهر أمر اتفاقي لا سنة مقصودة قال تلميذه ابن أمير حاج الحلبي في الحلية شرح المنية لكن الذي في سنن ابن ماجه عن المستورد بن شداد قال رأيت رسول الله صلى الله عليه وسلم توضأ فخلل أصابع رجليه بخنصره وأما كونه بخنصر يده اليسرى وكونه من أسفل فالله أعلم به ويشكل كونه بخنصر اليسرى أنه من الطهارة والمستحب في فعلها اليمين ولعل الحكمة في كونه بالخنصر كونها أدق الأصابع فهي بالتخليل أنسب وفي كونه من أسفل أنه أبلغ في إيصال الماء اه ثم نقل ندب هذه الكيفية عن الشافعي قلت ويجاب عن قوله ويشكله الخ بأن الرجلين محل الوسخ والقذر ولذا سيذكر الشارح أن من الآداب غسلهما باليسار (رد المحتار ١١٧/١)

انظر أيضا 68

[77] وقال الترمذي رحمه الله: هذا حديث حسن غريب لا نعرفه إلا من حديث ابن لهيعة

وعن المستورد بضم الميم وسكون السين وفتح التاء فوقها نقطتان وبكسر الراء وبالدال المهملة كذا في جامع الأصول قال في التقريب له ولأبيه صحبة قال الطيبي قرشي من بني محارب بن فهر عداده في أهل الكوفة ثم سكن مصر ويعد فيهم يقال إنه كان غلاما يوم قبض رسول الله إلا أنه سمع منه ووعى عنه زاد المصنف وقال وروى (المستورد) عنه (عن النبي صلى الله علي وسلم) وروى عنه (المستورد) جماعة قال رأيت رسول الله إذا توضأ يدلك أصابع رجليه أي يخلل كما في رواية أحمد في مسنده بخنصره كما تقدم قال الأبهري لأنه أصغر والخدمة بالصغار أليق والدخول في الخلال أيسر وقال ابن حجر إن أراد المستورد بالدلك التخليل فهو حجة لما مر من ندبه بالخنصر وخصت اليسرى بذلك لأنها أليق به إذ لا تكرمة في ذلك بالنسبة للرجلين (مرقاة المفاتيح ١١٦/٢)

(بخنصره) أي بخنصر يده اليسرى قوله (هذا حديث غريب لا نعرفه إلا من حديث ابن لهيعة) غرابة هذا الحديث والذي قبله ترجع إلى الإسناد فلا ينافي قوله الحسن قاله ابن سيد الناس وقد شارك ابن لهيعة في روايته عن يزيد بن عمرو الليث وعمرو بن الحارث فالحديث إذن صحيح سالم عن الغرابة كذا في النيل (تحفة الأحوذي ١٢٥/١)

Hazrat Mustawrid bin Shaddaad رَضِيَ اللهُ عَنْهُ reports, "I saw Hazrat Rasulullah صَلَّى اللهُ عَلَيْهِ وَسَلَّمَ making khilaal of his toes with the small finger (of his left hand) whilst making wudhu."

19. Upon completing the wudhu, recite the shahaadah. If you are in an open place, look towards the sky when reciting the shahaadah.[78] Similarly, recite the other masnoon duas which are reported in the Hadith.

Below are some of the various masnoon duas which are reported in the Hadith to be recited upon the completion of wudhu:

Dua One:

The one who recites the following dua, the eight doors of Jannah are opened for him and he may enter from whichever door he wishes:[79]

أَشْهَدُ أَنْ لَّا إِلٰهَ إِلَّا اللهُ وَحْدَهُ لَا شَرِيْكَ لَهُ وَأَشْهَدُ أَنَّ مُحَمَّدًا عَبْدُهُ وَرَسُوْلُهُ اَللّٰهُمَّ اجْعَلْنِيْ مِنَ التَّوَّابِيْنَ وَاجْعَلْنِيْ مِنَ الْمُتَطَهِّرِيْنَ

---

[78] عن عقبة بن عامر رضي الله عنه يقول قال رسول الله صلى الله عليه وسلم من توضأ فأحسن الوضوء ثم رفع نظره إلى السماء فقال أشهد أن لا إله إلا الله وحده لا شريك له وأن محمدا عبده ورسوله فتحت له ثمانية أبواب من الجنة يدخل من أيها شاء (مسند أحمد، الرقم: ١٧٣٦٥)

[79] عن عمر بن الخطاب رضي الله عنه قال قال رسول الله صلى الله عليه وسلم من توضأ فأحسن الوضوء ثم قال أشهد أن لا إله إلا الله وحده لا شريك له وأشهد أن محمدا عبده ورسوله اللهم اجعلني من التوابين واجعلني من المتطهرين فتحت له ثمانية أبواب الجنة يدخل من أيها شاء (سنن الترمذي، الرقم: ٥٥)

انظر أيضا: صحيح مسلم، الرقم: ٢٣٤ ، مجمع الزوائد، الرقم: ١٢٢٩، ١٢٣٠

I testify that there is no deity besides Allah تَبَارَكَوَتَعَالَى *who is alone and has no partner, and I testify that Hazrat Muhammad* صَلَّىٱللَّهُعَلَيْهِوَسَلَّمَ *is His servant and messenger. O Allah* تَبَارَكَوَتَعَالَى*, include me from among those who constantly repent and among those who are extremely pure.*

Dua Two:

The one who recites the following dua, the reward of the dua will be recorded for him on a scroll which will be kept sealed until the Day of Qiyaamah:[80]

سُبْحَانَكَ اللَّهُمَّ وَبِحَمْدِكَ أَشْهَدُ أَنْ لَّا إِلَهَ إِلَّا أَنْتَ أَسْتَغْفِرُكَ وَأَتُوْبُ إِلَيْكَ

Glory and praise be for You O Allah تَبَارَكَوَتَعَالَى*. I testify that there is none worthy of worship besides You. I seek Your forgiveness and I repent to You.*

20. Make wudhu in sequence.[81]

21. Wash the right limbs before the left limbs.[82]

---

[80] عن أبي سعيد الخدري رضي الله عنه قال قال رسول الله صلى الله عليه وسلم من قرأ سورة الكهف كانت له نورا يوم القيامة من مقامه إلى مكة ومن قرأ عشر آيات من آخرها ثم خرج الدجال لم يضره ومن توضأ فقال سبحانك اللهم وبحمدك لا إله إلا أنت أستغفرك وأتوب إليك كتب في رق ثم جعل في طابع فلم يكسر إلى يوم القيامة رواه الطبراني في الأوسط ورجاله رجال الصحيح إلا أن النسائي قال بعد تخرجه في اليوم والليلة هذا خطأ والصواب موقوفا ثم رواه من رواية الثوري وغندر عن شعبة موقوفا (مجمع الزوائد، الرقم: ١٢٣١)

[81] (و) يسن (الترتيب) سنة مؤكدة في الصحيح وهو (كما نص الله في كتابه) (حاشية الطحطاوي على مراقي الفلاح صـ ٧٣)

[82] الفصل الثالث في المستحبات والمذكور منها في المتون اثنان الأول التيامن وهو أن يبدأ باليد اليمنى قبل اليسرى وبالرجل اليمنى قبل اليسرى وهو فضيلة على الصحيح وليس في أعضاء الطهارة عضوان لا يستحب تقديم الأيمن منهما على الأيسر إلا الأذنان ولو لم يكن له إلا يد واحدة أو بإحدى يديه علة ولا يمكنه مسحهما معا يبدأ بالأذن اليمنى ثم باليسرى كذا في الجوهرة النيرة (الفتاوى الهندية ١/٨)

عن أبي هريرة قال قال رسول الله صلى الله عليه وسلم إذا لبستم وإذا توضأتم فابدءوا
بأيامنكم (سنن أبي داود، الرقم: ٤١٤١)[83]

Hazrat Abu Hurairah رَضِيَٱللَّهُعَنْهُ reports that Hazrat Rasulullah صَلَّىٱللَّهُعَلَيْهِوَسَلَّمَ said, "When you wear a garment and when you perform wudhu, then commence from your right limbs".

عن عائشة رضي الله عنها قالت كان النبي صلى الله عليه وسلم ليعجبه التيمن فى تنعله
وترجله وطهوره وفي شأنه كله (صحيح البخاري، الرقم: ١٦٨)[84]

Hazrat Aaishah رَضِيَٱللَّهُعَنْهَا reports that Hazrat Rasulullah صَلَّىٱللَّهُعَلَيْهِوَسَلَّمَ would like commencing from the right side when wearing his shoes, combing his hair, performing wudhu and when carrying out all other works (i.e. all other noble works which require respect being shown to the right side e.g. entering the musjid and Ka'bah with the right foot, commencing from the right when wearing clothing, using the right hand to receive or give an item, etc.).

22. Rub each limb thoroughly when washing it to ensure that water reaches each part of the limb.[85]

---

[83] عن أبي هريرة رضي الله عنه عن رسول الله صلى الله عليه وسلم قال إذا لبستم وإذا توضأتم فابدءوا بأيامنكم حديث حسن رواه أبو داود والترمذي وأبو عبد الله محمد بن يزيد هو ابن ماجه وأبو بكر أحمد بن الحسين البيهقي (الأذكار للإمام النووي، الرقم: ١٢٤)

[84] (يحب التيمن) أي البدء بالأيمن من اليد والرجل والجانب الأيمن لكن التيمن في اللغة المشهورة هو التبرك بالشيء من اليمن وهو البركة في القاموس اليمن بالضم البركة وفي مختصر النهاية اليمن البركة وضده الشؤم والتيمن الابتداء في الأفعال باليد اليمنى والرجل اليمنى والجانب الأيمن (ما استطاع) أي ما أمكنه وقدر عليه (في شأنه) أي في أمره (كله) تأكيد والمراد الأمور المكرمة (مرقاة المفاتيح ١١١/٢–١١٢)

[85] (ومن آدابه) ... (استقبال القبلة ودلك أعضائه) في المرة الأولى (الدر المختار ١٢٤/١) والدلك أيضا سنة (غنية المتملي صـ ٢٧)

23. All the limbs should be washed, one after the other, without any delay in between.[86]

24. While making wudhu, do not speak of worldly affairs.[87]

25. Do not waste water while making wudhu.[88]

عن عبد الله بن عمرو رضي الله عنهما أن رسول الله صلى الله عليه وسلم مر بسعد وهو يتوضأ فقال ما هذا السرف فقال أفي الوضوء إسراف قال نعم وإن كنت على نهر جار (سنن ابن ماجة، الرقم: ٤٢٥)[89]

Hazrat Abdullah bin Amr ﵁ reports that Hazrat Rasulullah ﷺ passed by Hazrat Sa'd ﵁ whilst he was performing wudhu. Hazrat Rasulullah ﷺ asked him, "What is this wastage (of water in your wudhu)?" He replied, "Is there also wastage in wudhu?" Hazrat Rasulullah ﷺ replied, "Yes, even if you are performing wudhu at the bank of a flowing river (then too, be mindful of not wasting water)."

---

[86] الفصل الثاني في سنن الوضوء ... ومنها الموالاة وهي التتابع وحده أن لا يجف الماء على العضو قبل أن يغسل ما بعده في زمان معتدل ولا اعتبار بشدة الحر والرياح ولا شدة البرد ويعتبر أيضا استواء حالة المتوضئ كذا في الجوهرة النيرة وإنما يكره التفريق في الوضوء إذا كان بغير عذر أما إذا كان بعذر بأن فرغ ماء الوضوء فيذهب لطلب الماء أو ما أشبه ذلك فلا بأس بالتفريق على الصحيح وهكذا إذا فرق في الغسل والتيمم كذا في السراج الوهاج (الفتاوى الهندية ١/٨)

[87] (ومن آدابه) ... (و) عدم (التكلم بكلام الناس) الا لحاجة تفوته (الدر المختار ١/١٢٦)

[88] وفي الأصل من الادب أن لا يسرف في الماء ولا يقتر كذا في الخلاصة وهذا إذا كان ماء نهر أو مملوكا له فإن كان ماء موقوفا على من يتطهر أو يتوضأ حرمت الزيادة والإسراف بلا خلاف كذا في البحر الرائق (الفتاوى الهندية ١/٨)

[89] في الزوائد للبوصيري (١/١٤٧): إسناده ضعيف لضعف حيي بن عبد الله وابن لهيعة

لهذا الحديث شاهد صحيح من حديث أبي نعامة أن عبد الله بن مغفل سمع ابنه يقول اللهم إني أسألك القصر الأبيض عن يمين الجنة إذا دخلتها فقال أي بني سل الله الجنة وتعوذ به من النار فإني سمعت رسول الله صلى الله عليه وسلم يقول إنه سيكون في هذه الأمة قوم يعتدون في الطهور والدعاء (سنن أبي داود، الرقم: ٩٦) وصححه ابن حبان (الرقم: ٦٧٦٣)

26. If any part of a limb which is fardh to wash in wudhu is left
    dry, the wudhu will be incomplete.[90]

عن عمر بن الخطاب رضي الله عنه أن رجلا توضأ فترك موضع ظفر على قدمه

فأبصره النبي صلى الله عليه وسلم فقال ارجع فأحسن وضوءك (صحيح مسلم، الرقم:

(٢٤٣

Hazrat Umar رَضِيَٱللَّهُعَنْهُ *reports that a man made wudhu and left out*
washing an area on his foot equivalent to a nail. Upon observing
the portion that was left dry, Hazrat Rasulullah صَلَّىٱللَّهُعَلَيْهِوَسَلَّمَ *said to*
him, "Go and complete your wudhu."

27. If you are making wudhu from a utensil, then after
    completing the wudhu, if any water remains, it is mustahab
    for one to drink it while standing, as this is established in the
    Hadith.[91]

28. Sprinkle water on the clothing around the private area. This
    is in order to remove doubts that may enter the mind later
    on regarding whether any urine drops had come out after
    making wudhu. However, if one is certain that urine drops

---

[90] في فتاوى ما وراء النهر إن بقي من موضع الوضوء قدر رأس إبرة أو لزق بأصل ظفره طين يابس أو رطب لم يجز (الفتاوى الهندية ١/٤)

[91] عن أبي حية قال رأيت عليا رضي الله عنه توضأ فغسل كفيه حتى أنقاهما ثم مضمض ثلاثا واستنشق ثلاثا وغسل وجهه ثلاثا وذراعيه ثلاثا

ومسح برأسه مرة ثم غسل قدميه إلى الكعبين ثم قام فأخذ فضل طهوره فشربه وهو قائم ثم قال: أحببت أن أريكم كيف كان طهور رسول الله

صلى الله عليه وسلم (سنن الترمذي، الرقم: ٤٨)

قال العلامة ابن عابدين رحمه الله (ومن آدابه) ... (... وأن يشرب بعده من فضل وضوئه) كماء زمزم (مستقبل القبلة قائما) أو قاعدا وفيما

عداها يكره قائما تنزيها (الدر المختار ١/١٢٩)

had come out after wudhu, he should wash the soiled area of the clothing and repeat his wudhu.[92]

29. If there is a need to use a towel to dry the limbs after wudhu, you may do so. It is reported in the Hadith that at times, Hazrat Rasulullah ﷺ would use a towel, and at times, he would not use a towel.[93]

30. If you are able to remain in the state of wudhu, you should do so, as remaining in the state of wudhu is a sign of imaan.[94]

31. After performing wudhu, it is recommended that one performs two rakaats of Tahiyyatul Wudhu. The one who

---

[92] عن الحكم أو ابن الحكم عن أبيه أن رسول الله صلى الله عليه وسلم بال ثم توضأ ونضح فرجه (سنن أبي داود، الرقم: ١٦٨)

(قال كان النبي صلى الله عليه وسلم إذا بال توضأ ونضح فرجه) أي ورش إزراه بقليل من الماء أو سرواله به لدفع الوسوسة تعليما للأمة (مرقاة المفاتيح ٢/٧٧)

وزاد في الخزائن ... ورش الماء على الفرج وعلى السروال بعد الوضوء (رد المحتار ١/١٢٥)

[93] عن ابن عباس رضي الله عنهما عن خالته ميمونة رضي الله عنها قالت وضعت للنبي صلى الله عليه وسلم غسلا يغتسل من الجنابة فأكفأ الإناء على يده اليمنى فغسلها مرتين أو ثلاثا ثم صب على فرجه فغسل فرجه بشماله ثم ضرب بيده الأرض فغسلها ثم تمضمض واستنشق وغسل وجهه ويديه ثم صب على رأسه وجسده ثم تنحى ناحية فغسل رجليه فناولته المنديل فلم يأخذه وجعل ينفض الماء عن جسده (سنن أبي داود، الرقم: ٢٤٥)

عن سلمان الفارسي رضي الله عنه أن رسول الله صلى الله عليه وسلم توضأ فقلب جبة صوف كانت عليه فمسح بها وجهه (سنن ابن ماجة، الرقم: ٤٦٨)

قال البوصيري في الزوائد (١/١٥٨): إسناده صحيح ورواته ثقات وفي سماع محفوظ من سليمان نظر

(ومن آدابه) ... والتمسح بمنديل

قال العلامة ابن عابدين رحمه الله (قوله والتمسح بمنديل) ذكره صاحب المنية في الغسل وقال في الحلية ولم أر من ذكره غيره وإنما وقع الخلاف في الكراهة ففي الخانية ولا بأس للمتوضئ والمغتسل روي عن رسول الله صلى الله عليه وسلم أنه كان يفعله ومنهم من كره ذلك ومنهم من كره للمتوضئ دون المغتسل والصحيح ما قلنا إلا أنه ينبغي أن لا يبالغ ولا يستقصي فيبقي أثر الوضوء على أعضائه اه وكذا وقع بلفظ لا بأس في خزانة الأكمل وغيرها وعزاه في الخلاصة إلى الأصل اه ما في الحلية (رد المحتار ١/١٣١)

[94] عن عبد الله بن عمرو رضي الله عنهما قال قال رسول الله صلى الله عليه وسلم استقيموا ولن تحصوا واعلموا أن من أفضل أعمالكم الصلاة ولا يحافظ على الوضوء إلا مؤمن (سنن ابن ماجة، الرقم: ٢٧٨)

performs two rakaats of Tahiyyatul Wudhu, his previous minor sins are forgiven.[95]

---

[95] عن أبي هريرة رضي الله عنه قال قال رسول الله صلى الله عليه وسلم لبلال عند صلاة الغداة يا بلال حدثني بأرجى عمل عملته عندك في الإسلام منفعة فإني سمعت الليلة خشف نعليك بين يدي في الجنة قال بلال: ما عملت عملا في الإسلام أرجى عندي منفعة من أني لا أتطهر طهورا تاما في ساعة من ليل ولا نهار إلا صليت بذلك الطهور ما كتب الله لي أن أصلي (صحيح مسلم، الرقم: ٢٤٥٨)

عن عقبة بن عامر رضي الله عنه قال كانت علينا رعاية الإبل فجاءت نوبتي فروحتها بعشي فأدركت رسول الله صلى الله عليه وسلم قائما يحدث الناس فأدركت من قوله ما من مسلم يتوضأ فيحسن وضوءه ثم يقوم فيصلي ركعتين مقبل عليهما بقلبه ووجهه إلا وجبت له الجنة قال فقلت ما أجود هذه فإذا قائل بين يدي يقول التي قبلها أجود فنظرت فإذا عمر قال إني قد رأيتك جئت آنفا قال ما منكم من أحد يتوضأ فيبلغ أو فيسبغ الوضوء ثم يقول أشهد أن لا إله إلا الله وأن محمدا عبد الله ورسوله إلا فتحت له أبواب الجنة الثمانية يدخل من أيها شاء (صحيح مسلم، الرقم: ٢٣٤)

عن ثعلبة بن عباد عن أبيه رضي الله عنه قال ما أدري كم حدثنيه رسول الله صلى الله عليه وسلم أزواجا أو أفرادا قال ما من عبد يتوضأ فيحسن الوضوء فيغسل وجهه حتى يسيل الماء على ذقنه ثم يغسل ذراعيه حتى يسيل الماء على مرفقيه ثم غسل رجليه حتى يسيل الماء من كعبيه ثم يقوم فيصلي إلا غفر له ما سلف من ذنبه رواه الطبراني في الكبير بإسناد لين (الترغيب والترهيب، الرقم: ٣٠١)

وقال الهيثمي في مجمع الزوائد (الرقم: ١١٣٤): رواه الطبراني في الكبير ورواه بإسناد آخر فقال عن ثعلبة بن عمارة وقال هكذا رواه إسحاق الدبري عن عبد الرزاق ووهم في اسمه والصواب ثعلبة بن عباد ورجاله موثقون

General Masaail Pertaining to Wudhu

1. **Q:** What are the faraaidh of wudhu?

    A: The faraaidh of wudhu are as follows:

    1. Washing the entire face once.
    2. Washing the arms including the elbows once.
    3. Making masah of at least one quarter of the head.
    4. Washing both the feet including the ankles once.[96]

2. **Q:** Which parts of the face should be washed in wudhu?

    A: The entire face should be washed in wudhu i.e. from the top of the forehead till beneath the chin, and from one ear to the other.[See 64]

3. **Q:** Is it necessary to wash the area between the sideburns and ears in wudhu?

    A: Yes, it is fardh (compulsory).[See 64]

4. **Q:** Is it necessary for one to repeat the masah in the case where one had his hair cut after making wudhu?

    A: No, it is not necessary.[97]

---

[96] أركان الوضوء أربعة وهى فرائضه الأول غسل الوجه ... والثاني غسل يديه مع مرفقيه والثالث غسل رجليه مع كعبيه والرابع مسح ربع رأسه

(نور الايضاح صـ ٣٠)

5. **Q:** Is it necessary to remove rings, bangles and watches when making wudhu?

    A: If water reaches the area beneath the rings, bangles and watches without removing them, it will not be necessary to remove them.[98]

6. **Q:** What is the method of making khilaal of the beard?

    A: Khilaal of the beard should be made by passing the wet fingers of the hand through the beard from beneath the chin.[See 65]

7. **Q:** What are the sunnats of wudhu?

    A: The sunnats of wudhu are as follows:

    1. To make niyyah (intention of wudhu).
    2. To make miswaak.
    3. To recite the tasmiyah (bismillah).
    4. To wash the hands up to the wrists.
    5. To gargle the mouth.
    6. To put water into the nostrils.
    7. To make khilaal of the beard.
    8. To make khilaal of the fingers and toes.

---

[97] (ولا يعاد الوضوء) بل ولا بل المحل (بحلق رأسه ولحيته كما لا يعاد) الغسل للمحل ولا الوضوء (بحلق شاربه وحاجبه و قلم ظفره) وكشط جلده (الدر المختار ١٠١/١)

[98] وفي مجموع النوازل تحريك الخاتم سنة إن كان واسعا وفرض إن كان ضيقا بحيث لم يصل الماء تحته كذا في الخلاصة وهو ظاهر الرواية هكذا في المحيط (الفتاوى الهندية ١/٥)

9. To wash each limb thrice.

10. To make masah of the entire head once.

11. To make masah of the ears.

12. To make wudhu in sequence.

13. To wash each limb, one after the other, without a delay, in such a manner that the limbs do not dry before the wudhu is completed.[99]

8. **Q:** Is it necessary to remove ointment from wounds or cracks in the feet or hands at the time of wudhu?

A: If passing water over the wounds or cracks will be harmful (or delay the process of healing), it will not be necessary to remove the ointment. Making masah (i.e. merely passing wet hands over the wound or crack) of that limb will suffice.[100]

9. **Q:** If a person's hand is amputated below the elbow, does he have to wash the remaining portion of his hand till the elbow in wudhu?

---

[99] (وسننه) ... (البداية بالنية) ... (و) البداية (بالتسمية) ... (و) البداية (بغسل اليدين) ... (إلى الرسغين) ... (والسواك) ... (وغسل الفم) أي استيعابه ولذا عبر بالغسل أو للاختصار (بمياه) ثلاثة (والأنف) ببلوغ الماء المارن (بمياه) وهما سنتان مؤكدتان مشتملتان على سنن خمس الترتيب والتثليث وتجديد الماء وفعلهما باليمنى (والمبالغة فيهما) بالغرغرة ومجاوزة المارن (لغير الصائم) لاحتمال الفساد ... (وتخليل اللحية) لغير المحرم بعد التثليث ويجعل ظهر كفه إلى عنقه (و) تخليل (الأصابع) اليدين بالتشبيك والرجلين بخنصر يده اليسرى بادئا بخنصر رجله اليمنى وهذا بعد دخول الماء خلالها فلو منضمة فرض (وتثليث الغسل) المستوعب ... (ومسح كل رأسه مرة) ... (وأذنيه) معا ولو (بمائه) ... (والترتيب) المذكور في النص ... (والولاء) (الدر المختار ١ / ١٠٢–١٢٢)

[100] فروع في أعضائه شقاق غسله إن قدر وإلا مسحه وإلا تركه ولو بيده ولا يقدر على الماء تيمم

قال العلامة ابن عابدين رحمه الله (قوله تيمم) زاد في الخزائن وصلاته جائزة عنده خلافا لهما ولو كان في رجله فجعل فيه الدواء يكفيه إمرار الماء فوقه ولا يكفيه المسح ولو أمره فسقط إن عن برء يعيده وإلا فلا كما في الصغرى اه ابن عبد الرزاق (رد المحتار ١٠٢/١)

A: He will have to wash the remaining portion of his hand which is below the elbow, including the elbow.[101]

10. **Q:** Is it sunnah to take new water for making masah of the head or can one make masah with the water that remains on the hands after washing the hands?

A: It is not sunnah to take new water for making masah of the head. One should make masah with the water that remains on the hands after washing the hands.[102]

11. **Q:** If one is performing wudhu in the bathroom, and there is also a toilet in the same bathroom, then should one recite the duas of wudhu?

A: If the basin where one is making wudhu is close to the toilet then one should not recite the duas of wudhu.[103]

---

[101] ولو قطع من المرفق غسل محل القطع

قال العلامة ابن عابدين رحمه الله (قوله ولو قطع الخ) قال في البحر ولو قطعت يده أو رجله فلم يبق من المرفق والكعب شيئ سقط الغسل ولو بقي وجب (رد المحتار ١٠٢/١)

[102] ولو كان في كفه بلل فمسح به أجزأه سواء كان أخذ الماء من الأناء أو غسل ذراعيه وبقي بلل في كفه هو الصحيح (الفتاوى الهندية ٧/١)

عن الربيع رضي الله عنه أن النبي صلى الله عليه وسلم مسح برأسه من فضل ماء كان في يده (سنن أبي داود، الرقم: ١٣٠)

وقال ابن قدامة رحمه الله في المغني روي عن علي وابن عمر وأبي أمامة فيمن نسي مسح رأسه إذا وجد بللا في لحيته أجزأه أن يمسح رأسه بذلك البلل انتهى (المغني ١٧/١)

[103] وفي محل نجاسة فيسمي بقلبه

قال العلامة ابن عابدين رحمه الله: الظاهر أن المراد أنه يسمي قبل رفع ثيابه إن كان في غير المكان المعد لقضاء الحاجة وإلا فقبل دخوله فلو نسي فيهما سمى بقلبه ولا يحرك لسانه تعظيما لاسم الله تعالى (رد المحتار ١٠٩/١)

CHAPTER THREE

GHUSL

SUNNAH METHOD OF MAKING GHUSL

1. Do not face the qiblah while performing ghusl.[104]

2. Bath in such a place where no one can see you. It is better to perform ghusl with the satr area covered. However, if one is in an enclosed area (e.g. bathroom) and one performs ghusl without the satr covered, it will be permissible.[See 104]

عن يعلى أن رسول الله صلى الله عليه وسلم رأى رجلا يغتسل بالبراز بلا إزار فصعد المنبر فحمد الله وأثنى عليه ثم قال صلى الله عليه وسلم إن الله عز وجل حيي ستير يحب الحياء والستر فإذا اغتسل أحدكم فليستتر (سنن أبي داود، الرقم: ٤٠١٢)[105]

---

[104] (وههنا سنن وآداب ذكرها بعض المشايخ) يسن أن يبدأ بالنية بقلبه ويقول بلسانه نويت الغسل لرفع الجنابة أو للجنابة ثم يسمي الله تعالى عند غسل اليدين ثم يستنجي كذا في الجوهرة النيرة وأن لا يسرف في الماء ولا يقتر وأن لا يستقبل القبلة وقت الغسل وأن يدلك كل أعضائه في المرة الأولى وأن يغتسل في موضع لا يراه أحد ويستحب أن لا يتكلم بكلام قط وأن يمسح بمنديل بعد الغسل كذا في المنية في الفتاوى الهندية (١/١٤)

[105] سكت الحافظ عن هذا الحديث في الفصل الثاني من هداية الرواة (١/٢٣٦) فالحديث حسن عنده

Hazrat Ya'laa رَضِيَ اللَّهُ عَنْهُ reports that on one occasion, Hazrat Rasulullah صَلَّى اللَّهُ عَلَيْهِ وَسَلَّمَ saw a person performing ghusl in the open, without a lower garment (i.e. with his private parts exposed). Later on, Hazrat Rasulullah صَلَّى اللَّهُ عَلَيْهِ وَسَلَّمَ ascended the mimbar, praised Allah تَبَارَكَ وَتَعَالَى and glorified Him, and thereafter said, "Indeed Allah تَبَارَكَ وَتَعَالَى is modest (i.e. He deals with His servants with the highest level of modesty and respect) and He is concealed (from the eyes of His servants), He likes (His servants to adopt) hayaa and concealment (when relieving themselves or bathing, etc). Hence, when any one of you performs ghusl, he should conceal his body."

3. Preferably use a bucket to bath.[106]

4. If you are performing ghusl in the shower then ensure that you do not waste water. Do not engage in soaping yourself or removing unwanted hair, etc. while the water is running. This is a serious waste of water and is a cause of great sin.[See 104]

5. Preferably perform ghusl while sitting.[107]

6. Commence the ghusl by washing both hands up to the wrists thrice.[108]

---

[106] حدثتني ميمونة قالت كنت أغتسل أنا ورسول الله صلى الله عليه وسلم من إناء واحد من الجنابة هذا حديث حسن صحيح (سنن الترمذي، الرقم: ٦٢)

[107] (وسننه) أي سنن الغسل كسنن الوضوء سوى الترتيب وآدابه كآدابه سوى استقبال القبلة لأنه يكون غالبا مع كشف عورة (الدر المختار ١٥٦/١)

(ومن آدابه) أي آداب الوضوء ... (استقبال القبلة ودلك أعضائه) ... (والجلوس في مكان مرتفع) (الدر المختار ١٢٧/١)

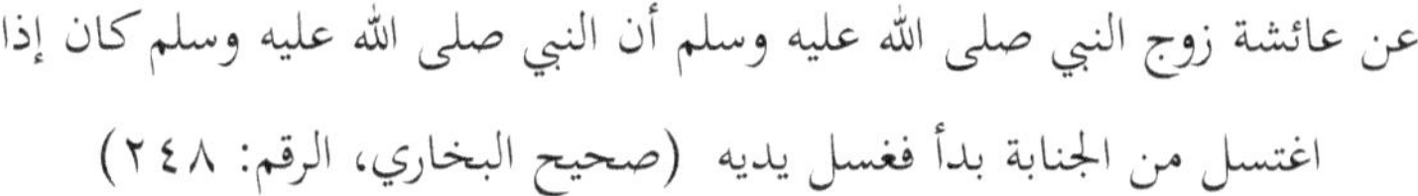

عن عائشة زوج النبي صلى الله عليه وسلم أن النبي صلى الله عليه وسلم كان إذا اغتسل من الجنابة بدأ فغسل يديه (صحيح البخاري، الرقم: ٢٤٨)

Hazrat Aaishah رَضِيَ اللّٰهُ عَنْهَا, *the respected wife of Hazrat Rasulullah* صَلَّى اللّٰهُ عَلَيْهِ وَسَلَّمَ, *reports that when Hazrat Rasulullah* صَلَّى اللّٰهُ عَلَيْهِ وَسَلَّمَ *would perform fardh ghusl, he would commence by washing his mubaarak hands."*

7. Wash the private parts with the left hand. The hands and private parts should be washed irrespective of whether there is any impurity on them or not.[109]

عن ابن عباس قال قالت ميمونة وضعت للنبي صلى الله عليه وسلم ماء للغسل فغسل يديه مرتين أو ثلاثا ثم أفرغ على شماله فغسل مذاكيره (صحيح البخاري، الرقم: ٢٥٧)

Hazrat Ibnu Abbaas رَضِيَ اللّٰهُ عَنْهُمَا *reports that Hazrat Maimoonah* رَضِيَ اللّٰهُ عَنْهَا *said, "I placed water for Hazrat Rasulullah* صَلَّى اللّٰهُ عَلَيْهِ وَسَلَّمَ *to perform ghusl. Hazrat Rasulullah* صَلَّى اللّٰهُ عَلَيْهِ وَسَلَّمَ *washed his mubaarak hands twice or thrice, and thereafter poured water onto his left hand and (using his left hand,) washed his private area."*

8. Wash any impurity found on the rest of the body.[See 108]

9. Perform the complete wudhu. If you are bathing in a place where the water collects on the ground and there is no water

---

[108] (الفصل الثاني في سنن الغسل) وهي أن يغسل يديه إلى الرسغ ثلاثا ثم فرجه ويزيل النجاسة إن كانت على بدنه ثم يتوضأ وضوءه للصلاة إلا رجليه هكذا في الملتقط (الفتاوى الهندية ١/١٤)

[109] (و) كذا (غسل فرجه) وإن لم يكن به نجاسة كما فعله النبي صلى الله عليه وسلم ليطمئن بوصول الماء إلى الجزء الذي ينضم من فرجه حال القيام وينفرج حال الجلوس (حاشية الطحطاوي على مراقي الفلاح صـ ١٠٤)

outlet, then postpone the washing of your feet to the end of the ghusl. After completing the other acts of the ghusl, you should move to another place and wash your feet.[110]

عن عائشة قالت كان رسول الله صلى الله عليه وسلم إذا أراد أن يغتسل من الجنابة بدأ فغسل يديه قبل أن يدخلهما الإناء ثم غسل فرجه ويتوضأ وضوءه للصلاة (سنن الترمذي، الرقم: ١٠٤)[111]

Hazrat Aaishah رَضِيَ اللّٰهُ عَنْهَا *reports that when Hazrat Rasulullah* صَلَّى اللّٰهُ عَلَيْهِ وَسَلَّمَ *would intend to perform fardh ghusl, he would commence by washing his mubaarak hands before submerging them in the utensil of water. Then, he would wash his private parts and perform wudhu, just as he would perform wudhu for salaah."*

عن ابن عباس قال قالت ميمونة وضعت لرسول الله صلى الله عليه وسلم ماء يغتسل به ... ثم تنحى من مقامه فغسل قدميه (صحيح البخاري، الرقم: ٢٦٥)

Hazrat Ibnu Abbaas رَضِيَ اللّٰهُ عَنْهُ *reports that Hazrat Maimoonah* صَلَّى اللّٰهُ عَلَيْهِ وَسَلَّمَ *said, "I placed water for Hazrat Rasulullah* رَضِيَ اللّٰهُ عَنْهَا *to perform ghusl ... (After completing the ghusl,) Hazrat Rasulullah* صَلَّى اللّٰهُ عَلَيْهِ وَسَلَّمَ *moved away from the place where he had performed ghusl and then washed his mubaarak feet."*

10. Pour water on the head thrice.[112]

---

[110] (ثم يتوضأ كوضوئه للصلاة فيثلث الغسل ويمسح الرأس) في ظاهر الرواية وقيل لا يمسحها لأنه يصب عليها الماء والأول أصح لأنه صلى الله عليه وسلم توضأ قبل الاغتسال وضوءه للصلاة وهو اسم للغسل والمسح (ولكنه يؤخر غسل الرجلين إن كان يقف) حال الاغتسال (في محل يجتمع فيه الماء) لاحتياجه لغسلهما ثانيا من الغسالة (حاشية الطحطاوي على مراقي الفلاح ص ١٠٥)

[111] قال أبو عيسى: هذا حديث حسن صحيح

عن عائشة قالت كان رسول الله صلى الله عليه وسلم إذا أراد أن يغتسل من الجنابة بدأ فغسل يديه قبل أن يدخلهما الإناء ثم غسل فرجه ويتوضأ وضوءه للصلاة ثم يشرب شعره الماء ثم يحثي على رأسه ثلاث حثيات (سنن الترمذي، الرقم: ١٠٤)[113]

Hazrat Aaishah رَضِيَاللَّهُعَنْهَا reports that when Hazrat Rasulullah صَلَّىاللَّهُعَلَيْهِوَسَلَّمَ would intend to perform fardh ghusl, he would commence by washing his mubaarak hands before submerging them in the utensil of water. Then, he would wash his private parts and perform wudhu, just as he would perform wudhu for salaah. Thereafter, he would wet his hair, after which he would pour three handfuls of water over his mubaarak head."

11. Pour water over the right side of the body thrice from top to bottom and thereafter pour water over the left side of the body thrice from top to bottom. Ensure that water reaches every part of the body.[See 112]

12. If you are performing a fardh ghusl, then ensure that water reaches every part of the body, especially the mouth, inside the nose, the corner of the eyes, inside the navel, etc. No part

---

[112] (بادئا بمنكبه الأيمن ثم الأيسر ثم رأسه) على (بقية بدنه مع دلكه) ندبا وقيل يثني بالرأس وقيل يبدأ بالرأس وهو الأصح وظاهر الرواية والأحاديث قال في البحر وبه يضعف تصحيح الدرر

قال العلامة ابن عابدين رحمه الله: (قوله وظاهر الرواية) كذا عبر في النهر والذي في البحر وغيره التعبير بظاهر الهداية (قوله والأحاديث) قال الشيخ إسماعيل في شرح البرجندي وهو الموافق لعدة أحاديث أوردها البخاري في صحيحه اه فافهم (قوله تصحيح الدرر) هو ما مشى عليه المصنف في متنه هنا (رد المحتار ١/١٥٩)

[113] قال أبو عيسى: هذا حديث حسن صحيح

should be left dry. Even if an area equal to a hair's breadth is left dry, the fardh ghusl will not be complete.[114]

عن علي رضي الله عنه أن رسول الله صلى الله عليه وسلم قال من ترك موضع شعرة من جنابة لم يغسلها فعل بها كذا وكذا من النار قال علي فمن ثم عاديت رأسي ثلاثا وكان يجز شعره (سنن أبي داود، الرقم: ٢٤٩)[115]

Hazrat Ali رَضِيَاللَّهُعَنْهُ reports that Hazrat Rasulullah صَلَّىاللَّهُعَلَيْهِوَسَلَّمَ said, "The one who is in janaabah (requires a fardh ghusl) and leaves a portion (of his body) equal to a hair without washing it, that portion of his body will be subjected to such-and-such punishment in Jahannum." Hazrat Ali رَضِيَاللَّهُعَنْهُ thereafter said thrice, "That is why I dislike keeping hair." It is reported that Hazrat Ali رَضِيَاللَّهُعَنْهُ would shave his head (out of the fear that during the ghusl, no hair should remain dry, thereby causing the ghusl to be incomplete).

13. Do not waste water during the ghusl. Too much of water should not be used, nor should so little be used, that one is unable to wash thoroughly.[See 104]

عن عبد الله بن محمد بن عقيل بن أبي طالب عن أبيه عن جده قال قال رسول الله صلى الله عليه وسلم يجزئ من الوضوء مد ومن الغسل صاع فقال رجل لا يجزئنا فقال

---

[114] (وأما) ركنه فهو إسالة الماء على جميع ما يمكن إسالته عليه من البدن من غير حرج مرة واحدة حتى لو بقيت لمعة لم يصبها الماء لم يجز الغسل وإن كانت يسيرة (بدائع الصنائع ٢٦٧/١)

ويجب إيصال الماء إلى داخل السرة وينبغي أن يدخل أصبعه فيها للمبالغة كذا في محيط السرخسي (الفتاوى الهندية ١٤/١)

[115] سكت الحافظ عن هذا الحديث في الفصل الثاني من هداية الرواة (٢٣٥/١) فالحديث حسن عنده

قد كان يجزئ من هو خير منك وأكثر شعرا يعني النبي صلى الله عليه وسلم (سنن ابن ماجة، الرقم: ٢٧٠)[116]

Hazrat Aqeel bin Abi Taalib رَضِيَٱللَّهُعَنْهُ *reported that Hazrat Rasulullah* صَلَّىٱللَّهُعَلَيْهِوَسَلَّمَ *said, "One mudd of water is sufficient for wudhu, and one saa' of water is sufficient for ghusl." Hearing this, a certain person remarked, "This amount of water will not suffice us." Hazrat Aqeel* رَضِيَٱللَّهُعَنْهُ *admonished this person and responded, "It would suffice the one who was better than you and who had more hair than you (referring to Hazrat Rasulullah* صَلَّىٱللَّهُعَلَيْهِوَسَلَّمَ*)."*

14. Do not engage in talking, singing or any type of conversation while performing ghusl.[See 104]

15. Do not recite any duas while bathing.[117]

16. Do not take too long in the bathroom, especially if it is a common bathroom which others also use.[See 88 and 107]

17. Do not mess the bathroom with unwanted hair.[118]

---

[116] قال البوصيري في الزوائد (٩٩/١): إسناده ضعيف لضعف حبان ويزيد

لهذا الحديث شاهد من حديث ابن عباس قال قال رجل كم يكفيني للوضوء قال كم مد قال كم يكفيني للغسل قال صاع قال فقال الرجل لا يكفيني فقال لا أم لك قد كفى من هو خير منك رسول الله صلى الله عليه وسلم رواه أحمد والبزار والطبراني في الكبير ورجاله ثقات (مجمع الزوائد الرقم: ١٠٩٩)

[117] أقول ويستثنى الدعاء أيضا فإنه مكروه كما في نور الإيضاح (قوله وآدابه كآدابه) نص عليه في البدائع قال الشرنبلالي ويستحب أن لا يتكلم بكلام مطلقا أما كلام الناس فلكراهته حال الكشف وأما الدعاء فلأنه في مصب المستعمل ومحل الأقذار والأوحال اه (رد المحتار ١٥٦/١)

[118] وإذا قص أظفاره أو حلق شعره ينبغي أن يدفنه قال تعالى ألم نجعل الأرض كفاتا أحياء وأمواتا وإن ألقاه فلا بأس به ويكره إلقاؤه في الكنيف والمغتسل قالوا لأنه يورث المرض (الاختيار ١٦٧/٤)

18. Be considerate when using hot water. Do not use so much that those coming after you are inconvenienced by not having enough hot water.[119]

19. After bathing, wipe the body with a cloth or towel.[See 104]

20. Hasten to cover the body after bathing.[120]

21. Do not urinate in the shower.[121]

---

[119] عن عبد الله بن عمرو رضي الله عنهما عن النبي صلى الله عليه وسلم قال المسلم من سلم المسلمون من لسانه ويده والمهاجر من هجر ما نهى الله عنه (صحيح البخاري، الرقم: ١٠)

[120] عن زرعة بن مسلم بن جرهد الأسلمي عن جده جرهد قال مر النبي صلى الله عليه وسلم بجرهد في المسجد وقد انكشف فخذه فقال إن الفخذ عورة هذا حديث حسن ما أرى إسناده بمتصل (سنن الترمذي، الرقم: ٢٧٩٥)

[121] عن عبد الله بن مغفل أن النبي صلى الله عليه وسلم نهى أن يبول الرجل في مستحمه وقال إن عامة الوسواس منه (سنن الترمذي، الرقم: ٢١)

ويكره أن يبول في موضع يتوضأ فيه أو يغتسل كذا في السراج الوهاج (الفتاوى الهندية ١/٥٠)

FARAAIDH OF GHUSL

1. Gargling the mouth in such a way that water reaches everywhere.

2. Inserting water into the nose upto the soft bone.

3. Pouring water over the entire body.[122]

---

[122] (الفصل الأول في فرائضه) وهي ثلاثة المضمضة والاستنشاق وغسل جميع البدن على ما في المتون (الفتاوى الهندية ١٣/١)

SUNNATS OF GHUSL

1. Making the intention to wash off impurities and become paak (pure).

2. If the satr area is covered then you should recite bismillah before commencing.

3. Washing the hands upto the wrists thrice.

4. Washing the private parts, whether they have impurity on them or not.

5. Making wudhu before washing the entire body.

6. Pouring water on the head thrice.

7. Pouring water over the right side of the body thrice from top to bottom.

8. Pouring water over the left side of the body thrice from top to bottom.

9. Rubbing the body when pouring the water to ensure that the water reaches every part of the body.

10. Not using so little water that you will not be able to perform the ghusl properly, but not wasting water.

11. Not facing the qiblah.

12. Performing ghusl in a secluded place where you will not be seen by anyone.[See 104, 108 and 112]

SUNNAH OCCASIONS OF GHUSL

There are numerous occasions when it is sunnah for one to perform ghusl. Some of these occasions are:

1. The Day of Jumuah.[123]

عن عبد الله بن عمر رضي الله عنهما أن رسول الله صلى الله عليه وسلم قال إذا جاء أحدكم الجمعة فليغتسل (صحيح البخاري، الرقم: ٨٧٧)

Hazrat Abdullah bin Umar رَضِيَٱللَّهُعَنْهَا *reports that Hazrat Rasulullah* صَلَّىٱللَّهُعَلَيْهِوَسَلَّمَ *said, "When any of you come for Jumuah then he should perform ghusl."*

2. The two days of Eid i.e. Eidul Fitr and Eidul Adha.[See 123]

عن ابن عباس رضي الله عنهما قال كان رسول الله صلى الله عليه وسلم يغتسل يوم الفطر ويوم الأضحى (سنن ابن ماجة، الرقم: ١٣١٥)[124]

Hazrat Ibnu Abbaas رَضِيَٱللَّهُعَنْهَا *reports that Hazrat Rasulullah* صَلَّىٱللَّهُعَلَيْهِوَسَلَّمَ *would have a bath on the Day of Eidul Fitr and the Day Eidul Adha.*

3. The Day of Arafah.[See 123]

---

[123] (وسن رسول الله صلى الله عليه وسلم الغسل للجمعة والعيدين وعرفة والإحرام) نص على السنية (الهداية ٢٠/١)

[124] قال البوصيري في الزوائد (٤١٧/١): هذا إسناد فيه جبارة وهو ضعيف وحجاج بن تميم ضعيف أيضا

لهذا الحديث شاهد من حديث عبد الله بن عمر: مالك عن نافع أن عبد الله بن عمر كان يغتسل يوم الفطر قبل أن يغدو إلى المصلى (الموطأ للإمام مالك، الرقم: ٦٠٩)

وكذا له شاهد من حديث زاذان قال سأل رجل عليا عن الغسل قال اغتسل كل يوم إن شئت فقال الغسل الذي هو الغسل يوم الجمعة ويوم عرفة ويوم النحر ويوم الفطر (مسند الشافعي على ترتيب السندي، الرقم: ١١٤)

عن زاذان قال سأل رجل عليا عن الغسل قال اغتسل كل يوم إن شئت فقال الغسل
الذي هو الغسل قال يوم الجمعة ويوم عرفة ويوم النحر ويوم الفطر (مسند الشافعي
على ترتيب السندي، الرقم: ١١٤)[125]

Hazrat Zaazaan رَحِمَهُٱللَّهُ reports that on one occasion, a certain person asked Hazrat Ali رَضِیَٱللَّهُعَنْهُ regarding (when he should perform) ghusl. Hazrat Ali رَضِیَٱللَّهُعَنْهُ replied, "You may perform ghusl daily if you wish." The person then asked, "(I am asking about) the ghusl which is the most important ghusl." Hazrat Ali رَضِیَٱللَّهُعَنْهُ answered, "(The most important occasions of ghusl are) the Day of Jumuah, the Day of Arafah, the Day of Eidul Adha and the Day of Eidul Fitr."

4.   For entering into ihraam.[See 123]

عن خارجة بن زيد بن ثابت عن أبيه عن أنه رأى النبي صلى الله عليه وسلم تجرد لإهلاله
واغتسل (سنن الترمذي، الرقم: ٨٣٠)[126]

Hazrat Zaid bin Thaabit رَضِیَٱللَّهُعَنْهُ reports that he had seen that Hazrat Rasulullah صَلَّیٱللَّهُعَلَیْهِوَسَلَّمَ removed his clothing for (entering into) ihraam and he performed ghusl.

---

[125] عن زاذان قال سألت عليا رضي الله عنه عن الغسل فقال اغتسل إذا شئت فقلت إنما أسألك عن الغسل الذي هو الغسل قال يوم الجمعة ويوم عرفة ويوم الفطر ويوم الأضحى (شرح معاني الآثار للطحاوي، الرقم: ٧٢٤)

[126] قال أبو عيسى: هذا حديث حسن غريب

عن ابن عمر قال من السنة أن يغتسل الرجل إذا أراد أن يحرم رواه البزار والطبراني في الكبير إلا أنه قال عند إحرامه وعند دخول مكة ورجال البزار ثقات كلهم (مجمع الزوائد، الرقم: ٥٣٢٣)

Note: Apart from these sunnah occasions of ghusl, there are certain mustahab occasions of ghusl which are mentioned by the Fuqahaa. Among these occasions are:

a)   For entering Makkah Mukarramah.[127]

b)   For a person who accepts Islam in the state of purity.[128]

c)   After cupping.[129]

---

[127] (كما يجب على من أسلم جنبا أو حائضا) ... (وإلا) بأن أسلم طاهرا أو بلغ بالسن (فمندوب) ... (وندب لمجنون أفاق) ... (وعند حجامة وفي ليلة براءة) ... و (عند دخول مكة لطواف الزيارة ولصلاة كسوف) (الدر المختار ١٦٧/١–١٦٩)

[128] عن أبي هريرة قال بعث النبي صلى الله عليه وسلم خيلا قبل نجد فجاءت برجل من بني حنيفة يقال له ثمامة بن أثال فربطوه بسارية من سواري المسجد فخرج إليه النبي صلى الله عليه وسلم فقال أطلقوا ثمامة فانطلق إلى نخل قريب من المسجد فاغتسل ثم دخل المسجد فقال أشهد أن لا إله إلا الله وأن محمدا رسول الله (صحيح البخاري، الرقم: ٤٦٢)

انظر أيضا 127

[129] حدثنا وكيع عن الأعمش عن مجاهد عن عبد الله بن عمرو قال اغتسل من الحجامة (المصنف لابن أبي شيبة، الرقم: ٤٨٠)

حدثنا المحاربي عن ليث عن مجاهد عن علي في الرجل يحتجم أو يحلق عانته أو ينتف إبطيه قال يغتسل (المصنف لابن أبي شيبة، الرقم: ٤٨٢)

حدثنا عبيد الله قال أخبرنا إسرائيل عن أبي إسحاق عن سعيد بن جبير عن ابن عباس قال إذا احتجم الرجل فليغتسل ولم يره واجبا (المصنف لابن أبي شيبة، الرقم:٤٨٤)

انظر أيضا 127

CHAPTER FOUR

MISWAAK

VIRTUES OF USING THE MISWAAK

1. Using the miswaak increases the reward of the salaah seventy times.

عن عائشة رضي الله عنها قالت قال رسول الله صلى الله عليه وسلم فضل الصلاة التي يستاك لها على الصلاة التي لا يستاك لها سبعين ضعفا (المستدرك على الصحيحين للحاكم، الرقم: ٥١٥)[130]

Hazrat Aaishah رَضِيَ اللهُ عَنْهَا *reports that Hazrat Rasulullah* صَلَّى اللهُ عَلَيْهِ وَسَلَّمَ *said, "The salaah performed after making miswaak is seventy times more virtuous than the salaah performed without making miswaak."*

2. Miswaak purifies the mouth and earns the pleasure of Allah تَبَارَكَ وَتَعَالَى.

---

[130] هذا حديث صحيح على شرط مسلم ولم يخرجاه

قال الذهبي في التلخيص: على شرط مسلم

عن عائشة رضي الله عنها قالت قال رسول الله صلى الله عليه وسلم السواك مطهرة للفم مرضاة للرب (صحيح البخاري تعليقا، ٢٥٩/١)

Hazrat Aaishah ﵂ reports that Hazrat Rasulullah ﷺ said, "Miswaak is a means of purifying the mouth, and a means of earning the pleasure of Allah ﵎."

3. Using the miswaak is from the sunnats of all the Ambiyaa ﵇.

عن أبي أيوب رضي الله عنه قال قال رسول الله صلى الله عليه وسلم أربع من سنن المرسلين الحياء والتعطر والسواك والنكاح (سنن الترمذي، الرقم: ١٠٨٠)

Hazrat Abu Ayyoob Ansaari ﵁ reports that Hazrat Rasulullah ﷺ said, "Four actions are from the sunnats of all the Ambiyaa ﵇; adopting hayaa (modesty in all spheres of human living), applying itr, using the miswaak, and making nikaah (getting married)." [See 6]

4. Apart from pleasing Allah ﵎, using the miswaak also causes the malaa'ikah (angels) to be happy and also contains numerous health benefits.

عن ابن عباس رضي الله عنهما قال قال رسول الله صلى الله عليه وسلم عليكم بالسواك فإنه مطهرة للفم مرضاة للرب مفرحة للملائكة يزيد في الحسنات وهو من

السنة ويجلو البصر ويذهب الحفر ويشد اللثة ويذهب البلغم ويطيب الفم ورواه غيره

وزاد فيه: ويصلح المعدة (شعب الإيمان للبيهقي، الرقم: ٢٥٢١)[131]

Hazrat Abdullah bin Abbaas رَضِيَ ٱللَّهُ عَنْهُمَا reports that Hazrat Rasulullah صَلَّى ٱللَّهُ عَلَيْهِ وَسَلَّمَ said, "Use the miswaak, for it purifies the mouth, is a means of pleasing Allah تَبَارَكَ وَتَعَالَى, a cause of pleasure to the malaa'ikah (angels), increases good deeds, it is from the sunnah practices, sharpens the eyesight, helps in removing scurvy (a disease affecting the gums), strengthens the gums, removes phlegm and gives the mouth a good smell." In some narrations, it has also been mentioned that using the miswaak helps the stomach and improves digestion."

---

[131] قال البيهقي: تفرد به الخليل بن مرة وليس بالقوي في الحديث

قال ابن الملقن في البدر المنير (٢٣/٢): هو كما قال فقد ضعفه يحيى بن معين والنسائي وقال البخاري منكر الحديث وقال ابن حبان منكر الحديث عن المشاهير كثير الرواية عن المجاهيل وقال أبو زرعة شيخ صالح وقال أبو حاتم ليس بالقوي وقال ابن عدي ليس بمتروك

قال السيوطي رحمه الله: كتصانيف البيهقي فقد التزم أن لا يخرج فيها حديثا يعلمه موضوعا انتهى (تدريب الراوي ٢٣٧/١)

وقد اعتمد السيوطي وابن عراق رحمهما الله على قول البيهقي هذا كما في اللآلئ المصنوعة في الأحاديث الموضوعة ١٢/١

قال الشيخ محمد عوامة: والشرط الرابع أن يكون لهذا الحديث الضعيف أصل يندرج تحته وهو أمر ملاحظ جدا في واقع علمائنا رحمهم الله فهم كما نبهت إليه يروون هذا الحديث الضعيف مع جملة أحاديث تشهد له إما صحيحة بذاتها فتعضد هذا الضعيف وإما ضعيفة أيضاً فتتعاضد مع بعضها وقد لاحظتُ هذا الامر كثيراً وأنا أستقرئ هذا الاستقراء من الكتب التي نقلت عنها فوجدته والحمد لله متوفراً مستوفٍ ... (حكم العمل بالحديث الضعيف ص ١٠٤-١٠٦)

SUNNAH METHOD OF USING THE MISWAAK

1. The method of holding the miswaak is for one to place his thumb and small finger under the miswaak with his remaining fingers on the upper-side of the miswaak.[132]

2. Hold the miswaak with the right hand and commence cleansing the teeth from the right.[133]

3. Make miswaak of the teeth horizontally and of the tongue vertically.[See 56]

عن أبي موسى رضي الله عنه قال دخلت على رسول الله صلى الله عليه وسلم وهو يستاك وهو واضع طرف السواك على لسانه يستن إلى فوق فوصف حماد كأنه يرفع سواكه قال حماد ووصفه لنا غيلان قال كان يستن طولا (مسند أحمد، الرقم: ١٩٧٣٧)[134]

---

[132] ويستحب إمساكه باليد اليمنى والسنة في كيفية أخذه أن تجعل الخنصر من يمينك أسفل السواك تحته والبنصر والوسطى والسبابة فوقه واجعل الإبهام أسفل رأسه تحته كما رواه ابن مسعود (البحر الرائق ٢١/١)

[133] قال العلامة ابن عابدين رحمه الله (قوله وندب إمساكه بيمناه) كذا في البحر والنهر قال في الدرر لأنه المنقول المتوارث اه وظاهره أنه منقول عن النبي صلى الله عليه وسلم لكن قال محشيه العلامة نوح أفندي: أقول دعوى النقل تحتاج إلى نقل ولم يوجد غاية ما يقال أن السواك إن كان من باب التطهير استحب باليمين كالمضمضة وإن كان من باب إزالة الأذى فباليسرى والظاهر الثاني كما روي عن مالك واستدل للأول بما ورد في بعض طرق حديث عائشة أنه صلى الله عليه وسلم كان يعجبه التيامن في ترجله وتنعله وطهوره وسواكه ورد بأن المراد البداءة بالجانب الأيمن من الفم اه ملخصا وفي البحر والنهر والسنة في كيفية أخذه أن يجعل الخنصر أسفله والإبهام أسفل رأسه وباقي الأصابع فوقه كما رواه ابن مسعود (رد المحتار ١١٤/١)

[134] سكت الحافظ عن هذا الحديث في التلخيص الحبير (٩٧/١) فالحديث حسن عنده (قواعد في علوم الحديث صـ ٥٥)

Hazrat Abu Moosa رَضِىَٱللَّهُعَنْهُ reports, "I once came to Rasulullah صَلَّىٱللَّهُعَلَيْهِوَسَلَّمَ while he was making miswaak and I found him making miswaak of his mubaarak tongue vertically."

عن عطاء بن أبي رباح رحمه الله قال قال رسول الله صلى الله عليه وسلم إذا شربتم فاشربوا مصا وإذا استكتم فاستاكوا عرضا (التلخيص الحبير ٩٦/١)[135]

Hazrat Ataa bin Abi Rabaah رَحِمَهُٱللَّهُ reports that Hazrat Rasulullah صَلَّىٱللَّهُعَلَيْهِوَسَلَّمَ said, "When you drink, then drink in sips (and avoid gulping the drink all at once), and when you make miswaak, then make miswaak (of the teeth) horizontally."

4. After using the miswaak, wash it and keep it upright.[See 56]

5. In the absence of a miswaak, the finger may be used as a substitute.[See 56]

عن أنس رضي الله عنه قال قال رسول الله صلى الله عليه وسلم يجزئ من السواك الأصابع (التلخيص الحبير ١٠٤/١)

---

[135] وفيه محمد بن خالد القرشي قال ابن القطان لا يعرف قلت وثقه ابن معين وابن حبان ورواه البغوي والعقيلي وابن عدي وابن منده والطبراني وابن قانع والبيهقي من حديث سعيد بن المسيب عن بهز بلفظ كان النبي صلى الله عليه وسلم يستاك عرضا الحديث وفي إسناده ثبيت بن كثير وهو ضعيف واليمان بن عدي وهو أضعف منه وذكر أبو نعيم في الصحابة ما يدل على أن هذا الحديث عن سعيد بن المسيب عن بهز بن حكيم بن معاوية القشيري وعلى هذا فهو منقطع فهو من رواية الأكابر عن الأصاغر وحكى ابن منده مما يؤيد ذلك أن مخيس بن تميم رواه عن بهز بن حكيم عن أبيه عن جده ورواه البيهقي والعقيلي أيضا من حديث ربيعة بن أكثم وإسناده ضعيف جدا وقد اختلف فيه على يحيى بن سعيد عن سعيد بن المسيب فرواه ثبيت بن كثير عنه فقال بهز ورواه علي بن ربيعة القرشي عنه فقال ربيعة بن أكثم قال ابن عبد البر ربيعة قتل بخيبر فلم يدركه سعيد وقال في التمهيد لا يصحان من جهة الإسناد ورواه أبو نعيم في كتاب السواك من حديث عائشة قالت: كان رسول الله صلى الله عليه وسلم يستاك عرضا ولا يستاك طولا وفي إسناده عبد الله بن حكيم وهو متروك (التلخيص الحبير ٩٦/١) قال الزبيدي في إتحاف السادة (٢٢٣/٥) وإذا استكتم فاستاكوا عرضا قال ابن القطان وفيه محمد بن خالد القرشي لا يعرف وقد رد عليه الحافظ ابن حجر بان محمد هذا وثقه ابن معين وابن حبان والحديث ورد من طرق عند البغوي والعقيلي وابن منده والطبراني وابن عدي وغيرهم بأسانيد وإن كانت مضطربة كما قاله ابن عبد البر لكن اجتماعها أحدث قوة صيرته حسنا

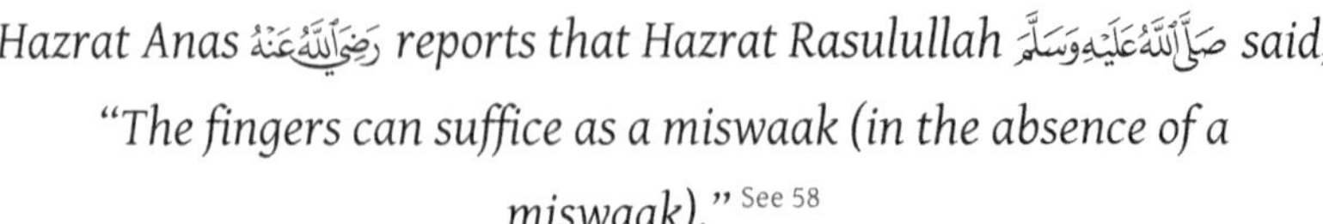

Hazrat Anas رَضِيَٱللَّهُ عَنْهُ *reports that Hazrat Rasulullah* صَلَّىٱللَّهُ عَلَيْهِ وَسَلَّمَ *said,
"The fingers can suffice as a miswaak (in the absence of a
miswaak)."* See 58

6. The miswaak should not exceed a hand-span in length, and
   should be equal to the small finger in thickness.[136]

7. Any stick that is useful for cleansing the mouth and is not
   harmful or poisonous can be used as a miswaak. The best
   miswaak is from the peelu tree *(salvadora persica)* and then
   the olive tree.[137]

عن معاذ بن جبل رضي الله عنه قال سمعت رسول الله صلى الله عليه وسلم يقول نعم
السواك الزيتون من شجرة مباركة تطيب الفم وتذهب بالحفر وهو سواكي وسواك
الأنبياء قبلي (مجمع الزوائد، الرقم: ٢٥٧٦)[138]

Hazrat Mu'aaz bin Jabal رَضِيَٱللَّهُ عَنْهُ *reports that Hazrat Rasulullah*
صَلَّىٱللَّهُ عَلَيْهِ وَسَلَّمَ *said, "How excellent is the miswaak taken from the olive
tree! It is from a blessed tree, cleanses the mouth and removes gum*

---

[136] كونه لينا مستويا بلا عقد في غلظ الخنصر وطول شبر

قال العلامة ابن عابدين رحمه الله (قوله في غلظ الخنصر) كذا في المعراج وفي الفتح الأصبع قوله (وطول شبر) الظاهر أنه في ابتداء استعماله فلا

يضر نقصه بعد ذلك بالقطع منه لتسويته تأمل وهل المراد شبر المستعمل أو المعتاد الظاهر الثاني لأنه محمل الإطلاق غالبا (رد المحتار ١١٤/١)

وليكن رطبا في غلظ الخنصر وطول الشبر (الفتاوى الهندية ٧/١)

[137] ويكره بمؤذ ويحرم بذي سم

قال العلامة ابن عابدين رحمه الله (قوله ويكره بمؤذ) قال في الحلية وذكر غير واحد من العلماء كراهته بقضبان الرمان والريحان اه وفي شرح الهداية

للعيني روى الحارث في مسنده عن ضمير بن حبيب قال نهى رسول له رسول الله عن السواك بعود الريحان وقال إنه يحرك عرق الجذام وفي النهر ويستاك

بكل عود إلا الرمان والقصب والأراك وأفضله الأراك ثم الزيتون روى الطبراني نعم السواك الزيتون من شجرة مباركة وهو سواكي وسواك الأنبياء من قبلي

(رد المحتار ١١٥/١)

[138] قال الهيثمي: رواه الطبراني في الأوسط وفيه معلل بن محمد ولم أجد من ذكره

sicknesses and maladies (and removes the yellowness of the teeth).
It is my miswaak as well as the miswaak of the previous Ambiyaa
عَلَيْهِمُ ٱلسَّلَامُ.”

عن ابن مسعود رضي الله عنه كنت أجتني لرسول الله صلى الله عليه وسلم سواكا من
أراك (إعلاء السنن ٧٥/١ ، التلخيص الحبير ٩٥/١)[139]

Hazrat Abdullah bin Mas'ood  reports, "I used to break twigs
from the peelu tree (salvadora persica) for the miswaak of
Rasulullah صَلَّى ٱللَّهُ عَلَيْهِ وَسَلَّمَ.”

---

[139] قال الحافظ في التلخيص: أخرجه ابن حبان والطبراني أيضا وصححه الضياء في أحكامه ورواه أحمد موقوفا على ابن مسعود أنه كان يجتني
سواكا من أراك الحديث ولم يقل فيه أنه كان يجتنيه للنبي صلى الله عليه وسلم

OCCASIONS WHEN THE MISWAAK SHOULD BE USED

1. Upon awakening.

عن عائشة رضي الله عنها أن النبي صلى الله عليه وسلم كان لا يرقد من ليل ولا نهار فيستيقظ إلا تسوك قبل أن يتوضأ (سنن أبي داود، الرقم: ٥٧)[140]

Hazrat Aaishah رَضِيَٱللَّهُعَنْهَا reports, "Whenever Nabi صَلَّىٱللَّهُعَلَيْهِوَسَلَّمَ awoke from his sleep, whether in the night or day, he would make miswaak before performing wudhu."

It should be borne in mind that the use of the miswaak upon awakening is a separate sunnah and using the miswaak at the time of wudhu is a separate sunnah. Hence, if one does not intend making wudhu to perform salaah upon awakening from one's sleep (or a woman is in menses), then one should use the miswaak upon awakening. However, if one makes wudhu immediately upon awakening and uses the miswaak during this wudhu, then using the miswaak during the wudhu will suffice on behalf of both sunnats.[141]

2. When entering the home.

عن عائشة رضي الله عنها أن النبي صلى الله عليه وسلم كان إذا دخل بيته بدأ

بالسواك (صحيح مسلم، الرقم: ٢٥٣)

Hazrat Aaishah رَضِيَٱللَّهُعَنْهَا reports, "Whenever Nabi صَلَّىٱللَّهُعَلَيْهِوَسَلَّمَ used

to enter his home, he would make miswaak."

3. Before reciting the Quraan Majeed.[142]

عن علي بن أبي طالب رضي الله عنه قال إن أفواهكم طرق للقرآن فطيبوها بالسواك

(سنن ابن ماجة، الرقم: ٢٩١)[143]

It is reported that Hazrat Ali رَضِيَٱللَّهُعَنْهُ said, "Indeed your mouths are

passages for the Quraan (your mouths are used to recite the

Quraan). Hence, cleanse your mouths through using the miswaak."

عن علي رضي الله عنه أنه أمر بالسواك وقال قال النبي صلى الله عليه وسلم إن العبد

إذا تسوك ثم قام يصلي قام الملك خلفه فتسمع لقراءته فيدنو منه أو كلمة نحوها حتى

---

[142] كما يندب لاصفرار سن وتغير رائحة وقراءة قرآن

قال العلامة ابن عابدين رحمه الله ... قال في إمداد الفتاح وليس السواك من خصائص الوضوء فإنه يستحب في حالات منها تغير الفم والقيام من النوم وإلى الصلاة ودخول البيت والاجتماع بالناس وقراءة القرآن لقول أبي حنيفة إن السواك من سنن الدين فتستوي فيه الأحوال كلها اه وفي القهستاني ولا يختص بالوضوء كما قيل بل سنة على حدة على ما في ظاهر الرواية وفي حاشية الهداية أنه مستحب في جميع الأوقات ويؤكد استحبابه عند قصد التوضؤ فيسن أو يستحب عند كل صلاة اه وممن صرح باستحبابه عند صلاة أيضا الحلبي في شرح المنية الصغير وفي هدية ابن عماد أيضا وفي التتارخانية عن التتمة ويستحب السواك عندنا عند كل صلاة ووضوء وكل ما يغير الفم وعند اليقظة اه فاغتنم هذا التحرير الفريد (رد المحتار ١١٤/١)

[143] عن علي رضي الله عنه أنه أمر بالسواك وقال قال رسول الله صلى الله عليه وسلم إن العبد إذا تسوك ثم قام يصلي قام الملك خلفه فيستمع لقراءته فيدنو منه أو كلمة نحوها حتى يضع فاه على فيه فما يخرج من فيه شيء من القرآن إلا صار في جوف الملك فطهروا أفواهكم للقرآن رواه البزار بإسناد جيد لا بأس به وروى ابن ماجه بعضه موقوفا ولعله أشبه (الترغيب والترهيب، الرقم: ٣٣٣)

يضع فاه على فيه فما يخرج من فيه شيء من القرآن إلا صار في جوف الملك فطهروا أفواهكم للقرآن (مسند البزار، الرقم: ٥٥٠)[144]

Hazrat Ali رَضِيَٱللَّهُعَنْهُ *reports that Hazrat Rasulullah* صَلَّىٱللَّهُعَلَيْهِوَسَلَّمَ *said, "When a person uses the miswaak and then stands to perform salaah, an angel stands behind him and listens attentively to his recitation of the Quraan. The angel then draws close to him until it places its mouth upon his mouth. Whatever portion of the Quraan he then recites is protected in the belly of the angel (and thereafter secured by Allah* تَبَارَكَوَتَعَالَى*). Hence, ensure that you cleanse your mouth before reciting the Quraan."*

4. At the time of wudhu.[See 56]

عن أبي هريرة رضي الله عنه عن النبي صلى الله عليه وسلم لولا أن أشق على أمتي لأمرتهم بالسواك عند كل وضوء (صحيح البخاري تعليقا ١/٢٥٩)

Hazrat Abu Hurairah رَضِيَٱللَّهُعَنْهُ *reports that Hazrat Rasulullah* صَلَّىٱللَّهُعَلَيْهِوَسَلَّمَ *said, "Had it not been for the fear of my Ummah experiencing difficulty, I would have certainly commanded them (and made it compulsory upon them) to use the miswaak at the time of every wudhu (however, using the miswaak is not compulsory but an emphasized sunnah)."*

5. When the teeth become discoloured or a bad odour emanates from the mouth.[See 142]

---

[144] وقال الهيثمي: رواه البزار ورجاله ثقات وروى ابن ماجه بعضه إلا أنه موقوف وهذا مرفوع (مجمع الزوائد، الرقم: ٢٥٦٤)

عن جعفر بن أبي طالب رضي الله عنه عن النبي صلى الله عليه وسلم أنه قال ما لي أراكم تدخلون علي قلحا استاكوا ولولا أن أشق على أمتي لأمرتهم أن يستاكوا عند كل صلاة (كتاب الآثار، الرقم: ٤١)

It is reported from Hazrat Ja'far رَضِيَٱللَّهُعَنْهُ that on one occasion, Hazrat Rasulullah صَلَّىٱللَّهُعَلَيْهِوَسَلَّمَ addressed certain people saying, "What is the matter that you come to me in the condition where I see your teeth to be yellow? I advise you to cleanse your teeth with the miswaak." Hazrat Rasulullah صَلَّىٱللَّهُعَلَيْهِوَسَلَّمَ then said, "Had it not been for the fear of my Ummah experiencing difficulty, I would have certainly commanded them (and made it compulsory upon them) to use the miswaak at the time of every salaah (however, using the miswaak is not compulsory but an emphasized sunnah at the time of wudhu)."

عن عبد الله بن بشر المازني رضي الله عنه قال قال رسول الله صلى الله عليه وسلم قصوا أظافيركم وادفنوا قلاماتكم ونقوا براجمكم ونظفوا لثاتكم من الطعام وتسننوا ولا تدخلوا علي قخرا بخرا (نوادر الأصول تحت الأصل التاسع والعشرين في باب النظافة)[145]

Hazrat Abdullah bin Bishr رَضِيَٱللَّهُعَنْهُ reports that Hazrat Rasulullah صَلَّىٱللَّهُعَلَيْهِوَسَلَّمَ said, "Trim your nails and bury your nails, cleanse your joints thoroughly, keep your gums clean from food particles, make

---

[145] قال صاحب نوادر الأصول: وقوله لا تدخلوا علي قخرا بخرا المحفوظ عندي قلحا وفحلا والأقلح الذي اصفرت أسنانه حتى بخرت من باطنها ولا نعرف القخر والبخر إلا الذي نجد له رائحة منكرة يقال رجل أبخر ورجال بخر

miswaak, and do not come to me in the condition that I find your teeth to be yellow and your mouths emitting a bad odour."

6. Before and after eating.

عن أبي هريرة رضي الله عنه أن رسول الله صلى الله عليه وسلم قال إن كان قاله لولا أن أشق على أمتي لأمرتهم بالسواك مع الوضوء وقال أبو هريرة رضي الله عنه لقد كنت أستن قبل أن أنام وبعد ما أستيقظ وقبل ما آكل وبعد ما آكل حين سمعت رسول الله صلى الله عليه وسلم يقول ما قال (مسند أحمد، الرقم: ٩١٩٤)[146]

Hazrat Abu Hurairah رَضِىَٱللَّهُعَنْهُ reports that Hazrat Rasulullah صَلَّىٱللَّهُعَلَيْهِوَسَلَّمَ said, and most certainly he had said, "Had it not been for the fear of my Ummah experiencing difficulty, I would have certainly commanded them (and made it compulsory upon them) to use the miswaak at the time of every wudhu (however, using the miswaak is not compulsory but an emphasized sunnah)." Hazrat Abu Hurairah رَضِىَٱللَّهُعَنْهُ further said, "On account of Rasulullah صَلَّىٱللَّهُعَلَيْهِوَسَلَّمَ emphasising the use of the miswaak, I made it a habit to use the miswaak before going to sleep, upon awakening, before eating and after eating."

7. When one perceives the pangs of death (sakaraatul maut).

عن عائشة رضي الله عنها قالت دخل عبد الرحمن بن أبي بكر ومعه سواك يستن به فنظر إليه رسول الله صلى الله عليه وسلم فقلت له أعطني هذا السواك يا عبد الرحمن

---

[146] قال الهيثمي: رواه أحمد ورجاله ثقات (مجمع الزوائد، الرقم: ١١١٩)

فأعطانيه فقصمته (وفي رواية وطيبته) ثم مضغته فأعطيته رسول الله صلى الله عليه
وسلم فاستن به وهو مستند إلى صدري (صحيح البخاري، الرقم: ٨٩٠)

Hazrat Aaishah رَضِيَ ٱللَّهُ عَنْهَا reports, "(When Hazrat Rasulullah صَلَّى ٱللَّهُ عَلَيْهِ وَسَلَّمَ was about to pass away,) my brother, Abdur Rahmaan رَضِيَ ٱللَّهُ عَنْهُ, entered the room with a miswaak which he was using to clean his teeth. The mubaarak sight of Rasulullah صَلَّى ٱللَّهُ عَلَيْهِ وَسَلَّمَ fell on the miswaak (but due to weakness, he was unable to ask for it. I understood that Hazrat Rasulullah صَلَّى ٱللَّهُ عَلَيْهِ وَسَلَّمَ wished to use the miswaak at this time), so I said to my brother, 'O Abdur Rahmaan, lend me your miswaak.' I took it from him, broke off the top portion, (cleansed it, softened it,) and then gave it to Hazrat Rasulullah صَلَّى ٱللَّهُ عَلَيْهِ وَسَلَّمَ. Hazrat Rasulullah صَلَّى ٱللَّهُ عَلَيْهِ وَسَلَّمَ then used the miswaak while he was reclining on my chest."

8. If one had made wudhu earlier and the time of salaah approaches, then it is mustahab for one to use the miswaak for salaah to remove any odour from the mouth. Similarly, it is mustahab to make miswaak when joining a gathering.[See 142]

9. When making tayammum due to illness, or water not being available or being insufficient, one should cleanse one's mouth with miswaak and perform salaah.[See 142]

CHAPTER FIVE

AZAAN AND IQAAMAH

Azaan – Its Inception and Origin

When Hazrat Rasulullah ﷺ made hijrah (migrated) to Madinah Munawwarah, he constructed the musjid. After constructing the musjid, he consulted the Sahaabah رضي الله عنهم regarding the method to be adopted to call people for salaah. It was the burning desire within the heart of Hazrat Rasulullah ﷺ that all the Sahaabah رضي الله عنهم congregate and perform their salaah together in the musjid. Hazrat Rasulullah ﷺ was neither pleased with the Sahaabah رضي الله عنهم performing their salaah in the musjid at different times nor in their homes.

The Sahaabah رضي الله عنهم presented various suggestions in regard to how people could be called for salaah. Some of the suggestions of the Sahaabah رضي الله عنهم were that a fire be lit or a flag be hoisted. On seeing the fluttering flag or the flames and smoke of the fire, people would understand that it is the time of salaah and thereby inform others to come to the musjid for salaah.

Other suggestions were that a horn be sounded or that the naaqoos (two sticks) be struck upon each other to alert people that it is the time for salaah.

Hazrat Rasulullah ﷺ was not pleased with these suggestions. Hazrat Rasulullah ﷺ did not want his Ummah to emulate the Christians, Jews and kuffaar in aspects of their Deen or their worldly life. If the Muslims were to adopt these methods, it would result in them resembling the disbelievers in their Deen, and furthermore, it would lead to confusion coming about in the salaah times as the disbelievers were calling people to their places of worship at other times through these same methods.

No conclusion was reached in that gathering and the matter was thus left undecided.

Prior to the Sahaabah ﷺ dispersing from the gathering of Hazrat Rasulullah ﷺ, Hazrat Umar ﷺ presented a suggestion before Hazrat Rasulullah ﷺ that, as no method has yet been decided, then for the time being, perhaps a person could be appointed to go around calling people for salaah whenever the time of salaah enters.

Hazrat Rasulullah ﷺ accepted the suggestion of Hazrat Umar ﷺ and appointed Hazrat Bilaal ﷺ to carry out this task. Hence, at the time of salaah, Hazrat Bilaal رَضِىَ اللّٰهُ عَنْهُ would go around informing the people that the jamaat (congregational salaah) in the musjid was about to commence.

The heart of each Sahaabi رَضِىَ اللّٰهُ عَنْهُ was filled with the concern of Hazrat Rasulullah صَلَّى اللّٰهُ عَلَيْهِ وَسَلَّمَ in regard to how the people should be called to perform salaah together in the musjid.

Nevertheless, it was not long thereafter that, one night, after Hazrat Abdullah bin Zaid رَضِىَ اللّٰهُ عَنْهُ went to sleep; he was shown a dream by Allah تَبَارَكَ وَتَعَالَى. In the dream, he saw an angel, in the form of a human being, who was dressed in two garments of green and was carrying a naaqoos. He asked the angel, "O servant of Allah! Are you selling the naaqoos?" The angel replied by asking him, "What do you wish to do with it?" Hazrat Abdullah bin Zaid رَضِىَ اللّٰهُ عَنْهُ answered, "I will use it to call people for salaah." The angel then said, "Should I not show you a method for calling people to salaah which is better than striking this naaqoos?" Hazrat Abdullah رَضِىَ اللّٰهُ عَنْهُ asked, "What method is better?" The angel replied, "You will call out the azaan." after which the angel taught him the words of the azaan.

When he awoke the following morning, he went to Hazrat Rasulullah صَلَّى اللّٰهُ عَلَيْهِ وَسَلَّمَ and related the entire dream. On hearing the dream, Hazrat Rasulullah صَلَّى اللّٰهُ عَلَيْهِ وَسَلَّمَ mentioned, "Certainly it is a true dream. Stand beside Bilaal رَضِىَ اللّٰهُ عَنْهُ and inform him of the words (of the azaan) that you were taught in the dream so that he may call out the azaan with these words. Allow Bilaal رَضِىَ اللّٰهُ عَنْهُ to call out the azaan as his voice is louder than your voice. Thus, his voice will reach further."

When Hazrat Umar رَضِىَ اللّٰهُ عَنْهُ heard the azaan of Hazrat Bilaal رَضِىَ اللّٰهُ عَنْهُ, he hastily took his shawl and rushed to the gathering of Hazrat Rasulullah صَلَّى اللّٰهُ عَلَيْهِ وَسَلَّمَ. On reaching the gathering of Hazrat Rasulullah صَلَّى اللّٰهُ عَلَيْهِ وَسَلَّمَ, he respectfully exclaimed, "O Rasul of Allah صَلَّى اللّٰهُ عَلَيْهِ وَسَلَّمَ! I take an oath by that Being who appointed you as His messenger to convey the truth of Islam, I was shown a dream in which I was taught the words of the azaan." When Hazrat Rasulullah صَلَّى اللّٰهُ عَلَيْهِ وَسَلَّمَ heard this, he became pleased and said, "This has been further confirmed as a true dream from the side of Allah تَبَارَكَ وَتَعَالَى."

It has been narrated that more than ten Sahaabah رَضِىَ اللّٰهُ عَنْهُمْ had been shown dreams wherein they were taught the words of the azaan. Among them were Hazrat Abu Bakr رَضِىَ اللّٰهُ عَنْهُ and Hazrat Umar رَضِىَ اللّٰهُ عَنْهُ.[147]

---

[147] مرقاة المفاتيح ٣٣١/٢ ، الدر المنضود ٨٦/٢ ، درس ترمذي ٤٥١/١ ، السعاية ٤/٢

VIRTUES OF THE MUAZZIN

Azaan is among the salient features of the Deen of Islam. Islam has afforded great honour to all those who call out the azaan, inviting people towards salaah. On the Day of Qiyaamah, people will admire those who used to call out the azaan in the world on account of their esteemed position and lofty status in the Hereafter. Numerous Ahaadith highlight the great virtues and immense rewards in store for those who call out the azaan.

1. The muazzin will enjoy an esteemed position on the Day of Qiyaamah.

عن معاوية رضي الله عنه قال سمعت رسول الله صلى الله عليه وسلم يقول المؤذنون أطول الناس أعناقا يوم القيامة (صحيح مسلم، الرقم: ٣٨٧)

Hazrat Mu'aawiyah رَضِيَٱللَّهُعَنْهُ *reports, "I heard Rasulullah* صَلَّىٱللَّهُعَلَيْهِوَسَلَّمَ *say, 'Verily the muazzins will have the 'longest necks' on the Day of Qiyaamah.'"*

In this Hadith, the literal meaning of having the 'longest necks' is not intended. Rather, the meaning of having the 'longest necks' is that they will occupy distinct positions of honour.

2. The muazzins will be on mountains of musk on the Day of Qiyaamah.

عن عبد الله بن عمر رضي الله عنهما قال قال رسول الله صلى الله عليه وسلم ثلاثة على كثبان المسك أراه قال يوم القيامة يغبطهم الأولون والآخرون رجل ينادي

بالصلوات الخمس في كل يوم وليلة ورجل يؤم قوما وهم به راضون وعبد أدى حق الله وحق مواليه (سنن الترمذي، الرقم: ٢٥٦٦)[148]

Hazrat Abdullah bin Umar رَضِىَاللهُعَنْهُمَا reports that Hazrat Rasulullah صَلَّىاللهُعَلَيْهِوَسَلَّمَ said, "Three groups of people will be on mountains of musk (on the Day of Qiyaamah), and the former and latter people will envy their position. The first is the person who used to call out the azaan every day for the five daily salaah. The second is the person who led the people in salaah while they were pleased with him (i.e. he fulfilled the obligation of salaah in its proper manner). The third is the slave who fulfilled the rights of Allah تَبَارَكَوَتَعَالَى and the rights of his masters."

3. There are great rewards in store in the Hereafter for those who call out the azaan.

عن أبي هريرة رضي الله عنه أن رسول الله صلى الله عليه وسلم قال لو يعلم الناس ما في النداء والصف الأول ثم لم يجدوا إلا أن يستهموا عليه لاستهموا (صحيح البخاري، الرقم: ٦١٥)

---

[148] قال أبو عيسى: هذا حديث حسن غريب

قال المنذري في الترغيب والترهيب (الرقم: ٣٧٤): رواه أحمد والترمذي من رواية سفيان عن أبي اليقظان عن زاذان عنه وقال حديث حسن غريب قال الحافظ وأبو اليقظان واه وقد روى عنه الثقات واسمه عثمان بن قيس قاله الترمذي وقيل عثمان بن عمير وقيل عثمان بن أبي حميد وقيل غير ذلك ورواه الطبراني في الأوسط والصغير بإسناد لا بأس به ولفظه (الرقم: ٣٧٥) قال رسول الله صلى الله عليه وسلم ثلاثة لا يهولهم الفزع الأكبر ولا ينالهم الحساب هم على كثب من مسك حتى يفرغ من حساب الخلائق رجل قرأ القرآن ابتغاء وجه الله وأم به قوما وهم به راضون وداع يدعو إلى الصلاة ابتغاء وجه الله وعبد أحسن فيما بينه وبين ربه وفيما بينه وبين مواليه ورواه في الكبير ولفظه (الرقم: ٣٧٦) عن ابن عمر رضي الله عنهما قال لو لم أسمعه من رسول الله صلى الله عليه وسلم إلا مرة ومرة ومرة حتى عد سبع مرات لما حدثت به سمعت رسول الله صلى الله عليه وسلم يقول ثلاثة على كثبان المسك يوم القيامة لا يهولهم الفزع ولا يفزعون حين يفزع الناس رجل علم القرآن فقام به يطلب به وجه الله وما عنده ورجل نادى في كل يوم وليلة خمس صلوات يطلب وجه الله وما عنده ومملوك لم يمنعه رق الدنيا من طاعة ربه

Hazrat Abu Hurairah رَضِيَ اللّٰهُ عَنْهُ *reports that Hazrat Rasulullah* صَلَّى اللّٰهُ عَلَيْهِ وَسَلَّمَ *said, "If the people only know the great reward for calling out the azaan and performing salaah in the first saff, and thereafter they could find no alternative to decide who would be granted that honour besides drawing lots, they would definitely draw lots to decide."*

4. Every creation (whether jinn, human or any other creation) that hears the voice of the muazzin calling out the azaan will testify on his behalf on the Day of Qiyaamah.

عن عبد الرحمن بن عبد الله بن عبد الرحمن بن أبي صعصعة الأنصاري ثم المازني عن أبيه أنه أخبره أن أبا سعيد الخدري رضي الله عنه قال له إني أراك تحب الغنم والبادية فإذا كنت في غنمك أو باديتك فأذنت بالصلاة فارفع صوتك بالنداء فإنه لا يسمع مدى صوت المؤذن جن ولا إنس ولا شيء إلا شهد له يوم القيامة قال أبو سعيد سمعته من رسول الله صلى الله عليه وسلم (صحيح البخاري، الرقم: ٦٠٩)

It is reported regarding Hazrat Abdullah bin Abdir Rahmaan bin Abi Sa'sa'ah رَحِمَهُ اللّٰهُ *that on one occasion, Hazrat Abu Sa'eed Khudri* رَضِيَ اللّٰهُ عَنْهُ *said to him, "I see that you like to remain with your livestock (grazing them) in the open fields. When you are among your livestock or in the open fields, (and the time of salaah enters) and you wish to call out the azaan, then you should raise your voice and call out the azaan, for certainly the jinn, humans or any other creation that hears the voice of the muazzin as far as it reaches will testify on his behalf on the Day of Qiyaamah." Hazrat Abu Sa'eed* رَضِيَ اللّٰهُ عَنْهُ *said, "I heard this from Rasulullah* صَلَّى اللّٰهُ عَلَيْهِ وَسَلَّمَ*."*

5. Forgiveness has been declared for the muazzin. Similarly, glad tidings have been given regarding the muazzin that he is blessed with the reward of all those who performed salaah due to responding to his call.

عن البراء بن عازب رضي الله عنه أن نبي الله صلى الله عليه وسلم قال إن الله وملائكته يصلون على الصف المقدم والمؤذن يغفر له بمد صوته ويصدقه من سمعه من رطب ويابس وله مثل أجر من صلى معه (سنن النسائي، الرقم: ٦٤٥)[149]

Hazrat Baraa bin Aazib رَضِيَٱللَّهُعَنْهُ *reports that Hazrat Rasulullah* صَلَّىٱللَّهُعَلَيْهِوَسَلَّمَ *said, "Certainly Allah* تَبَارَكَوَتَعَالَى *showers His special mercy upon those (who perform salaah) in the first saff and the malaa'ikah (angels) make special dua for them. The muazzin will receive forgiveness from Allah* تَبَارَكَوَتَعَالَى *for the distance his voice covers (if he had so many sins that they cover the distance from the place he calls out the azaan till the furthest point his voice reaches, all those sins will be forgiven, or for the duration of time it takes his voice to reach the furthest point, he will receive the forgiveness of Allah* تَبَارَكَوَتَعَالَى *for that same duration of time in his life in which he committed sins), and every creation, whether possessing life or not, will bear testimony on his behalf (on the Day of Qiyaamah), and he will receive the reward of all those people who performed salaah*

---

[149] قال المنذري في الترغيب والترهيب (١/٢٤٣): رواه أحمد والنسائي بإسناد حسن جيد

قوله بمدى صوته وفي نسخة بمد صوته قيل معناه بقدر صوته وحده فإن بلغ الغاية من الصوت بلغ الغاية من المغفرة وان كان صوته دون ذلك فمغفرته على قدره أو المعنى لو كان له ذنوب تملأ ما بين محله الذي يؤذن فيه إلى ما ينتهي إليه صوته لغفر له وقيل يغفر له من الذنوب ما فعله في زمان مقدر بهذه المسافة (حاشية السندي ١/١٠٦)

with him (i.e. all those people who performed salaah on account of his call)."

6.   The muazzin has been described in the Hadith as being from the best servants of Allah تَبَارَكَ وَتَعَالَى.

عن ابن أبي أوفى رضي الله عنه قال قال رسول الله صلى الله عليه وسلم إن خيار عباد الله الذين يراعون الشمس والقمر والنجوم والأظلة لذكر الله (المستدرك على الصحيحين للحاكم، الرقم: ١٦٣)[150]

Hazrat Ibnu Abi Awfaa رَضِيَ ٱللَّهُ عَنْهُ *reports that Hazrat Rasulullah* صَلَّى ٱللَّهُ عَلَيْهِ وَسَلَّمَ *said, "Certainly the best servants of Allah* تَبَارَكَ وَتَعَالَى *are those who observe the rising and setting of the sun, the moon, the stars and the (length of the) shadows for the remembrance of Allah* تَبَارَكَ وَتَعَالَى *(i.e. they fulfil their ibaadaat in its proper time according to the command of Allah* تَبَارَكَ وَتَعَالَى, *while keeping track of time through observing the sun, moon, stars and the length of the shadows, as explained in the Ahaadith. The muazzin is included in this glad tiding on account of him keeping track of time so that he can call out the azaan of each salaah at its proper time)."*

7.   Freedom from the fire of Jahannum is promised for the one who calls out the azaan for seven years.

عن ابن عباس رضي الله عنهما أن النبي صلى الله عليه وسلم قال من أذن سبع سنين محتسبا كتبت له براءة من النار (سنن الترمذي، الرقم: ٢٠٦)[151]

---

[150] قال بشر بن موسى: ولم يكن هذا الحديث عند الحميدي في مسنده هذا إسناد صحيح وعبد الجبار العطار ثقة وقد احتج مسلم والبخاري بإبراهيم السكسكي وإذا صح هذه الاستقامة لم يضره توهين من أفسد إسناده وقال الذهبي في التلخيص: إسناده صحيح

Hazrat Ibnu Abbaas رَضِيَ ٱللَّهُ عَنْهُمَا reports that Hazrat Rasulullah صَلَّى ٱللَّهُ عَلَيْهِ وَسَلَّمَ said, "The one who calls out the azaan for seven years with sincerity and the hope of attaining reward receives the guarantee of freedom from the fire of Jahannum."

8. Hazrat Rasulullah صَلَّى ٱللَّهُ عَلَيْهِ وَسَلَّمَ made dua for the forgiveness of those who call out the azaan.

عن أبي هريرة رضي الله عنه قال قال رسول الله صلى الله عليه وسلم الإمام ضامن والمؤذن مؤتمن اللهم أرشد الأئمة واغفر للمؤذنين (سنن أبي داود، الرقم: ٥١٧)[152]

Hazrat Abu Hurairah رَضِيَ ٱللَّهُ عَنْهُ reports that Hazrat Rasulullah صَلَّى ٱللَّهُ عَلَيْهِ وَسَلَّمَ said, "The imaam is responsible (for the salaah of the entire congregation) and the muazzin is one who is entrusted with a trust (i.e. he has been entrusted with the duty of calling out the azaan on its prescribed time). O Allah تَبَارَكَ وَتَعَالَى, guide the imaams

---

[151] سكت الحافظ عن هذا الحديث في الفصل الثاني من هداية الرواة (٣١٨/١) فالحديث حسن عنده

وعن ابن عمر رضي الله عنهما أن النبي صلى الله عليه وسلم قال من أذن اثنتي عشرة سنة وجبت له الجنة وكتب له بتأذينه في كل يوم ستون حسنة وبكل إقامة ثلاثون حسنة رواه ابن ماجه والدارقطني والحاكم وقال صحيح على شرط البخاري

قال الحافظ وهو كما قال فإن عبد الله بن صالح كاتب الليث وإن كان فيه كلام فقد روى عنه البخاري في الصحيح (الترغيب والترهيب، الرقم: ٣٨٥)

[152] سكت الحافظ عن هذا الحديث في الفصل الثاني من هداية الرواة (٣١٨/١) فالحديث حسن عنده

قال المنذري في الترغيب والترهيب وعن أبي هريرة رضي الله عنه قال قال رسول الله صلى الله عليه وسلم الإمام ضامن والمؤذن مؤتمن اللهم أرشد الأئمة واغفر للمؤذنين رواه أبو داود والترمذي وابن خزيمة وابن حبان في صحيحيهما إلا أنهما قالا فأرشد الله الأئمة وغفر للمؤذنين ولابن خزيمة رواية كرواية أبي داود (الترغيب والترهيب، الرقم: ٣٦٥)

وفي أخرى له قال رسول الله صلى الله عليه وسلم المؤذنون أمناء والأئمة ضمناء اللهم اغفر للمؤذنين وسدد الأئمة ثلاث مرات ورواه أحمد من حديث أبي أمامة بإسناد حسن (الترغيب والترهيب، الرقم: ٣٦٦)

وعن عائشة رضي الله عنها قالت سمعت رسول الله صلى الله عليه وسلم يقول الإمام ضامن والمؤذن مؤتمن فأرشد الله الأئمة وعفا عن المؤذنين رواه ابن حبان في صحيحه (الترغيب والترهيب، الرقم: ٣٦٧)

(towards fulfilling their obligation of leading the salaah correctly) and forgive the muazzins (for their shortcomings)."

9. It was the desire of the Sahaabah رَضِىَٱللَّهُعَنْهُمْ to call out the azaan and they desired that their children also call out the azaan.

Below are some of the Ahaadith which illustrate the eagerness of the Sahaabah رَضِىَٱللَّهُعَنْهُمْ to call out the azaan:

❖ The eagerness of Hazrat Ali رَضِىَٱللَّهُعَنْهُ for Hazrat Hasan رَضِىَٱللَّهُعَنْهُ and Hazrat Husain رَضِىَٱللَّهُعَنْهُ to call out the azaan:

عن علي رضي الله عنه قال ندمت أن لا أكون طلبت إلى رسول الله صلى الله عليه وسلم فيجعل الحسن والحسين مؤذنين (مجمع الزوائد، الرقم: ١٨٣٦)[153]

It is reported that Hazrat Ali رَضِىَٱللَّهُعَنْهُ said, "I feel remorseful over the fact that I did not request Rasulullah صَلَّىٱللَّهُعَلَيْهِوَسَلَّمَ to appoint my two sons, Hasan and Husain رَضِىَٱللَّهُعَنْهُمَا, as muazzins to call out the azaan."

---

[153] رواه الطبراني في الأوسط وفيه الحارث وهو ضعيف

قال أبو عيسى: وقد ضعف بعض أهل العلم الحارث الأعور (سنن الترمذي، الرقم: ٢٨٢)

قال العلامة ظفر أحمد التهانوي في إعلاء السنن (١٧/٢١٧): والحارث مختلف فيه احتج به أصحاب السنن ومنهم النسائي مع تعنته في الرجال

قال الذهبي في الميزان وحديث الحارث في السنن الأربعة والنسائي مع تعنته في الرجال فقد احتج به وقوى أمره والجمهور على توهين أمره مع روايتهم لحديثه في الأبواب هذا الشعبي يكذبه ثم يروي عنه والظاهر أنه كان يكذب في لهجته وحكايته وأما في الحديث النبوي فلا وكان من أوعية العلم قال مرة بن خالد أنبأنا محمد بن سيرين قال كان من أصحاب ابن مسعود خمسة يؤخذ عنهم أدركت منهم أربعة وفاتني الحارث فلم أره وكان يفضل عليهم وكان أحسنهم ويختلف في هؤلاء الثلاثة أيهم أفضل علقمة ومسروق وعبيدة وقال عباس عن ابن معين ليس به بأس وكذا قال النسائي وعنه قال ليس بالقوي (وهذا تليين هين) وقال عثمان الدارمي سألت يحيى بن معين عن الحارث الأعور فقال ثقة قال عثمان ليس يتابع يحيى على هذا اه

وخلاصة الكلام في الحارث الأعور كما قال الحافظ ابن حجر في التقريب (الرقم: ١٠٢٩) أن فيه ضعفا

❖ **The eagerness of Hazrat Umar** رَضِىَ ٱللَّهُ عَنْهُ **to call out the azaan:**

عن قيس بن أبي حازم قال قدمنا على عمر بن الخطاب فسأل من مؤذنكم فقلنا عبيدنا وموالينا فقال بيده هكذا يقلبها عبيدنا وموالينا إن ذلكم بكم لنقص شديد لو أطقت الأذان مع الخلافة لأذنت (السنن الكبرى للبيهقي، الرقم: ٢٠٠٢)[154]

Qais bin Abi Haazim رَحِمَهُ ٱللَّهُ *reports, "Once, we had come (to Madinah Munawwarah) to meet Umar* رَضِىَ ٱللَّهُ عَنْهُ*. During our conversation, he asked us, 'Who calls out the azaan in the place where you live?' We answered, 'We have appointed our slaves to call out the azaan.' Umar* رَضِىَ ٱللَّهُ عَنْهُ*, gesturing with his hands (in surprise, repeated our words) saying, 'We have appointed our slaves to call out the azaan.' He then remarked, 'Certainly this is a major shortcoming on your side (that you have appointed such people to call out the azaan who are not knowledgeable in Deen). (Azaan is such a great ibaadah and its reward is so abundant that) had I been able to call out the azaan together with managing the affairs of khilaafah, I would have certainly accepted the position of a muazzin and called out the azaan."'*

عن عمر رضي الله عنهما أنه قال لو كنت مؤذنا لكمل أمري وما باليت أن لا أنتصب لقيام ليل ولا لصيام نهار سمعت رسول الله صلى الله عليه وسلم يقول اللهم اغفر للمؤذنين ثلاثا قلت يا رسول الله تركتنا ونحن نجتلد على الأذان

---

[154] حدثنا يزيد ووكيع قالا حدثنا إسماعيل عن شبيل بن عوف قال قال عمر من مؤذنوكم قالوا عبيدنا وموالينا قال إن ذلك لنقص بكم كبيرا إلا أن وكيعا قال كثير أو كبير حدثنا يزيد ووكيع عن إسماعيل قال قال قيس قال عمر لو كنت أطيق الأذان مع الخليفى لأذنت (المصنف لابن أبي شيبة، الرقم: ٢٣٥٩، ٢٣٦٠)

سكت عليه الحافظ في التلخيص الحبير (الرقم: ٣١٣)

بالسيوف فقال كلا يا عمر إنه سيأتي زمان يتركون الأذان على ضعفائهم تلك

لحوم حرمها الله على النار لحوم المؤذنين (كشف الخفاء، الرقم: ٢١١٨)[155]

It is reported regarding Hazrat Umar رَضِيَ ٱللَّهُ عَنْهُ that he had said, "Had I been able to call out the azaan (together with managing the affairs of khilaafah), certainly my happiness would have been completed. (The reward of calling out the azaan is so great that if I had the honour of being a muazzin and) if I had not performed any nafl salaah during the night (tahajjud) nor kept any nafl fast during the day, it would have not grieved me. I heard Rasulullah صَلَّى ٱللَّهُ عَلَيْهِ وَسَلَّمَ making special dua for the muazzins of this Ummah saying, 'O Allah تَبَارَكَ وَتَعَالَى, forgive the sins of the muazzins!' Rasulullah صَلَّى ٱللَّهُ عَلَيْهِ وَسَلَّمَ made this dua three times. In surprise, I said, 'O Rasulullah صَلَّى ٱللَّهُ عَلَيْهِ وَسَلَّمَ! (You have elevated the position of the muazzin to such an extent that) you have now left us in the condition that we will be prepared to fight amongst ourselves with our swords in order to call out the azaan.' Hazrat Nabi صَلَّى ٱللَّهُ عَلَيْهِ وَسَلَّمَ said, 'No, O Umar رَضِيَ ٱللَّهُ عَنْهُ! A time will come where the desire of calling out the azaan will no longer be in the hearts of people, to such an extent that people will rely on the weak among them to call out the azaan. Those people (the muazzins) are such that Allah تَبَارَكَ وَتَعَالَى

---

[155] لولا الخليفى لأذنت رواه أبو الشيخ ثم البيهقي عن عمر من قوله ورواه سعيد بن منصور عنه أنه قال لو أطيق مع الخليفى لأذنت ولأبي الشيخ ثم الديلمي عنه أنه قال لو كنت مؤذنا لكمل أمري وما باليت أن لا أنتصب لقيام ليل ولا لصيام نهار سمعت رسول الله صلى الله عليه وسلم يقول اللهم اغفر للمؤذنين ثلاثا قلت يا رسول الله تركتنا ونحن نجتلد على الأذان بالسيوف فقال كلا يا عمر إنه سيأتي زمان يتركون الأذان على ضعفائهم تلك لحوم حرمها الله على النار لحوم المؤذنين والخليفى بكسر المعجمة واللام المشددة والقصر الخلافة وهو وأمثاله من الأبنية الدليلي مصدر يدل على الكثرة يعني هنا لولا كثرة الاشتغال بأمر الخلافة وضبط أحوالها لأذنت (كشف الخفاء، الرقم: ٢١١٨)

has made the fire of Jahannum haraam on their flesh, the flesh of the muazzins.'"

The Qualities of a Muazzin

1. The muazzin should be a male.[156]

عن ابن عمر رضي الله عنهما قال ليس على النساء أذان ولا إقامة (السنن الكبرى للبيهقي، الرقم: ١٩٩٦)[157]

It is reported that Hazrat Ibnu Umar ﷺ said, "Calling out the azaan and iqaamah is not the responsibility of women."

2. He should be sane.[158]

3. He should be of the age of understanding. The azaan of a small child who has not reached the age of understanding is not valid.[See 158]

4. He should be able to pronounce the words of azaan correctly.[See 158]

5. He should have knowledge of the salaah times.[See 158]

6. He should be a pious and upright Muslim.[See 158]

---

[156] (ويكره أذان جنب وإقامته وإقامة محدث لا أذانه) على المذهب (و) أذان (امرأة) وخنثى (وفاسق) ولو عالما لكنه أولى بإمامة وأذان من جاهل تقي (وسكران) ولو بمباح كمعتوه وصبي لا يعقل (وقاعد إلا إذا أذن لنفسه) وراكب إلا لمسافر (ويعاد أذان جنب) ندبا وقيل وجوبا (لا إقامته) لمشروعية تكراره في الجمعة دون تكرارها (وكذا) يعاد (أذان امرأة ومجنون ومعتوه وسكران وصبي لا يعقل) (الدر المختار ٣٩٢/١) وأما الذي يرجع إلى صفات المؤذن فأنواع أيضا منها أن يكون رجلا فيكره أذان المرأة باتفاق الروايات (بدائع الصنائع ١٥٠/١)

[157] لهذا الحديث شاهد مرسل من حديث إبراهيم النخعي حدثنا محمد بن الحسن الشيباني قال أخبرنا أبو حنيفة عن حماد عن إبراهيم قال ليس على النساء أذان ولا إقامة (كتاب الآثار، الرقم: ٦٤)

[158] وأهلية الأذان تعتمد بمعرفة القبلة والعلم بمواقيت الصلاة كذا في فتاوى قاضي خان وينبغي أن يكون المؤذن رجلا عاقلا صالحا تقيا عالما بالسنة كذا في النهاية وينبغي أن يكون مهيبا ويتفقد أحوال الناس ويزجر المتخلفين عن الجماعات كذا في القنية وأن يكون مواظبا على الأذان هكذا في البدائع والتتارخانية (الفتاوى الهندية ٥٣/١)

عن ابن عباس رضي الله عنهما قال قال رسول الله صلى الله عليه وسلم ليؤذن لكم

خياركم وليؤمكم قراؤكم (سنن أبي داود، الرقم: ٥٩٠)[159]

Hazrat Ibnu Abbaas  reports that Hazrat Rasulullah
ﷺ said, "The best (most righteous) from amongst you
should be appointed to call out the azaan, and the best qaari from
amongst you (i.e. the most learned in regard to recitation and the
masaail of salaah) should lead you in your salaah."

---

[159] سكت الحافظ عن هذا الحديث في الفصل الثاني من هداية الرواة (٤/٢) فالحديث حسن عنده

قال صاحب بذل المجهود (٤٦٧/٣) (خياركم) أي من هو أكثر صلاحًا ليحفظ نظره عن العورات ويبالغ في محافظة الأوقات (وليؤمكم قراؤكم)

بضم القاف وتشديد الراء جمع قارئ وكل ما يكون أقرأ فهو أفضل إذا كان عالما بمسائل الصلاة

Sunnah Method of Calling Out the Azaan

1. Ensure that your intention for calling out the azaan is solely to please Allah تَبَارَكَ وَتَعَالَى.

عن ابن عباس رضي الله عنهما أن النبي صلى الله عليه وسلم قال من أذن سبع سنين محتسبا كتبت له براءة من النار (سنن الترمذي، الرقم: ٢٠٦)[160]

Hazrat Ibnu Abbaas رَضِيَ اللّٰهُ عَنْهُمَا reports that Hazrat Rasulullah صَلَّى اللّٰهُ عَلَيْهِ وَسَلَّمَ said, "The one who calls out the azaan for seven years with sincerity and the hope of attaining reward receives the guarantee of freedom from the fire of Jahannum." See 151

2. Call out the azaan on time with punctuality.

عن أبي محذورة رضي الله عنه قال قال رسول الله صلى الله عليه وسلم أمناء المسلمين على صلاتهم وسحورهم المؤذنون (السنن الكبرى للبيهقي، الرقم: ١٩٩٩)[161]

Hazrat Abu Mahzoorah رَضِيَ اللّٰهُ عَنْهُ reports that Hazrat Rasulullah صَلَّى اللّٰهُ عَلَيْهِ وَسَلَّمَ said, "The trustees of the Muslims over their salaah and sehri are the muazzins (i.e. the muazzins have been entrusted with

---

[160] قال أبو عيسى: حديث ابن عباس حديث غريب

[161] عن الحسن أن النبي صلى الله عليه وسلم قال المؤذنون أمناء المسلمين على صلاتهم قال وذكر معها غيرها قال وهذا المرسل شاهد لما تقدم (السنن الكبرى للبيهقي، الرقم: ٢٠٠٠)

عن الحسن أن النبي صلى الله عليه وسلم قال المؤذنون أمناء الناس على صلاتهم (لأن الناس متى سمعوا الأذان أدوا الفريضة اعتمادا عليه والغرض من الحديث إشعار المؤذنين بمسؤليتهم ليحتفلوا بها ويتحروا الأوقات حتى لا يضلوا الناس ويحملوهم على الصلاة قبل وقتها) وذكر معها غيرها (مسند الشافعي، الرقم: ١٧٣)

the task of alerting the Muslims to the correct salaah time and sehri time).”

3. Call out the azaan outside the musjid, preferably from an elevated place so that the voice will travel further.[162]

عن عروة بن الزبير عن امرأة من بني النجار قالت كان بيتي من أطول بيت حول المسجد وكان بلال يؤذن عليه الفجر فيأتي بسحر فيجلس على البيت ينظر إلى الفجر فإذا رآه تمطى ثم قال اللهم إني أحمدك وأستعينك على قريش أن يقيموا دينك قالت ثم يؤذن قالت والله ما علمته كان تركها ليلة واحدة تعني هذه الكلمات (سنن أبي داود، الرقم: ٥١٩)[163]

Hazrat Urwah bin Zubair رَحِمَهُٱللَّهُ reports that a woman from the tribe of Banu Najjaar relates, “My house was one of the highest houses around the Musjid (Musjid-e-Nabawi), and Hazrat Bilaal رَضِيَٱللَّهُعَنْهُ would call out the azaan of Fajr from the top of my house. He would arrive at the time of sehri and sit on the roof, looking at the horizon and waiting for the time of Fajr to set in. When he would see the time set in, he would stretch (due to sitting for a long time, waiting to see the time of Fajr set in) and make the following dua, ‘O Allah, I praise You (for allowing me to call out the azaan) and I seek Your assistance and beseech You to guide the Quraish (the family of Hazrat Rasulullah صَلَّىٱللَّهُعَلَيْهِوَسَلَّمَ who had not yet

---

162 ينبغي أن يؤذن على المأذنة أو خارج المسجد ولا يؤذن في المسجد كذا في فتاوى قاضي خان والسنة أن يؤذن في موضع عال يكون أسمع لجيرانه ويرفع صوته ولا يجهد نفسه كذا في البحر الرائق (الفتاوى الهندية ٥٥/١)

163 قال الحافظ: أخرجه أبو داود وإسناده حسن (فتح الباري ١٢١/٢)

embraced Islam) to Islam so that they may uphold and establish Your Deen (in the world).'" The woman further said, "He would then call out the azaan. I take a qasm by the name of Allah تَبَارَكَ وَتَعَالَى, I cannot remember him leaving out this dua for even a single day (i.e his dua for the Quraish before calling out the azaan)."

4. Call out the azaan in a loud voice.[See 162]

عن عبد الله بن زيد رضي الله عنه قال... فأخبرته بما رأيت فقال إنها لرؤيا حق إن شاء الله فقم مع بلال فألق عليه ما رأيت فليؤذن به فإنه أندى صوتا منك (سنن أبي داود، الرقم: ٤٩٩)[164]

Hazrat Abdullah bin Zaid رَضِيَ اللَّهُ عَنْهُ reports, "... I then informed Rasulullah صَلَّى اللَّهُ عَلَيْهِ وَسَلَّمَ about the dream that I had seen (and the manner of calling out the azaan that I was taught in the dream). Hazrat Rasulullah صَلَّى اللَّهُ عَلَيْهِ وَسَلَّمَ replied, 'Certainly it is a true dream insha-Allah. Stand up with Bilaal رَضِيَ اللَّهُ عَنْهُ and tell him the words of azaan which you had heard in your dream so that he may call out the azaan with these words, since his voice is louder than yours.'"

عن عبد الرحمن بن عبد الله بن عبد الرحمن بن أبي صعصعة الأنصاري ثم المازني عن أبيه أنه أخبره أن أبا سعيد الخدري رضي الله عنه قال له إني أراك تحب الغنم والبادية فإذا كنت في غنمك أو باديتك فأذنت بالصلاة فارفع صوتك بالنداء فإنه لا يسمع مدى صوت المؤذن جن ولا إنس ولا شيء إلا شهد له يوم القيامة قال أبو سعيد

---

[164] هذا الحديث سكت عنه أبو داود والمنذري (مختصر سنن أبي داود ٢٠٢/١)

رضي الله عنه سمعته من رسول الله صلى الله عليه وسلم (صحيح البخاري، الرقم: ٦٠٩)

It is reported from Hazrat Abdullah bin Abdir Rahmaan bin Abi Sa'sa'ah رَحِمَهُٱللَّهُ that on one occasion, Hazrat Abu Sa'eed Khudri رَضِيَٱللَّهُعَنْهُ said to him, "I see that you like to remain with your livestock (grazing them) in the open fields. When you are among your livestock or in the open fields, (and the time of salaah enters) and you wish to call out the azaan, then you should raise your voice and call out the azaan, for certainly the jinn, humans or any other creation that hears the voice of the muazzin as far as it reaches will testify on his behalf on the Day of Qiyaamah." Hazrat Abu Sa'eed رَضِيَٱللَّهُعَنْهُ said, "I heard this from Rasulullah صَلَّىٱللَّهُعَلَيْهِوَسَلَّمَ."

5. Call out the azaan in the state of wudhu.[165]

عن أبي هريرة رضي الله عنه عن النبي صلى الله عليه وسلم قال لا يؤذن إلا متوضئ (سنن الترمذي، الرقم: ٢٠٠)[166]

Hazrat Abu Hurairah رَضِيَٱللَّهُعَنْهُ reports that Hazrat Rasulullah صَلَّىٱللَّهُعَلَيْهِوَسَلَّمَ said, "The one calling out the azaan should be in the state of wudhu."

6. Face the qiblah when calling out the azaan.[167]

---

[165] ويستحب أن يكون المؤذن صالحا عالما بالسنة وأوقات الصلاة وعلى وضوء

(و) أن يكون (على وضوء) لقوله صلى الله عليه وسلم لا يؤذن إلا متوضئ (مراقي الفلاح صـ ١٩٧)

[166] قال أبو هريرة رضي الله عنه لا ينادي بالصلاة إلا متوضئ قال أبو عيسى: وهذا أصح من الحديث الأول قال أبو عيسى وحديث أبي هريرة لم يرفعه ابن وهب وهو أصح من حديث الوليد بن مسلم والزهري لم يسمع من أبي هريرة (سنن الترمذي، الرقم: ٢٠١)

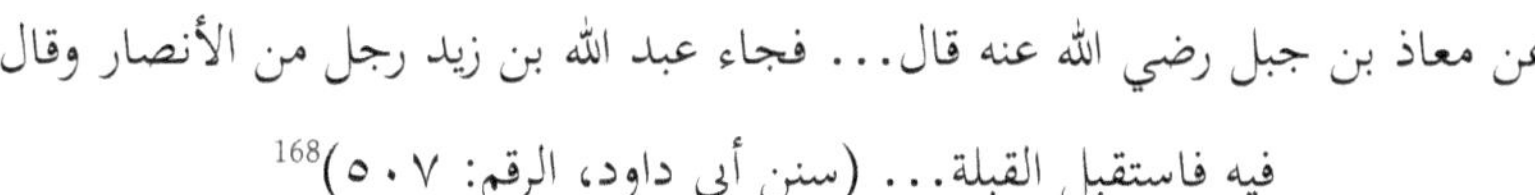

عن معاذ بن جبل رضي الله عنه قال… فجاء عبد الله بن زيد رجل من الأنصار وقال فيه فاستقبل القبلة… (سنن أبي داود، الرقم: ٥٠٧)[168]

Hazrat Mu'aaz bin Jabal ﷺ reports, "… Hazrat Abdullah bin Zaid ﷺ, who was from the Ansaar, came (and related his dream to Hazrat Rasulullah ﷺ wherein he was taught the words of the azaan), and he (the angel in the dream) faced the qiblah (and called out the azaan)."

عن الحسن ومحمد قالا إذا أذن المؤذن استقبل القبلة (المصنف لابن أبي شيبة، الرقم: ٢٢٤٣)

It is reported from Hazrat Hasan Basri رحمه الله and Hazrat Muhammad bin Munkadir رحمه الله that when the muazzin calls out the azaan, he should face the qiblah.

7. Call out the azaan while standing.[169]

---

[167] قوله (ويستقبل بهما القبلة) أي بالأذان والإقامة لفعل الملك النازل من السماء وللتوارث عن بلال ولو ترك الاستقبال جاز لحصول المقصود ويكره لمخالفة السنة كذا في الهداية والظاهر أنها كراهة تنزيه لما في المحيط وإذا انتهى إلى الصلاة والفلاح حول وجهه يمنة ويسرة ولا يحول قدميه لأنه في حالة الذكر والثناء على الله تعالى والشهادة له بالوحدانية ولنبيه بالرسالة فالأحسن أن يكون مستقبلا فأما الصلاة والفلاح دعاء إلى الصلاة وأحسن أحوال الداعي أن يكون مقبلا على المدعوين ويستثنى من سنية الاستقبال ما إذا أذن راكبا فإنه لا يسن الاستقبال بخلاف ما إذا كان ماشيا ذكره في الظهيرية عن محمد (البحر الرائق ٢٧٢/١)

[168] قال المنذري: ذكر الترمذي ومحمد بن إسحاق بن خزيمة أن عبد الرحمن بن أبي ليلى لم يسمع من معاذ بن جبل وما قالاه ظاهر جدا فإن ابن أبي ليلى قال ولدت لست بقين من خلافة عمر فيكون مولده سنة سبع عشرة من الهجرة ومعاذ توفي في سنة سبع عشرة أو ثمان عشرة وقد قيل إن مولده لست مضين من خلافة عمر فيكون مولده على هذا بعد موت معاذ ولم يسمع ابن أبي ليلى أيضا من عبد الله بن زيد وقول ابن أبي ليلى حدثنا أصحابنا إن أراد الصحابة فهو قد سمع من جماعة من الصحابة فيكون الحديث مسندا وإلا فهو مرسل (مختصر سنن أبي داود ٢٠٥/١)

قال الحافظ في التلخيص الحبير (٣٣٣/١): قال المنذري إلا أن قوله في رواية أبي داود حدثنا أصحابنا إن أراد به الصحابة فيكون مسندا وإلا فهو مرسل قلت في رواية أبي بكر بن أبي شيبة وابن خزيمة والطحاوي والبيهقي ثنا أصحاب محمد فتعين الاحتمال الأول ولهذا صححها ابن حزم وابن دقيق العيد

عبد الجبار بن وائل عن أبيه قال حق وسنة أن لا يؤذن الرجل إلا وهو طاهر ولا يؤذن إلا وهو قائم (التلخيص الحبير، الرقم: ٣٠١)[170]

Abdul Jabbaar bin Waail ﷻ relates from his father, Hazrat Waail ﵁, "It is established in the sunnah that the muazzin should call out the azaan in the state of wudhu and whilst he is standing."

8. Call out the azaan slowly and pause after calling out each phrase of the azaan.[171]

---

[169] ومنها أن يؤذن قائما إذا أذن للجماعة ويكره قاعدا لأن النازل من السماء أذن قائما حيث وقف على حذم حائط وكذا الناس توارثوا ذلك فعلا فكان تاركه مسيئا لمخالفته النازل من السماء وإجماع الخلق ولأن تمام الإعلام بالقيام ويجزئه لحصول أصل المقصود وإن أذن لنفسه قاعدا فلا بأس به لأن المقصود مراعاة سنة الصلاة لا الإعلام وأما المسافر فلا بأس أن يؤذن راكبا لما روي أن بلالا رضي الله عنه ربما أذن في السفر راكبا ولأن له أن يترك الأذان أصلا في السفر فكان له أن يأتي به راكبا بطريق الأولى وينزل للإقامة لما روي أن بلالا أذن وهو راكب ثم نزل وأقام على الأرض ولأنه لو لم ينزل لوقع الفصل بين الإقامة والشروع في الصلاة بالنزول وإنه مكروه وأما في الحضر فيكره الأذان راكبا في ظاهر الرواية وعن أبي يوسف أنه قال لا بأس به (بدائع الصنائع ١٥١/١)

[170] إسناده حسن إلا أن فيه انقطاعا لأن عبد الجبار ثبت عنه في صحيح مسلم أنه قال كنت غلاما لا أعقل صلاة أبي ونقل النووي اتفاق أئمة الحديث على أنه لم يسمع من أبيه ونقل عن بعضهم أنه ولد بعد وفاة أبيه ولا يصح ذلك لما يعطيه ظاهر سياق مسلم (التلخيص الحبير، الرقم: ٣٠١)

واعلم أن لوائل بن حجر ابنان أحدهما عبد الجبار وثانيهما علقمة والصحيح أن عبد الجبار لم يسمع من أبيه وأنه ولد في حياة أبيه وائل وما قال الترمذي في باب ما جاء في المرأة إذا استكرهت على الزنى سمعت محمدا يقول عبد الجبار بن وائل بن حجر لم يسمع من أبيه ولا أدركه يقال إنه ولد بعد موت أبيه بأشهر فضعفه المزي وقال في تهذيب الكمال هذا القول ضعيف جدا فإنه قد صح أنه قال كنت غلاما لا أعقل صلاة أبي ولو مات أبوه وهو حمل لم يقل هذا القول قال الذهبي وهذا القول مردود بما صح عنه أنه قال كنت غلاما لا أعقل صلاة أبي وأما علقمة فالحق أنه سمع من أبيه أخرج المؤلف أبو داود في باب الإمام يأمر بالعفو في الدم حدثنا عبيد الله بن عمر بن ميسرة الجشمي أخبرنا يحيى بن سعيد عن عوف أخبرنا حمزة أبو عمرو العائذي حدثني علقمة بن وائل قال حدثني وائل بن حجر كنت عند النبي صلى الله عليه وسلم الحديث فقوله حدثني أبي يدل على سماعه من أبيه وكذا قال علقمة حدثني أبي في روايات أخرى قال الترمذي في ذلك الباب وعلقمة بن وائل بن حجر سمع من أبيه وهو أكبر من عبد الجبار بن وائل وعبد الجبار بن وائل لم يسمع من أبيه انتهى فما قال الحافظ في التقريب في ترجمة علقمة بن وائل صدوق إلا أنه لم يسمع من أبيه ليس بصحيح (عون المعبود ٢٩٢/٢–٢٩٣)

(قوله كنت غلاما الخ) أى كنت صبيا لا أفهم صلاة أبي وهو صريح في أن قائله عبد الجبار فيقتضى وجوده حال حياة أبيه لكن قد علمت أن أباه مات قبل أن يولد قال الحافظ نص البزار على أن القائل كنت غلاما لا أعقل صلاة أبي هو علقمة بن وائل لا أخوه عبد الجبار (المنهل العذب المورود ١٢٤/٥)

عن جابر رضي الله عنه أن رسول الله صلى الله عليه وسلم قال لبلال إذا أذنت فترسل... (سنن الترمذي، الرقم: ١٩٥)[172]

Hazrat Jaabir رَضِيَاللَّهُعَنْهُ reports that Hazrat Rasulullah صَلَّىاللَّهُعَلَيْهِوَسَلَّمَ addressed Hazrat Bilaal رَضِيَاللَّهُعَنْهُ saying, "When you call out the azaan then call it out with tarassul (gradually, with pausing after each phrase) ..."

9. Insert the index fingers into the ears or cover both ears entirely with all the fingers.[173]

---

[171] ويترسل في الأذان ويحدر في الإقامة وهذا بيان الاستحباب كذا في الهداية حتى لو ترسل فيهما أو حدر فيهما أو ترسل في الإقامة وحدر في الأذان جاز كذا في الكافي وقيل يكره وهو الحق هكذا في فتح القدير والترسل أن يقول الله أكبر ويقف ثم يقول مرة أخرى مثله وكذلك يقف بين كل كلمتين إلى آخر الأذان (الفتاوى الهندية ٥٦/١)

[172] قال أبو عيسى: حديث جابر هذا حديث لا نعرفه إلا من هذا الوجه من حديث عبد المنعم وهو إسناد مجهول قال الحافظ في هداية الرواة (٣١١/١) ضعيف

قال النبي صلى الله عليه وسلم إذا أذنت فترسل وإذا أقمت فاحدر قلت أخرجه الترمذي عن عبد المنعم بن نعيم ثنا يحيى بن مسلم عن الحسن وعطاء عن جابر أن رسول الله صلى الله عليه وسلم قال لبلال يا بلال إذا أذنت فترسل وإذا أقمت فاحدر واجعل بين أذانك وإقامتك قدر ما يفرغ الآكل من أكله والشارب من شربه والمعتصر إذا دخل لقضاء حاجته انتهى قال الترمذي هذا حديث لا نعرفه إلا من هذا الوجه من حديث عبد المنعم وهو إسناد مجهول انتهى وعبد المنعم هذا ضعفه الدارقطني وقال أبو حاتم منكر الحديث جدا لا يجوز الاحتجاج به وأخرجه الحاكم في مستدركه عن عمرو بن فائد الأسواري ثنا يحيى بن مسلم به سواء ثم قال هذا حديث ليس في إسناده مطعون فيه غير عمرو بن فائد ولم يخرجاه انتهى قال الذهبي في مختصره وعمرو بن فائد قال الدارقطني متروك انتهى وأخرجه ابن عدي عن يحيى بن مسلم به وقال فيه فاحذم بحاء مهملة وذال معجمة مكسورة وأسند عن يحيى قال يحيى بن مسلم بصري متروك الحديث انتهى ومن أحاديث الباب ما أخرجه الدارقطني في سننه عن سويد بن غفلة قال سمعت علي بن أبي طالب يقول كان رسول الله صلى الله عليه وسلم يأمرنا أن نرتل الأذان ونحذف الإقامة انتهى وأخرج أيضا عن مرحوم بن عبد العزيز عن أبيه عن أبي الزبير مؤذن بيت المقدس قال جاءنا عمر بن الخطاب فقال إذا أذنت فترسل وإذا أقمت فاحذم انتهى وعبد العزيز مولى آل معاوية بن أبي سفيان القرشي البصري ذكر ابن أبي حاتم أنه روى عنه ابنه مرحوم ولم يعرف بحاله ولا ذكره غيره قال في الإمام وروى الطبراني في معجمه الوسط عن عمرو بن بشير عن عمران بن مسلم عن سعيد بن علقمة عن علي قال كان رسول الله صلى الله عليه وسلم يأمر بلالا أن يرتل الأذان ويحدر في الإقامة انتهى (نصب الراية ٢٧٥/١-٢٧٦)

[173] (ويجعل) ندبا (أصبعيه في) صماخ (أذنيه) فأذانه بدونه حسن وبه أحسن

قال العلامة ابن عابدين رحمه الله (قوله ويجعل أصبعيه الخ) لقوله لبلال رضي الله عنه اجعل أصبعيك في أذنيك فإنه أرفع لصوتك وإن جعل يديه على أذنيه فحسن لأن أبا محذورة رضي الله عنه ضم أصابعه الأربعة ووضعها على أذنيه وكذا على ما روي عن الإمام إمداد وقهستاني عن التحفة قوله (فأذانه) تفريع على قوله ندبا قال في البحر والأمر أي في الحديث المذكور للندب بقرينة التعليل فلذا لو لم يفعل كان

عن عبد الرحمن بن سعد بن عمار بن سعد مؤذن رسول الله صلى الله عليه وسلم قال حدثني أبي عن أبيه عن جده أن رسول الله صلى الله عليه وسلم أمر بلالا أن يجعل أصبعيه في أذنيه وقال إنه أرفع لصوتك (سنن ابن ماجه، الرقم: ٧١٠)[174]

Hazrat Sa'd Al-Quraz رَضِيَٱللَّهُعَنْهُ reports that Hazrat Rasulullah صَلَّىٱللَّهُعَلَيْهِوَسَلَّمَ commanded Hazrat Bilaal رَضِيَٱللَّهُعَنْهُ to place his fingers in his ears (at the time of calling out the azaan) and said, "This will enable you to call out the azaan in a louder tone."

10. Turn the face to the right when saying حَيَّ عَلَى الصَّلَاةِ (hayya alas salaah) and to the left when saying حَيَّ عَلَى الْفَلَاحِ (hayya alal

---

حسنا فإن قيل ترك السنة كيف يكون حسنا قلنا إن الأذان معه أحسن فإذا تركه بقي الأذان حسنا كذا في الكافي اه فافهم (رد المحتار ٣٨٨/١)

وفيه جعل إصبعيه في أذنيه ونادى وقد روى ذلك أيضا في حديث أبي محذورة قاله ابن المنذر في كتاب الأشراف وزاد صاحب الغاية في شرح الهداية أنه ضمّ أصابعه الأربع وجعلها على أذنيه (شرح سنن ابن ماجه للإمام مغلطاي ٥٣/٣-٥٤)

قال (ويجعل أصابعه مضمومة على أذنيه) المشهور عن أحمد أنه يجعل إصبعيه في أذنيه وعليه العمل عند أهل العلم يستحبون أن يجعل المؤذن إصبعيه في أذنيه لما روى الترمذي قال أبو جحيفة أن بلالا أذن ووضع إصبعيه في أذنيه متفق عليه وعن سعد مؤذن رسول الله صلى الله عليه وسلم أن رسول الله صلى الله عليه وسلم أمر بلالا أن يجعل إصبعيه في أذنيه وقال إنه أرفع لصوتك وروى أبو طالب عن أحمد أنه قال أحب إلي أن يجعل يديه على أذنيه على حديث أبي محذورة وضم أصابعه الأربع ووضعها على أذنيه وحكى أبو حفص عن ابن بطة قال سألت أبا القاسم الخرقي عن صفة ذلك فأرانيه بيديه فضم أصابعه على راحتيه ووضعهما على أذنيه

واحتج لذلك القاضي بما روى أبو حفص بإسناده عن ابن عمر أنه كان أنه كان إذا بعث مؤذنا يقول له اضمم أصابعك مع كفيك واجعلها مضمومة على أذنيك وبما روى أبو محذورة أنه كان يضم أصابعه والأول أصح لصحة الحديث وشهرته وعمل أهل العلم به وأيهما فعل فحسن وإن ترك الكل فلا بأس (المغني لابن قدامة ٨١/٢-٨٢)

[174] قال البوصيري في الزوائد (٢٣٦/١): رواه الترمذي بإسناد صححه وإسناد المصنف ضعيف لضعف أولاد سعد

باب ما جاء في إدخال الإصبع في الأذن عند الأذان

لهذا الحديث شاهد من حديث أبي جحيفة: حدثنا محمود بن غيلان قال حدثنا عبد الرزاق قال أخبرنا سفيان الثوري عن عون بن أبي جحيفة عن أبيه قال رأيت بلالا يؤذن ويدور ويتبع فاه هاهنا وهاهنا وإصبعاه في أذنيه ورسول الله صلى الله عليه وسلم في قبة له حمراء أراه قال من أدم فخرج بلال بين يديه بالعنزة فركزها بالبطحاء فصلى إليها رسول الله صلى الله عليه وسلم يمر بين يديه الكلب والحمار وعليه حلة حمراء كأني أنظر إلى بريق ساقيه قال سفيان نراه حبرة حديث أبي جحيفة حديث حسن صحيح وعليه العمل عند أهل العلم يستحبون أن يدخل المؤذن إصبعيه في أذنيه في الأذان (سنن الترمذي، الرقم: ١٩٧)

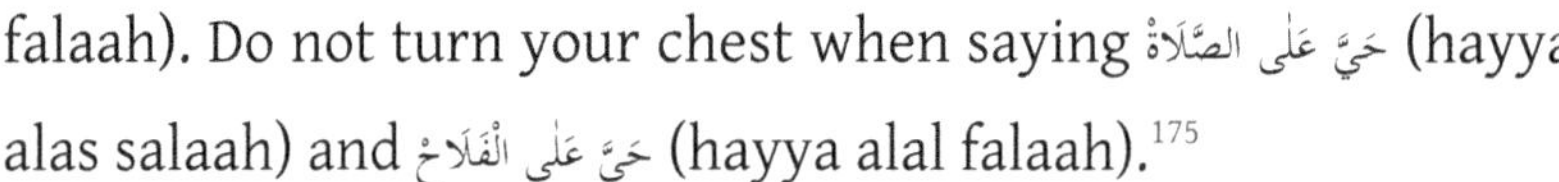

falaah). Do not turn your chest when saying حَيَّ عَلَى الصَّلَاةِ (hayya alas salaah) and حَيَّ عَلَى الْفَلَاحِ (hayya alal falaah).[175]

عن عون بن أبي جحيفة عن أبيه قال أتيت النبي صلى الله عليه وسلم بمكة وهو فى قبة حمراء من أدم فخرج بلال فأذن ... فلما بلغ حي على الصلاة حي على الفلاح لوى عنقه يمينا وشمالا ولم يستدر (سنن أبي داود، الرقم: ٥٢٠)[176]

Hazrat Abu Juhaifah رَضِيَاللَّهُعَنْهُ *reports, "On one occasion, I came to Rasulullah* صَلَّىاللَّهُعَلَيْهِوَسَلَّمَ *in Makkah Mukarramah. At that time, Rasulullah* صَلَّىاللَّهُعَلَيْهِوَسَلَّمَ *was in a red coloured tent made of leather. Hazrat Bilaal* رَضِيَاللَّهُعَنْهُ *came out to call the azaan ... When he reached 'hayya alas salaah' and 'hayya alal falaah', he turned his face towards the right and left, and he did not turn his chest."*

عن أبي جحيفة رضي الله عنه قال رأيت بلالا يؤذن ويدور ويتبع فاه هاهنا وهاهنا وإصبعاه في أذنيه (سنن الترمذي، الرقم: ١٩٧)[177]

Hazrat Abu Juhaifah رَضِيَاللَّهُعَنْهُ *reports, "I had seen Hazrat Bilaal* رَضِيَاللَّهُعَنْهُ *calling out the azaan and turning his face towards the right and left (when saying 'hayya alas salaah' and 'hayya alal falaah'),*

---

[175] قوله (ويلتفت يمينا وشمالا بالصلاة والفلاح) لما قدمناه ولفعل بلال رضي الله عنه على ما رواه الجماعة ثم أطلقه فشمل ما إذا كان وحده على الصحيح لكونه سنة الأذان فلا يتركه خلافا للحلواني لعدم الحاجة إليه وفي السراج الوهاج إنه من سنن الأذان فلا يخل المنفرد بشيء منها حتى قالوا في الذي يؤذن للمولود ينبغي أن يحول اه وقيد باليمين والشمال لأنه لا يحول وراءه لما فيه من استدبار القبلة ولا أمامه لحصول الإعلام في الجملة بغيرها من كلمات الأذان وقوله بالصلاة والفلاح لف ونشر مرتب يعني أنه يلتفت يمينا بالصلاة وشمالا بالفلاح وهو الصحيح خلافا لمن قال إن الصلاة باليمين والشمال والفلاح كذلك (البحر الرائق ٢٧٢/١)

[176] سكت عن هذا الحديث أبو داود والمنذري (مختصر سنن أبي داود ٢٠٨/١)

[177] قال أبو عيسى: حديث أبي جحيفة حديث حسن صحيح

and his two fingers were inserted into his ears (while he was calling out the azaan)."

11. Do not speak while calling out the azaan.[178]

12. Do not distort the words of the azaan, nor call out the azaan with such a tune that the words of the azaan become distorted.[179]

عن يحيى البكاء قال قال رجل لابن عمر رضي الله عنهما إني لأحبك في الله فقال ابن عمر رضي الله عنهما لكني أبغضك في الله قال ولم قال إنك تتغنى في أذانك وتأخذ عليه أجرا (مجمع الزوائد، الرقم: ١٩٠٩)[180]

Yahya Al-Bakkaa رَحِمَهُٰاللّٰه reports that on one occasion, a man came to Hazrat Abdullah bin Umar رَضِىَاللّٰهُعَنْهُ and said, "I most definitely love you for the sake of Allah تَبَارَكَوَتَعَالَى." Hearing this, Hazrat Abdullah bin Umar رَضِىَاللّٰهُعَنْهُ replied, "However, I dislike you for the sake of Allah تَبَارَكَوَتَعَالَى." When the man enquired as to why Hazrat Abdullah bin Umar رَضِىَاللّٰهُعَنْهُ disliked him, he answered, "(The reason

---

[178] عن الشعبي أنه كره الكلام في الأذان (المصنف لابن أبي شيبة، الرقم: ٢٢١٩)

عن إبراهيم أنه كره أن يتكلم المؤذن في أذانه حتى يفرغ (المصنف لابن أبي شيبة، الرقم: ٢٢٢٠)

[179] (ولا لحن فيه) أي تغني بغير كلماته فإنه لا يحل فعله وسماعه كالتغني بالقرآن وبلا تغيير حسن

قال العلامة ابن عابدين رحمه الله (قوله بغير كلماته) أي بزيادة حركة أو حرف أو مد أو غيرها في الأوائل والأواخر قوله (وبلا تغيير حسن) أي والتغني بلا تغيير حسن فإن تحسين الصوت مطلوب ولا تلازم بينهما بحر وفتح (رد المحتار ٣٨٧/١)

وأما بيان سنن الأذان فسنن الأذان في الصلاة نوعان نوع يرجع إلى نفس الأذان ونوع يرجع إلى صفات المؤذن (أما) الذي يرجع إلى نفس الأذان فأنواع ... (ومنها) ترك التلحين في الأذان لما روي أن رجلا جاء إلى ابن عمر رضي الله عنهما فقال إني أحبك في الله تعالى فقال ابن عمر إني أبغضك في الله تعالى فقال لم قال لأنه بلغني أنك تغني في أذانك يعني التلحين ... (بدائع الصنائع ٦٤٢/١-٦٤٤)

[180] رواه الطبراني في الكبير وفيه يحيى البكاء ضعفه أحمد وأبو زرعة وأبو حاتم ووثقه يحيى بن سعيد القطان وقال محمد بن سعد كان ثقة إن شاء الله

is that) you give the azaan in a singing tone (changing and distorting the words of the azaan) and you accept a fee for calling out the azaan."

13. The dua that is made after the azaan and between the azaan and iqaamah is accepted.

عن أنس بن مالك رضي الله عنه قال قال رسول الله صلى الله عليه وسلم الدعاء لا يرد بين الأذان والإقامة (سنن الترمذي، الرقم: ٢١٢)[181]

Hazrat Anas ﷺ reports that Hazrat Rasulullah ﷺ said, "The dua made between the azaan and iqaamah is not rejected."

عن عبد الله بن عمرو أن رجلا قال يا رسول الله إن المؤذنين يفضلوننا فقال رسول الله صلى الله عليه وسلم قل كما يقولون فإذا انتهيت فسل تعطه (سنن أبي داود، الرقم: ٥٢٤)[182]

Hazrat Abdullah bin Amr bin Aas ﷺ reports that a certain Sahaabi once said to Hazrat Rasulullah ﷺ, "O Rasul of Allah ﷺ! Indeed the muazzins have great virtue over us!" Hazrat Rasulullah ﷺ responded, "Repeat the words of the muazzin (when he calls out the azaan), and when you complete (replying to the azaan) then make dua, your dua will be accepted."

14. Leave a sufficient amount of time between the azaan and iqaamah so that people will be able to fulfill their needs and

---

[181] قال أبو عيسى: حديث أنس حديث حسن

[182] هذا الحديث سكت عنه أبو داود والمنذري (مختصر سنن أبي داود ١٦٣/١)

prepare for salaah. However, Maghrib Salaah should be performed immediately after the azaan.[183]

عن جابر رضي الله عنه أن رسول الله صلى الله عليه وسلم قال لبلال إذا أذنت فترسل وإذا أقمت فاحدر واجعل بين أذانك وإقامتك قدر ما يفرغ الآكل من أكله والشارب من شربه والمعتصر إذا دخل لقضاء حاجته ولا تقوموا حتى تروني (سنن الترمذي، الرقم: ١٩٥)[See 172]

Hazrat Jaabir رَضِيَٱللَّهُعَنْهُ *reports that Hazrat Rasulullah* صَلَّىٱللَّهُعَلَيْهِوَسَلَّمَ *addressed Hazrat Bilaal* رَضِيَٱللَّهُعَنْهُ *saying, "When you call out the azaan then call it out with tarassul (gradually, with pausing after each phrase), and when you call out the iqaamah then call it out quickly, and allow so much of time to pass between your azaan and iqaamah that a person who is eating can complete his meal, and the one who is drinking can finish his drink, and the person who has a need to relieve himself can do so, and do not stand up (to form the saffs and call out the iqaamah) until you see me."*

15. If you are in a place out of the town where there is no person present to perform salaah with you, then even though you will perform salaah alone, you should still call out the azaan and iqaamah. If you call out the azaan and iqaamah and

---

[183] وأما بيان سنن الأذان فسنن الأذان في الصلاة نوعان نوع يرجع إلى نفس الأذان ونوع يرجع إلى صفات المؤذن (أما) الذي يرجع إلى نفس الأذان فأنواع ... (ومنها) الفصل فيما سوى المغرب بين الأذان والإقامة لأن الإعلام المطلوب من كل واحد منهما لا يحصل إلا بالفصل والفصل فيما سوى المغرب بالصلاة أو بالجلوس مسنون والوصل مكروه وأصله ما روي عن رسول الله صلى الله عليه وسلم أنه قال لبلال إذا أذنت فترسل وإذا أقمت فاحدر وفي رواية فاحذف وفي رواية فاحذم وليكن بين أذانك وإقامتك مقدار ما يفرغ الآكل من أكله والشارب من شربه والمعتصر إذا دخل لقضاء حاجته ولا تقوموا في الصف حتى تروني ولأن الأذان لاستحضار الغائبين فلا بد من الإمهال ليحضروا (بدائع الصنائع ١/٦٤٢-٦٤٤)

thereafter perform salaah, the malaa'ikah (angels) will perform salaah with you.[184]

عن عقبة بن عامر رضي الله عنه قال سمعت رسول الله صلى الله عليه وسلم يقول يعجب ربك من راعي غنم في رأس شظية الجبل يؤذن بالصلاة ويصلي فيقول الله عز وجل انظروا إلى عبدي هذا يؤذن ويقيم الصلاة يخاف مني قد غفرت لعبدي وأدخلته الجنة (سنن النسائي، الرقم: ٦٦٦)[185]

Hazrat Uqbah bin Aamir رَضِيَاللَّهُعَنْهُ *reports, "I heard Rasulullah* صَلَّىاللَّهُعَلَيْهِوَسَلَّمَ *mentioning, 'Allah* تَبَارَكَوَتَعَالَى *becomes pleased when the shepherd of goats and sheep, who is (alone) on the peak of the mountain, calls out the azaan and then performs salaah. Hence, Allah* تَبَارَكَوَتَعَالَى *says, 'Look at this servant of mine! He is calling out the azaan and establishing salaah while fearing me! Indeed I have forgiven my servant and I (have decreed that I) will admit him into paradise!'""*

عن سلمان الفارسي رضي الله عنه قال قال رسول الله صلى الله عليه وسلم إذا كان الرجل قي بأرض فحانت الصلاة فليتوضأ فإن لم يجد ماء فليتيمم فإن أقام صلى معه ملكاه وإن أذن وأقام صلى خلفه من جنود الله ما لا يرى طرفاه (الترغيب والترهيب، الرقم: ٣٨٧)[186]

---

[184] وندب الأذان والإقامة للمسافر والمقيم في بيته (الفتاوى الهندية ٥٣/١)

[185] عن عقبة بن عامر قال سمعت رسول الله صلى الله عليه وسلم يقول يعجب ربكم من راعي غنم في رأس شظية بجبل يؤذن بالصلاة ويصلي فيقول الله عز وجل انظروا إلى عبدي هذا يؤذن ويقيم الصلاة يخاف مني قد غفرت لعبدي وأدخلته الجنة (سنن أبي داود: الرقم: ١٢٠٣)

قال المنذري: رجال إسناده ثقات (مختصر سنن أبي داود ٣٨٥/١)

[186] قال المنذري: رواه عبد الرزاق في كتابه عن ابن التميمي عن أبيه عن أبي عثمان النهدي عنه القي بكسر القاف وتشديد الياء هي الأرض القفر

Hazrat Salmaan Al-Faarsi رَضِيَاللَّهُعَنْهُ reports that Hazrat Rasulullah صَلَّىاللَّهُعَلَيْهِوَسَلَّمَ said, "When a person is (alone) in a deserted area and the time of salaah enters, then he should perform wudhu. If he cannot find water then he should perform tayammum. If he calls out the iqaamah (before performing salaah), his two angels will perform salaah with him, and if he calls out the azaan and iqaamah (before performing salaah), such large armies of Allah تَبَارَكَوَتَعَالَى (angels) will perform salaah behind him that both ends of these armies cannot be seen."

16. If many qadha salaahs are being performed together, it is permissible to call out a separate azaan for each missed salaah, as well as to suffice on one azaan for all the missed salaahs. However, a separate iqaamah should be called out for each salaah.[187]

عن أبي عبيدة بن عبد الله بن مسعود قال قال عبد الله إن المشركين شغلوا رسول الله صلى الله عليه وسلم عن أربع صلوات يوم الخندق حتى ذهب من الليل ما شاء الله فأمر بلالا فأذن ثم أقام فصلى الظهر ثم أقام فصلى العصر ثم أقام فصلى المغرب ثم أقام فصلى العشاء (سنن الترمذي، الرقم: ١٧٩)[188]

---

[187] (و) يسن أن (يؤذن ويقيم لفائتة) رافعا صوته لو بجماعة أو صحراء لا ببيته منفردا (وكذا) يسنان (لأولى الفوائت) لا لفاسدة (ويخير فيه للباقي) لو في مجلس وفعله أولى ويقيم للكل

قال العلامة ابن عابدين رحمه الله (قوله وفعله أولى) لأنه اختلفت الروايات في قضائه صلى الله عليه وسلم ما فاته يوم الخندق ففي بعضها أنه أمر بلالا فأذن وأقام للكل وفي بعضها أنه اقتصر على الإقامة فيما بعد الأولى فالأخذ بالزيادة أولى خصوصا في باب العبادات وتمامه في الإمداد (قوله ويقيم للكل) أي لا يخير في الإقامة للباقي بل يكره تركها كما في نور الإيضاح (رد المحتار ٣٩٠/١ -٣٩١)

[188] قال أبو عيسى: وفي الباب عن أبي سعيد وجابر حديث عبد الله ليس بإسناده بأس إلا أن أبا عبيدة لم يسمع من عبد الله

قال الحافظ في الفتح (٨٢/٢): وفي قوله أربع تجوز لأن العشاء لم تكن فاتت

Hazrat Abu Ubaidah ﺭﺣﻤﻪ ﺍﻟﻠﻪ reports that his father, Hazrat Abdullah bin Mas'ood ﺭﺿﻲ ﺍﻟﻠﻪ ﻋﻨﻪ, mentioned, "On the occasion of the Battle of Khandaq (the Battle of the Trench), the disbelievers kept Rasulullah ﺻﻠﻰ ﺍﻟﻠﻪ ﻋﻠﻴﻪ ﻭﺳﻠﻢ (and the believers) occupied (through fighting) until four salaahs were missed and a portion of the night had passed. Hazrat Rasulullah ﺻﻠﻰ ﺍﻟﻠﻪ ﻋﻠﻴﻪ ﻭﺳﻠﻢ then commanded Hazrat Bilaal ﺭﺿﻲ ﺍﻟﻠﻪ ﻋﻨﻪ to call out the azaan. After calling out the azaan, Hazrat Bilaal ﺭﺿﻲ ﺍﻟﻠﻪ ﻋﻨﻪ called out the iqaamah and they performed the qadha of the Zuhr Salaah. Thereafter, Hazrat Bilaal ﺭﺿﻲ ﺍﻟﻠﻪ ﻋﻨﻪ called out the iqaamah and they performed the qadha of the Asr Salaah. Thereafter, Hazrat Bilaal ﺭﺿﻲ ﺍﻟﻠﻪ ﻋﻨﻪ called out the iqaamah and they performed the qadha of the Maghrib Salaah. Finally, Hazrat Bilaal ﺭﺿﻲ ﺍﻟﻠﻪ ﻋﻨﻪ called out the iqaamah and they performed the Esha Salaah."

Note: The Esha Salaah was not missed but was performed later than the normal time. For this reason, the Esha Salaah was also included with the other missed salaahs.

THE WORDS OF THE AZAAN

There are seven phrases in the azaan. The seven phrases are:

1. First call out:

اَللّٰهُ أَكْبَرْ اللّٰهُ أَكْبَرْ

Allah تَبَارَكَوَتَعَالَى *is the greatest, Allah* تَبَارَكَوَتَعَالَى *is the greatest.*

اَللّٰهُ أَكْبَرْ اللّٰهُ أَكْبَرْ

Allah تَبَارَكَوَتَعَالَى *is the greatest, Allah* تَبَارَكَوَتَعَالَى *is the greatest.*

2. Secondly, call out:

أَشْهَدُ أَلَّا إِلٰهَ إِلَّا اللّٰهْ

I testify that there is none worthy of worship besides Allah تَبَارَكَوَتَعَالَى.

أَشْهَدُ أَلَّا إِلٰهَ إِلَّا اللّٰهْ

I testify that there is none worthy of worship besides Allah تَبَارَكَوَتَعَالَى.

3. Thirdly, call out:

أَشْهَدُ أَنَّ مُحَمَّدًا رَّسُوْلُ اللّٰه

I testify that Hazrat Muhammad صَلَّىاللّٰهُعَلَيْهِوَسَلَّمَ *is the messenger of Allah* تَبَارَكَوَتَعَالَى.

أَشْهَدُ أَنَّ مُحَمَّدًا رَّسُوْلُ اللّٰه

I testify that Hazrat Muhammad صَلَّىاللّٰهُعَلَيْهِوَسَلَّمَ *is the messenger of Allah* تَبَارَكَوَتَعَالَى.

4. Fourthly, call out:

حَيَّ عَلَى الصَّلَاةْ

Come to salaah.

حَيَّ عَلَى الصَّلَاةْ

Come to salaah.

5. Fifthly, call out:

حَيَّ عَلَى الْفَلَاحْ

Come to success.

حَيَّ عَلَى الْفَلَاحْ

Come to success.

6. Sixthly, call out:

اَللّٰهُ أَكْبَرْ اللّٰهُ أَكْبَرْ

Allah تَبَارَكَوَتَعَالَى *is the greatest, Allah* تَبَارَكَوَتَعَالَى *is the greatest.*

7. Finally, call out:

لَا إِلٰهَ إِلَّا اللّٰهْ

There is none worthy of worship besides Allah تَبَارَكَوَتَعَالَى.

THE CORRECT PRONUNCIATION OF THE WORDS OF THE AZAAN

When calling out the azaan, one should try to pronounce all the words correctly. In this regard, some of the important points to bear in mind are:

1. When reciting اَللهُ أَكْبَرُ اَللهُ أَكْبَرُ, the letter ر *(raa)* in the first أَكْبَرُ *(akbar)* can be read with a sukoon (ْ) without joining it to the word اَللهُ *(Allahu)*, or with a fat-hah (َ) by joining it to the word اَللهُ *(Allahu)*. To read it in any other way (with a dhammah ُ or kasrah ِ) is against the sunnah.[189]

2. When reciting أَشْهَدُ أَلَّا إِلَهَ إِلَّا اللهُ, the word أَلَّا *(al-laa)* should be pronounced with an empty mouth. Furthermore, the tashdeed (ّ) on the letter ل (laam) should not be over-emphasised by stretching the sound of the ل (laam).

    The sukoon (ْ) on the letter ش (sheen) should be clearly pronounced followed by the ه (haa). One should not omit the sukoon and haa ه (haa) by joining the ه (haa) to the ش (sheen) saying "ashadu" without pronouncing the ه (haa) at all. Rather, the correct way of pronouncing it is "ash-ha-du".

---

¹⁸⁹ وحاصلها أن السنة أن يسكن الراء من الله أكبر الأول أو يصلها بالله أكبر الثانية فإن سكنها كفى وإن وصلها نوى السكون فحرك الراء بالفتحة فإن ضمها خالف السنة لأن طلب الوقف على أكبر الأول صيره إصالة فحرك بالفتح (رد المحتار ٣٨٦/١)

3. When reciting أَشْهَدُ أَنَّ مُحَمَّدًا رَّسُوْلُ الله, the word أَنَّ (anna) should not be over-emphasised by stretching the sound of the ن (noon) for longer than the duration of a ghunnah. Similarly, the tashdeed (ّ) in the letter م (meem) and ر (raa) should not be over-emphasized by stretching them.

4. When reciting حَيَّ عَلَى الصَّلَاةِ, the tashdeed (ّ) on the letter ي (yaa) in the word حَيَّ (hayya) should be read completely. The ي (yaa) should not be read without the tashdeed (ّ) by saying "haya" instead of "hayya". Likewise, the letter ع (ain) in the word على (ala) should be pronounced clearly.

When stopping at the end of the word الصَّلَاةِ (salaah), the ة (taa) will be read with a sukoon (ْ) and thus produce the sound of a ه (haa). One will not pronounce the ة (taa) by saying hayya alas salaa**t**.

Similarly, one should ensure that the sound does not resemble that of a big haa (ح).

5. When reciting حَيَّ عَلَى الْفَلَاحْ, when stopping at the word الْفَلَاحْ (falaah), ensure that the ح (haa) is pronounced correctly by saying it as a big ح (haa), not as a small ه.[190]

THE MANNER OF CALLING OUT THE AZAAN OF FAJR

If one is calling out the azaan of Fajr, then one will give the azaan in the same manner explained above. The only difference is that one will recite the following words twice after saying حَيَّ عَلَى الْفَلَاحْ (hayya alal falaah):[191]

$$ اَلصَّلَاةُ خَيْرٌ مِّنَ النَّوْمْ $$

Salaah is better than sleep.

عن محمد بن عبد الملك بن أبي محذورة عن أبيه عن جده قال قلت يا رسول الله علمني سنة الأذان ... فإن كان صلاة الصبح قلت الصلاة خير من النوم الصلاة خير من النوم (سنن أبي داود، الرقم: ٥٠٠)[192]

Hazrat Abu Mahzoorah رَضِيَٱللَّهُعَنْهُ *reports that on one occasion, he said to Hazrat Rasulullah* صَلَّىٱللَّهُعَلَيْهِوَسَلَّمَ*, "O Rasulullah* صَلَّىٱللَّهُعَلَيْهِوَسَلَّمَ*, teach me the sunnah method of calling out the azaan." ... Hazrat Rasulullah* صَلَّىٱللَّهُعَلَيْهِوَسَلَّمَ *said, "If it is the azaan of Fajr, then add the words* اَلصَّلَاةُ خَيْرٌ مِّنَ النَّوْمْ *(assalaatu khairum minan nawm) twice (after* حَيَّ عَلَى الْفَلَاحْ - *hayya alal falaah)."*

---

[191] الأذان خمس عشرة كلمة وآخره عندنا لا إله إلا الله كذا في فتاوى قاضي خان وهي الله أكبر الله أكبر الله أكبر الله أكبر أشهد أن لا إله إلا الله أشهد أن لا إله إلا الله أشهد أن محمدا رسول الله أشهد أن محمدا رسول الله حي على الصلاة حي على الصلاة حي على الفلاح حي على الفلاح الله أكبر الله أكبر لا إله إلا الله هكذا في الزاهدي والإقامة سبع عشرة كلمة خمس عشرة منها كلمات الأذان وكلمتان قوله قد قامت الصلاة مرتين كذا في فتاوى قاضي خان ويزيد بعد فلاح أذان الفجر الصلاة خير من النوم مرتين كذا في الكافي (الفتاوى الهندية ٥٥/١)

[192] سكت عن هذا الحديث أبو داود والمنذري (مختصر سنن أبي داود ٢٠٢/١)

REPLYING TO THE AZAAN

Azaan is among the salient symbols of Islam. When azaan holds such great importance in Deen, then we should show respect to the azaan by replying to it and not being engaged in any worldly talk at that time. The Fuqahaa have written that it is incorrect to engage in worldly talk at the time of azaan.[193]

1. On hearing the azaan, reply to the azaan by repeating the words that the muazzin has called out.[194]

   For example, when one hears the muazzin saying, اَللهُ أَكْبَرُ اَللهُ أَكْبَرُ (Allahu Akbar, Allahu Akbar), he should reply by also saying, اَللهُ أَكْبَرُ اَللهُ أَكْبَرُ (Allahu Akbar, Allahu Akbar).

---

[193] ولا ينبغي أن يتكلم السامع في خلال الأذان والإقامة (الفتاوى الهندية ٥٧/١)

[194] (ويجيب) وجوبا وقال الحلواني ندبا والواجب الإجابة بالقدم (من سمع الأذان) ولو جنبا لا حائضا ونفساء وسامع خطبة وفي صلاة جنازة وجماع ومستراح وأكل وتعليم علم وتعلمه بخلاف قرآن (بأن يقول) بلسانه (كمقالته) إن سمع المسنون منه وهو ما كان عربيا لا لحن فيه ولو تكرر أجاب الأول (إلا في الحيعلتين) فيحوقل (وفي الصلاة خير من النوم) فيقول صدقت وبررت (الدر المختار ٣٩٦/١)

قال العلامة ابن عابدين رحمه الله (قوله إن سمع المسنون منه) الظاهر أن المراد ما كان مسنونا جميعه ف من لبيان الجنس لا للتبعيض فلو كان بعض كلماته غير عربي أو ملحونا لا تجب عليه الإجابة في الباقي لأنه حينئذ ليس مسنونا كما لو كان كله كذلك أو كان قبل الوقت أو من جنب أو امرأة ويحتمل أن المراد ما كان مسنونا من أفراد كلماته فيجيب المسنون منها دون غيره وهو بعيد لأنه يستلزم استماعه والإصغاء إليه وقد ذكر في البحر أنهم صرحوا بأنه لا يحل سماع المؤذن إذا لحن كالقارىء وقدمنا أنه لا يصح بالفارسية وإن علم أنه في الأصح

قال العلامة ابن عابدين رحمه الله (قوله فيحوقل) أي يقول لا حول ولا قوة إلا بالله وزاد في عمدة المفتي ما شاء الله كان وخير بينهما في الكافي وفصل في المحيط بأن يأتي بالحوقلة مكان الصلاة وبالمشيئة مكان الفلاح إسماعيل والمختار الأول نوح أفندي ثم إن الإتيان بالحوقلة وإن خالف ظاهر قوله عليه الصلاة والسلام فقولوا مثل ما يقول لكنه ورد فيه حديث مفسر لذلك رواه مسلم واختار في الفتح الجمع بينهما عملا بالأحاديث قال فإنه ورد في بعضها صريحا إذا قال حي على الصلاة قال حي على الصلاة إلخ وقولهم إنه يشبه الاستهزاء لا يتم إذ لا مانع من اعتباره مجيبا بهما داعيا نفسه مخاطبا لها وقد رأينا من مشايخ السلوك من كان يجمع بينهما فيدعو نفسه ثم يتبرأ من الحول والقوة ليعمل بالحديثين وقد أطال في ذلك وأقره في البحر والنهر وغيرهما قلت وهو مذهب سلطان العارفين سيدي محيي الدين نص عليه في الفتوحات المكية (رد المختار ٣٩٧/١)

عن عمر رضي الله عنه قال قال رسول الله صلى الله عليه وسلم إذا قال المؤذن الله أكبر

الله أكبر فقال أحدكم الله أكبر الله أكبر ... ثم قال لا إله إلا الله قال لا إله إلا الله

من قلبه دخل الجنة (صحيح مسلم، الرقم: ٣٨٥)

Hazrat Umar رَضِيَٱللَّهُعَنْهُ *reports that Hazrat Rasulullah* صَلَّىٱللَّهُعَلَيْهِوَسَلَّمَ *said, "When the muazzin calls out* اَللّٰهُ أَكْبَرْ اَللّٰهُ أَكْبَرْ *(Allahu Akbar, Allahu Akbar) and one of you replies* اَللّٰهُ أَكْبَرْ اَللّٰهُ أَكْبَرْ *(Allahu Akbar, Allahu Akbar) (and one thereafter replies to all the remaining phrases of the azaan called out by the muazzin) with a good and true heart, then he will enter Jannah."*

2. When the muazzin says حَيَّ عَلَى الصَّلَاةْ (hayya alas salaah) and حَيَّ عَلَى الْفَلَاحْ (hayya alal falaah), one should recite لَا حَوْلَ وَلَا قُوَّةَ إِلَّا بِاللهِ (la hawla wa la quwwata illa billaah). However, if one repeats the words of the muazzin by saying حَيَّ عَلَى الصَّلَاةْ (hayya alas salaah) and حَيَّ عَلَى الْفَلَاحْ (hayya alal falaah) and thereafter recites لَا حَوْلَ وَلَا قُوَّةَ إِلَّا بِاللهِ (la hawla wa la quwwata illa billaah), it will be better, as both have been mentioned in the Hadith.[195]

---

[195] واختار المحقق في الفتح الجمع بين الحيعلة والحوقلة عملا بالأحاديث الواردة وجمعا بينها ففي مسند أبي يعلى عن أبي أمامة عنه صلى الله عليه وسلم إذا نادى المنادي للصلاة فتحت أبواب السماء واستجيب الدعاء فمن نزل به كرب أو شدة فليتحر المنادي إذا كبر كبر وإذا تشهد تشهد وإذا قال حي على الصلاة قال حي على الصلاة وإذا قال حي على الفلاح قال حي على الفلاح ثم يقول يعني بعدما يتمه متابعا اللهم رب هذه الدعوة الحق المستجاب لها دعوة الحق وكلمة التقوى أحينا عليها وأمتنا عليها وابعثنا عليها واجعلنا من خيار أهلها محيانا ومماتنا ثم يسأل الله عز وجل حاجته رواه الطبراني في كتاب الدعاء وقال الحاكم صحيح الإسناد فهذا صريح في أنه يقول مثل ما يقول في جميع الكلمات ولا يقال أن ذلك يشبه الإستهزاء لأنا نقول لا مانع من صحة اعتبار المجيب بما آمر نفسه داعيا محركا إياها منها السواكن مخاطبا لها حثا وحضا على الإجابة بالفعل ثم يتبرأ من الحول والقوة وقد رأينا من مشايخ السلوك من يجمع بينهما (حاشية الطحطاوي على مراقي الفلاح صر ٢٠٣)

انظر أيضا 194

عن أبي سعيد الخدري رضي الله عنه أن رسول الله صلى الله عليه وسلم قال إذا سمعتم

النداء فقولوا مثل ما يقول المؤذن (صحيح البخاري، الرقم: ٦١١)

Hazrat Abu Sa'eed Khudri رضي الله عنه *reports that Hazrat Rasulullah*
صلى الله عليه وسلم *said, "When you hear the azaan, then reply by
repeating the words of the muazzin."*

عن عمر رضي الله عنه قال قال رسول الله صلى الله عليه وسلم إذا قال المؤذن الله أكبر

الله أكبر فقال أحدكم الله أكبر الله أكبر ... ثم قال حي على الصلاة قال لا حول

ولا قوة إلا بالله ثم قال حي على الفلاح قال لا حول ولا قوة إلا بالله (صحيح مسلم،

الرقم: ٣٨٥)

Hazrat Umar رضي الله عنه *reports that Hazrat Rasulullah* صلى الله عليه وسلم
said, "When the muazzin says اَللهُ أَكْبَرُ اَللهُ أَكْبَرُ *(Allahu Akbar, Allahu
Akbar), then you should say* اَللهُ أَكْبَرُ اَللهُ أَكْبَرُ *(Allahu Akbar, Allahu
Akbar)... and when he says* حَيَّ عَلَى الصَّلَاةِ *(hayya alas salaah), then you
should say* لَا حَوْلَ وَلَا قُوَّةَ إِلَّا بِاللهِ *(la hawla wa la quwwata illa billaah),
and when he says* حَيَّ عَلَى الْفَلَاحِ *(hayya alal falaah), then you should
say* لَا حَوْلَ وَلَا قُوَّةَ إِلَّا بِاللهِ *(la hawla wa la quwwata illa billaah)."*

3. During the Fajr azaan, when the muazzin calls out
اَلصَّلَاةُ خَيْرٌ مِّنَ النَّوْمِ, reply by saying صَدَقْتَ وَبَرَرْتَ.[196]

DUA AFTER THE AZAAN

1. After the azaan, one should recite durood upon Hazrat Rasulullah ﷺ and thereafter recite the following dua:[197]

اللّٰهُمَّ رَبَّ هٰذِهِ الدَّعْوَةِ التَّامَّةِ وَالصَّلَاةِ الْقَائِمَةِ آتِ مُحَمَّدَانِ الْوَسِيْلَةَ وَالْفَضِيلَةَ وَابْعَثْهُ مَقَامًا مَّحْمُوْدَانِ الَّذِيْ وَعَدْتَّهُ إِنَّكَ لَاتُخْلِفُ الْمِيْعَاذْ

O Allah تَبَارَكَوَتَعَالَى, *Rabb of this perfect call and of the established salaah, bestow upon Hazrat Muhammad* ﷺ *the 'waseelah' (an extremely high stage in Jannah) and 'fadheelah' (a lofty position that is above all the creation), and grant him the "Maqaam Mahmood" (i.e the honour of interceding to Allah* تَبَارَكَوَتَعَالَى *to commence the reckoning for the entire creation on the Day of Qiyaamah) which You have promised him, indeed You do not go against Your promise.*

عن عبد الله بن عمرو بن العاص رضي الله عنهما أنه سمع النبي صلى الله عليه وسلم يقول إذا سمعتم المؤذن مثل ما يقول فقولوا ثم صلوا علي فإنه من صلى علي صلاة

---

[197] ويدعو عند فراغه بالوسيلة لرسول لله صلى الله عليه وسلم

قال العلامة ابن عابدين رحمه الله (قوله ويدعو إلخ) أي بعد أن يصلي على النبي لما رواه مسلم وغيره إذا سمعتم المؤذن فقولوا مثل ما يقول ثم صلوا علي فإنه من صلى علي صلاة صلى الله عليه بها عشرا ثم سلوا لي الوسيلة فإنها منزلة في الجنة لا تنبغي إلا لعبد مؤمن من عباد الله وأرجو أن أكون أنا هو فمن سأل الله لي الوسيلة حلت له الشفاعة وروى البخاري وغيره من قال حين يسمع النداء اللهم رب هذه الدعوة التامة والصلاة القائمة آت محمدا الوسيلة والفضيلة وابعثه مقاما محمودا الذي وعدته حلت له شفاعتي يوم القيامة وزاد البيهقي في آخره إنك لا تخلف الميعاد وتمامه في الإمداد والفتح قال ابن حجر في شرح المنهاج والدرجة الرفيعة وختمه بيا أرحم الراحمين لا أصل لهما اه (رد المحتار ٣٩٨/١)

صلى الله عليه بها عشرا ثم سلوا الله لي الوسيلة فإنها منزلة في الجنة لا تنبغي إلا لعبد من عباد الله وأرجو أن أكون أنا هو فمن سأل لي الوسيلة حلت له الشفاعة (صحيح مسلم، الرقم: ٣٨٤)

Hazrat Abdullah bin Amr bin Aas رَضِيَ اللّٰهُ عَنْهُمَا reports that he heard Hazrat Rasulullah صَلَّى اللّٰهُ عَلَيْهِ وَسَلَّمَ saying, "When you hear the muazzin call out the azaan, then repeat the words of the azaan after him and thereafter recite durood upon me (before reciting the dua of azaan). Verily, whoever recites durood upon me once, Allah تَبَارَكَ وَتَعَالَى sends ten blessings on him. Then (recite the dua after the azaan in which you) supplicate to Allah تَبَارَكَ وَتَعَالَى to bless me with the honour of 'waseelah' which is a lofty position and rank in Jannah which will be exclusively granted to one of Allah's تَبَارَكَ وَتَعَالَى special servants. I earnestly hope that I am granted that position, and whoever supplicates to Allah تَبَارَكَ وَتَعَالَى to grant me the 'waseelah', he will receive my intercession on the Day of Qiyaamah."

عن جابر رضي الله عنه قال قال رسول الله صلى الله عليه وسلم من قال حين يسمع النداء اللهم رب هذه الدعوة التامة والصلاة القائمة آت محمدا الوسيلة والفضيلة وابعثه مقاما محمودا الذي وعدته حلت له شفاعتي يوم القيامة (صحيح البخاري، الرقم: ٦١٤) (وأما زيادة إنك لا تخلف الميعاد فقد ذكرها البيهقي في السنن الكبرى، ٤١٠/١)

Hazrat Jaabir رَضِيَ اللّٰهُ عَنْهُ reports that Hazrat Rasulullah صَلَّى اللّٰهُ عَلَيْهِ وَسَلَّمَ said, "Whosoever recites the following dua after azaan, he will receive my intercession on the Day of Qiyaamah."

اللّٰهُمَّ رَبَّ هٰذِهِ الدَّعْوَةِ التَّامَّةِ وَالصَّلَاةِ الْقَائِمَةِ آتِ مُحَمَّدَنِ الْوَسِيلَةَ وَالْفَضِيلَةَ وَابْعَثْهُ مَقَامًا مَحْمُودًانِ الَّذِي وَعَدْتَّهُ (إِنَّكَ لَاتُخْلِفُ الْمِيعَادْ)

2. After reciting the dua after azaan, the following dua should also be recited:

أَشْهَدُ أَنْ لَّا إِلٰهَ إِلَّا اللهُ وَحْدَهُ لَا شَرِيكَ لَهُ وَأَنَّ مُحَمَّدًا عَبْدُهُ وَرَسُولُهُ رَضِيْتُ بِاللهِ رَبًّا وَبِمُحَمَّدٍ رَسُوْلًا وَبِالْإِسْلَامِ دِيْنًا

I bear testimony that there is no deity except Allah تَبَارَكَوَتَعَالَ who is alone and has no partner, and that Hazrat Muhammad صَلَّىٱللَّهُعَلَيْهِوَسَلَّمَ is His servant and messenger. I am pleased with Allah تَبَارَكَوَتَعَالَ as my Rabb, Hazrat Muhammad صَلَّىٱللَّهُعَلَيْهِوَسَلَّمَ as a messenger of Allah تَبَارَكَوَتَعَالَ and Islam as my religion.

Note: This dua should be recited after the azaan as well as during the azaan, after the muazzin calls out the shahaadatain (أَشْهَدُ أَنَّ مُحَمَّدًا رَسُوْلُ الله).[198]

عن سعد بن أبي وقاص رضي الله عنه عن رسول الله صلى الله عليه وسلم أنه قال من قال حين يسمع المؤذن أشهد أن لا إله إلا الله وحده لا شريك له وأن محمدا عبده ورسوله رضيت بالله ربا وبمحمد رسولا وبالإسلام دينا غفر له ذنبه (صحيح مسلم، الرقم: ٣٨٦)

Hazrat Sa'd bin Abi Waqqaas ﷺ *reports that Hazrat Rasulullah* ﷺ *said, "Whoever recites the following dua at the time when the azaan is called out, his (minor) sins will be forgiven."*

أَشْهَدُ أَنْ لَّا إِلٰهَ إِلَّا اللهُ وَحْدَهُ لَا شَرِيْكَ لَهُ وَأَنَّ مُحَمَّدًا عَبْدُهُ وَرَسُوْلُهُ رَضِيْتُ بِاللهِ رَبًّا وَبِمُحَمَّدٍ رَسُوْلاً وَبِالْإِسْلَامِ دِيْنًا

3. The following duas of azaan may also be recited:

اللّٰهُمَّ رَبَّ هٰذِهِ الدَّعْوَةِ التَّامَّةِ وَالصَّلَاةِ الْقَائِمَةِ صَلِّ عَلٰى مُحَمَّدٍ وَأَعْطِهِ سُؤْلَهُ يَوْمَ الْقِيَامَةِ[199]

O Allah ﷻ *! Rabb of this perfect call and established salaah! Send salutations upon Hazrat Muhammad* ﷺ *(shower Your mercy upon him) and grant him his request (of interceding for all the creation) on the Day of Qiyaamah.*

اللّٰهُمَّ رَبَّ هٰذِهِ الدَّعْوَةِ التَّامَّةِ وَالصَّلَاةِ الْقَائِمَةِ صَلِّ عَلٰى عَبْدِكَ وَرَسُوْلِكَ وَاجْعَلْنَا فِيْ شَفَاعَتِهِ يَوْمَ الْقِيَامَةِ[200]

O Allah ﷻ *! Rabb of this perfect call and established salaah! Send salutations upon Your slave and Your Rasul* ﷺ

---

[199] عن أبي الدرداء رضي الله عنه أن رسول الله صلى الله عليه وسلم كان يقول إذا سمع المؤذن اللهم رب هذه الدعوة التامة والصلاة القائمة صل على محمد وأعطه سؤله يوم القيامة وكان يسمعها من حوله ويحب أن يقولوا مثل ذلك إذا سمعوا المؤذن قال ومن قال مثل ذلك إذا سمع المؤذن وجبت له شفاعة محمد صلى الله عليه وسلم يوم القيامة رواه الطبراني في الكبير وفيه صدقة بن عبد الله السمين ضعفه أحمد والبخاري ومسلم وغيرهم دحيم ووثقه وأبو حاتم وأحمد بن صالح المصري (مجمع الزوائد، الرقم: ١٨٧٨)

[200] عن أبي الدرداء رضي الله عنه قال كان رسول الله صلى الله عليه وسلم إذا سمع النداء قال اللهم رب هذه الدعوة التامة والصلاة القائمة صل على عبدك ورسولك واجعلنا في شفاعته يوم القيامة قال رسول الله صلى الله عليه وسلم من قال هذا عند النداء جعله الله في شفاعتي يوم القيامة رواه الطبراني في الأوسط وفيه صدقة المذكور قبل هذا الحديث (مجمع الزوائد، الرقم: ١٨٧٩)

(shower Your mercy upon him), and make us among those who will receive his intercession on the Day of Qiyaamah.

اللّٰهُمَّ رَبَّ هٰذِهِ الدَّعْوَةِ الْقَائِمَةِ وَالصَّلَاةِ النَّافِعَةِ صَلِّ عَلٰى مُحَمَّدٍ وَارْضَ عَنِّيْ رِضَاءً لَا سَخَطَ بَعْدَهُ[201]

O Allah تَبَارَكَ وَتَعَالٰى*! Rabb of this established call and beneficial salaah! Send salutations (shower Your mercy) upon Hazrat Muhammad* صَلَّى اللّٰهُ عَلَيْهِ وَسَلَّمَ *and grant me Your pleasure after which You will never be displeased with me.*

It is reported in the Hadith that if one recites the above dua and thereafter makes dua to Allah تَبَارَكَ وَتَعَالٰى, his dua will be accepted.[See 201]

---

[201] عن جابر رضي الله عنه أن رسول الله صلى الله عليه وسلم قال من قال حين ينادي المنادي اللهم رب هذه الدعوة القائمة والصلاة النافعة صل على محمد وارض عني رضاء لا سخط بعده استجاب الله له دعوته رواه أحمد والطبراني في الأوسط وفيه ابن لهيعة وفيه ضعف (مجمع الزوائد، الرقم: ١٨٧٥)

Dua at the Time of the Maghrib Azaan

Recite the following dua during the azaan of Maghrib or after the azaan:[202]

اَللّٰهُمَّ إِنَّ هٰذَا إِقْبَالُ لَيْلِكَ وَإِدْبَارُ نَهَارِكَ وَأَصْوَاتُ دُعَاتِكَ فَاغْفِرْ لِيْ

O Allah تَبَارَكَ وَتَعَالَىٰ*! This is the approach of the night and the departure of the day, and these are the voices of Your servants calling out (the muazzins), so forgive me (my sins).*

عن أم سلمة رضي الله عنها قالت علمني رسول الله صلى الله عليه وسلم أن أقول عند أذان المغرب اللهم إن هذا إقبال ليلك وإدبار نهارك وأصوات دعاتك فاغفر لي (سنن أبي داود، الرقم: ٥٣٠)[203]

Hazrat Ummu Salamah رَضِيَ اللهُ عَنْهَا *reports, "Rasulullah* صَلَّى اللهُ عَلَيْهِ وَسَلَّمَ *taught me to recite the following dua at the time of the Maghrib azaan:*

اَللّٰهُمَّ إِنَّ هٰذَا إِقْبَالُ لَيْلِكَ وَإِدْبَارُ نَهَارِكَ وَأَصْوَاتُ دُعَاتِكَ فَاغْفِرْ لِيْ

---

[202] الظاهر أن يقال هذا بعد جواب الأذان أو في أثنائه (مرقاة المفاتيح ٢/٣٦٥)

[203] قال الحاكم: هذا حديث صحيح ولم يخرجاه والقاسم بن معن بن عبد الرحمن بن عبد الله بن مسعود رضي الله عنه من أشراف الكوفيين وثقاهم ممن يجمع حديثه ولم أكتبه إلا عن شيخنا أبي عبد الله رحمه الله وأقره الذهبي وقال صحيح (المستدرك على الصحيحين للحاكم، الرقم: ٧١٤)

WORDS OF IQAAMAH

The words of the iqaamah are the same as the words of azaan. However, after حَيَّ عَلَى الْفَلَاحْ (hayya alal falaah), one will say:

قَدْ قَامَتِ الصَّلَاةْ قَدْ قَامَتِ الصَّلَاةْ

The salaah has been established, the salaah has been established

The words of iqaamah are as follows:

اَللهُ أَكْبَرْ اَللهُ أَكْبَرْ

Allah تَبَارَكَ وَتَعَالَى *is the greatest, Allah* تَبَارَكَ وَتَعَالَى *is the greatest.*

اَللهُ أَكْبَرْ اَللهُ أَكْبَرْ

Allah تَبَارَكَ وَتَعَالَى *is the greatest, Allah* تَبَارَكَ وَتَعَالَى *is the greatest.*

أَشْهَدُ أَلَّا إِلٰهَ إِلَّا اللهْ أَشْهَدُ أَلَّا إِلٰهَ إِلَّا اللهْ

I testify that there is none worthy of worship besides Allah تَبَارَكَ وَتَعَالَى, *I testify that there is none worthy of worship besides Allah* تَبَارَكَ وَتَعَالَى.

أَشْهَدُ أَنَّ مُحَمَّدًا رَّسُوْلُ اللهْ أَشْهَدُ أَنَّ مُحَمَّدًا رَّسُوْلُ اللهْ

I testify that Hazrat Muhammad صَلَّى اللهُ عَلَيْهِ وَسَلَّمَ *is the messenger of Allah* تَبَارَكَ وَتَعَالَى, *I testify that Hazrat Muhammad* صَلَّى اللهُ عَلَيْهِ وَسَلَّمَ *is the messenger of Allah* تَبَارَكَ وَتَعَالَى.

حَيَّ عَلَى الصَّلَاةْ حَيَّ عَلَى الصَّلَاةْ

Come to salaah, Come to salaah.

حَيَّ عَلٰى الْفَلَاحْ حَيَّ عَلٰى الْفَلَاحْ

Come to success, Come to success.

قَدْ قَامَتِ الصَّلَاةْ قَدْ قَامَتِ الصَّلَاةْ

The salaah has been established, the salaah has been established.

اَللّٰهُ أَكْبَرْ اَللّٰهُ أَكْبَرْ

Allah تَبَارَكَوَتَعَالَىٰ is the greatest, Allah تَبَارَكَوَتَعَالَىٰ is the greatest.

لَا إِلٰهَ إِلَّا اللّٰهْ

There is none worthy of worship besides Allah تَبَارَكَوَتَعَالَىٰ.

Note: The ة (taa) of the word الصَّلَاة (salaah) in حَيَّ عَلٰى الصَّلَاة (hayya alas salaah) and in قَدْ قَامَتِ الصَّلَاة (qad qaamatis salaah) will be read with a sukoon (ْ) and thus produce the sound of a هـ (haa). One will not pronounce the ة (taa) in both. Similarly, when reading both these phrases in the iqaamah, one will not say hayya alas salaa<u>ti</u> hayya alas salaa<u>t</u> and qad qaamatis salaa<u>tu</u> qad qaamatis salaa<u>t</u>. Rather, one will say hayya alas salaa<u>h</u> hayya alas salaa<u>h</u> and qad qaamatis salaa<u>h</u> qad qaamatis salaa<u>h</u>.[204]

---

[204] ويسكن كلماتهما على الوقف لكن في الأذان حقيقة وفي الإقامة ينوي الوقف كذا في التبيين (الفتاوى الهندية ١ / ٥٦) (سن الأذان) فليس بواجب على الأصح لعدم تعليمه الأعرابي (و) كذا (الإقامة سنة مؤكدة) ... ويجزم الراء في التكبير ويسكن كلمات الأذان والإقامة في الأذان حقيقة وينوي الوقف في الإقامة لقوله صلى الله عليه و سلم الأذان جزم والإقامة جزم والتكبير جزم أي لافتتاح الصلاة قال الطحطاوي قوله (ويسكن كلمات الأذان) يعني للوقف والأولى ذكره قوله (في الأذان حقيقة) أي الوقف الذي لأجله السكون حقيقة في الأذان لأجل الترسل فيه قوله (وينوي الوقف في الإقامة) لأنه لم يقف حقيقة لأن المطلوب فيها الحدر أفاده في الشرح قوله (لقوله صلى الله عليه وسلم) علة لقوله ويسكن الخ ويأتي بالشهادتين كل واحدة مرتين يفصل بينهما بسكتة وهكذا الخ (حاشية الطحطاوي على مراقي الفلاح صـ ١٩٥)

SUNNAH METHOD OF CALLING OUT THE IQAAMAH

1. Call out the iqaamah with hadr (reciting it in a swift manner).[205]

عن جابر رضي الله عنه أن رسول الله صلى الله عليه وسلم قال لبلال إذا أذنت فترسل وإذا أقمت فاحدر (سنن الترمذي، الرقم: ١٩٥)

Hazrat Jaabir رَضِيَٱللَّهُعَنْهُ *reports that Hazrat Rasulullah* صَلَّىٱللَّهُعَلَيْهِوَسَلَّمَ *addressed Hazrat Bilaal* رَضِيَٱللَّهُعَنْهُ *saying, "When you call out the azaan then call it out with tarassul (gradually, with pausing after each phrase), and when you call out the iqaamah then call it out quickly."* See 172

2. Each phrase of the words of the iqaamah will be recited in sets of two. When reciting the set, join the two phrases of the words of iqaamah and do not pause between the two phrases (i.e. only pause after completing both phrases).[206]

---

[205] (والإقامة كالأذان) فيما مر (لكن هي) أي الإقامة وكذا الإمامة (أفضل منه) فتح (ولا يضع) المقيم (أصبعيه في أذنيه) لأنها أخفض (ويحدر) بضم الدال أي يسرع فيها فلو ترسل لم يعدها في الأصح (ويزيد قد قامت الصلاة بعد فلاحها مرتين) (الدر المختار ٣٨٨/١)

[206] قوله (ويترسل فيه ويحدر فيها) أي يتمهل في الأذان ويسرع في الإقامة وحده أن يفصل بين كلمتي الأذان بسكتة بخلاف الإقامة للتوارث ولحديث الترمذي أنه قال لبلال إذا أذنت فترسل في أذانك وإذا أقمت فاحدر (البحر الرائق ٢٧١/١)

عن عبد الله بن زيد رضي الله عنه قال كان أذان رسول الله صلى الله عليه وسلم شفعا

شفعا في الأذان والإقامة (سنن الترمذي، الرقم: ١٩٤) [207]

Hazrat Abdullah bin Zaid رَضِيَ اللهُ عَنْهُ *reports that the (phrases of the)*
azaan and iqaamah of Hazrat Rasulullah صَلَّى اللهُ عَلَيْهِ وَسَلَّمَ *were in sets of*
two.

3. The iqaamah will be called out inside the musjid.[208]

4. It is preferable that the iqaamah be called out by the person
   who called out the azaan.[209]

---

[207] قال أبو عيسى: حديث عبد الله بن زيد رواه وكيع عن الأعمش عن عمرو بن مرة عن عبد الرحمن بن أبي ليلى قال حدثنا أصحاب محمد

صلى الله عليه وسلم أن عبد الله بن زيد رأى الأذان في المنام وقال شعبة عن عمرو بن مرة عن عبد الرحمن بن أبي ليلى أن عبد الله بن زيد رأى

الأذان في المنام وهذا أصح من حديث ابن أبي ليلى وعبد الرحمن بن أبي ليلى لم يسمع من عبد الله بن زيد وقال بعض أهل العلم الأذان مثنى

مثنى والإقامة مثنى مثنى وبه يقول سفيان الثوري وابن المبارك وأهل الكوفة ابن أبي ليلى هو محمد بن عبد الرحمن بن أبي ليلى كان قاضي الكوفة

ولم يسمع من أبيه شيئا إلا أنه يروي عن رجل عن أبيه

وله شواهد منها:

عن معاذ بن جبل قال جاء رجل من الأنصار إلى النبي صلى الله عليه وسلم فقال إني رأيت في النوم كأني مستيقظ أرى رجلا نزل من السماء

عليه بردان أخضران نزل على جذم حائط من المدينة فأذن مثنى مثنى ثم جلس ثم أقام مثنى مثنى فقال فقال نعم ما رأيت علمها بلالا قال قال

عمر قد رأيت مثل ذلك ولكنه سبقني (مسند أحمد، الرقم: ٢٢٠٢٧)

عن الأسود عن بلال أنه كان يثني الأذان ويثني الإقامة (شرح معاني الآثار للطحاوي، الرقم: ٨٢٦)

[208] والمكان هنا مختلف لأن السنة أن يكون الأذان في المنارة والإقامة في المسجد وكذا النغمة والهيئة بخلاف خطبتي الجمعة لاتحاد المكان والهيئة

فلا يقع الفصل إلا بالجلسة (البحر الرائق ٢٧٥/١)

[209] عن زياد بن الحارث الصدائي قال كنت مع رسول الله صلى الله عليه وسلم في سفر فأمرني فأذنت بلال أن يقيم فقال رسول الله

صلى الله عليه وسلم إن أخا صداء قد أذن ومن أذن فهو يقيم (سنن ابن ماجه، الرقم: ٧١٧)

(أقام غير من أذن بغيبته) أي المؤذن (لا يكره مطلقا) وإن بحضوره كره إن لحقه وحشة كما كره مشيه في إقامته

قال العلامة ابن عابدين رحمه الله (قوله مطلقا) أي لحقه وحشة أو لا قوله (كره إن لحقه وحشة) أي بأن لم يرض به وهذا اختيار خواهر زاده

ومشى عليه في الدرر والخانية لكن في الخلاصة إن لم يرض به يكره وجواب الرواية أنه لا بأس به مطلقا اه قلت وبه صرح الإمام الطحاوي في

مجمع الآثار معزيا إلى أئمتنا الثلاثة الأفضل أن يكون المؤذن هو المقيم من أذن فهو يقيم لحديث اه أي لحديث وتمامه في حاشية نوح وقال في البحر

ويدل عليه إطلاق قول المجمع ولا نكرهها من غيره فما في شرحه لابن ملك من أنه لو حضر ولم يرض يكره اه نظر فيه اتفاقا اه وكذا يدل عليه

إطلاق الكافي معللا بأن كل واحد ذكر فلا بأس بأن يأتي بكل واحد رجل آخر ولكن الأفضل أن يكون المؤذن هو المقيم اه أي لحديث من

أذن فهو يقيم وتمامه في حاشية نوح (رد المحتار ٣٩٥/١)

عن زياد بن الحارث الصدائي رضي الله عنه قال أمرني رسول الله صلى الله عليه وسلم أن أؤذن في صلاة الفجر فأذنت فأراد بلال أن يقيم فقال رسول الله صلى الله عليه وسلم إن أخا صداء قد أذن ومن أذن فهو يقيم (سنن الترمذي، الرقم: ١٩٩)[210]

Hazrat Ziyaad bin Haarith Sudaa'ee ﷺ reports, "On one occasion, I was with Rasulullah ﷺ on a journey. He commanded me to call out the azaan and I did so. Thereafter, Hazrat Bilaal ﷺ intended to call out the iqaamah. However, Hazrat Rasulullah ﷺ said to him, 'Your Sudaa'ee brother (from Sudaa', a famous tribe from Yemen,) has called out the azaan, and the one who calls out the azaan should give the iqaamah.'"

5. Turn your face to the right when saying حَيَّ عَلَى الصَّلَاةِ (hayya alas salaah) and to the left when saying حَيَّ عَلَى الْفَلَاحْ (hayya alal falaah).[211]

---

[210] قال أبو عيسى: وفي الباب عن ابن عمر وحديث زياد إنما نعرفه من حديث الإفريقي والإفريقي هو ضعيف عند أهل الحديث ضعفه يحيى بن سعيد القطان وغيره قال أحمد لا أكتب حديث الإفريقي ورأيت محمد بن إسماعيل يقوي أمره ويقول هو مقارب الحديث والعمل على هذا عند أكثر أهل العلم أن من أذن فهو يقيم

[211] وأطلق في الالتفات ولم يقيده بالأذان وقدمنا عن القنية أنه يحول في الإقامة أيضا وفي السراج الوهاج لا يحول فيها لأنها لإعلام الحاضرين بخلاف الأذان فإنه إعلام للغائبين وقيل يحول إذا كان الموضع متسعا (البحر الرائق ٢٧٢/١)

(ويلتفت فيه) وكذا فيها مطلقا وقيل إن المحل متسعا (يمنا ويسارا) فقط لئلا يستدبر القبلة (بصلاة وفلاح)

قال العلامة ابن عابدين رحمه الله قوله (ويلتفت) أي يحول وجهه لا صدره قهستاني ولا قدميه نهر قوله (وكذا فيها مطلقا) أي في الإقامة سواء كان المحل متسعا أو لا قوله (لئلا يستدبر) تعليل لقوله فقط أي انته عن القول بالالتفات خلفا لئلا يستدبر المؤذن أو المقيم القبلة ح قوله (بصلاة وفلاح) لف ونشر مرتب يعني يلتفت فيهما يمينا بالصلاة ويسارا بالفلاح وهو الأصح كما في القهستاني عن المنية وهو الصحيح كما في البحر والتبيين وقال مشايخ مرو يمنة ويسرة في كل كذا في القهستاني ح قال في الفتح والثاني أوجه ورده الرملي بأنه خلاف الصحيح المنقول عن السلف (رد المختار ٣٨٧/١)

6. Once the iqaamah is being called out for salaah, do not engage in performing the sunnah salaah. Rather, immediately join the fardh salaah. After the fardh salaah, perform the sunnah if it was not performed before the fardh salaah. However, Asr Salaah and Fajr Salaah are an exception. In the case of Asr Salaah, one will not perform the sunnats after the fardh, as nafl salaah cannot be performed after Asr Salaah until sunset.[212] In the case of Fajr Salaah, even if the fardh has commenced, one will perform the sunnats before joining the fardh, provided one is sure that he will be able to join the fardh before the imaam makes salaam.[213]

عن أبي هريرة رضي الله عنه عن النبي صلى الله عليه وسلم قال إذا أقيمت الصلاة فلا صلاة إلا المكتوبة (صحيح مسلم، الرقم: ٧١٠)

Hazrat Abu Hurairah ﷺ reports that Hazrat Nabi ﷺ said, "Once the iqaamah is called out, no salaah is to be performed besides the fardh salaah."

---

[212] (وكره نفل) قصدا ولو تحية مسجد (وكل ما كان واجبا) لا لعينه بل (لغيره) وهو ما يتوقف وجوبه على فعله (كمنذور وركعتي طواف) وسجدتي سهو (والذي شرع فيه) في وقت مستحب أو مكروه (ثم أفسده و) لو سنة الفجر (بعد صلاة فجر و) صلاة (عصر) ولو المجموعة بعرفة (لا) يكره (قضاء فائتة و) لو وترا أو (سجدة تلاوة وصلاة جنازة (الدر المختار ٣٧٥/١)

[213] عن حارثة بن مضرب أن ابن مسعود وأبا موسى خرجا من عند سعيد بن العاص فأقيمت الصلاة فركع ابن مسعود ركعتين ثم دخل مع القوم في الصلاة وأما أبو موسى فدخل في الصف رواه أبو بكر ابن أبي شيبة في مصنفه (الرقم ٦٤٧٦) وإسناده صحيح (آثار السنن ص ٣٥٩) عن أبي الدرداء أنه كان يدخل المسجد والناس صفوف في صلاة الفجر فيصلي الركعتين في ناحية المسجد ثم يدخل مع القوم في الصلاة رواه الطحاوي في شرح معاني الآثار (الرقم: ٢٢٠٥) وإسناده حسن (آثار السنن ص ٣٥٩) (وكذا يكره تطوع عند إقامة صلاة مكتوبة) أي إقامة إمام مذهبه لحديث إذا أقيمت الصلاة فلا صلاة إلا المكتوبة (إلا سنة فجر إن لم يخف فوت جماعتها) ولو بإدراك تشهدها فإن خاف تركها أصلا (الدر المختار ٣٧٧/١-٣٧٨)

REPLYING TO THE IQAAMAH

Reply to the iqaamah in the same way that you reply to the azaan. However, when replying to قَدْ قَامَتِ الصَّلَاةُ (qad qaamatis salaah) then say:

أَقَامَهَا اللهُ وَأَدَامَهَا

May Allah تَبَارَكَ وَتَعَالَى *establish it (salaah) and preserve it.*

عن أبي أمامة أو بعض أصحاب رسول الله صلى الله عليه وسلم أن بلالا أخذ في الإقامة فلما أن قال قد قامت الصلاة قال رسول الله صلى الله عليه وسلم أقامها الله وأدامها (سنن أبي داود، الرقم: ٥٢٨)[214]

Hazrat Abu Umaamah رَضِيَ اللهُ عَنْهُ *or another Sahaabi reports that on one occasion, Hazrat Bilaal* رَضِيَ اللهُ عَنْهُ *was calling out the iqaamah. When he reached the words* قَدْ قَامَتِ الصَّلَاةُ *(qad qaamatis salaah), Hazrat Rasulullah* صَلَّى اللَّهُ عَلَيْهِ وَسَلَّمَ *replied by saying* أَقَامَهَا اللهُ وَأَدَامَهَا *(aqaamahallaahu wa adaamahaa).*

---

[214] قال المنذري: في إسناده رجل مجهول وشهر بن حوشب تكلم فيه غير واحد ووثقه الإمام أحمد ويحيى بن معين (مختصر سنن أبي داود ٢١٠/١)

GENERAL MASAAIL PERTAINING TO AZAAN AND IQAAMAH

1. **Q:** Should the person calling out the iqaamah turn his head to the right and left when saying حَيَّ عَلَى الصَّلَاةِ and حَيَّ عَلَى الْفَلَاحْ?

   A: There are three opinions in this mas'alah:

   The first opinion is that the muazzin will not turn his head to the right and left when saying حَيَّ عَلَى الْفَلَاحْ and حَيَّ عَلَى الصَّلَاةِ in the iqaamah.

   The second opinion is that if the area where the salaah is being performed is a big area, then the muazzin should turn his head to the right and left when saying حَيَّ عَلَى الصَّلَاةِ and حَيَّ عَلَى الْفَلَاحْ.

   The third opinion is that the muazzin should turn his head to the right and left, regardless of whether the area is big or small.

   It is permissible for one to act upon any of the above three opinions in the Hanafi Mazhab.[See 211]

2. **Q:** Is it permissible to call out the azaan in the musjid?

   A: It is makrooh to call out the azaan in the musjid. The azaan should be called out outside the musjid e.g. in the sehn.[215]

---

[215] ويكره أن يؤذن في المسجد كما في القهستاني عن النظم (حاشية الطحطاوي على مراقي الفلاح صـ ١٩٧)

انظر أيضا 162

3. **Q:** When calling out the azaan in the musjid is makrooh, then why is the azaan before the jumuah khutbah called out in the musjid?

    A: The law of the azaan given before the khutbah is different to the azaan given for the five daily salaah. In regard to this azaan, the sunnah is that it should be given in the musjid. The purpose of this azaan which is called out near the mimbar is to conscientize the people who are in the musjid that the khutbah is about to commence and that they should complete their salaah and zikr and listen attentively to the khutbah.[216]

4. **Q:** If the words of the azaan have been distorted and changed (e.g. the azaan of the Shias), should one still reply to the azaan?

    A: If the azaan is distorted then do not reply to the azaan.[See 194]

5. **Q:** If during the azaan, one forgets to call out a certain phrase then what should one do?

    A: If one remembers during the azaan or immediately upon completing the azaan before speaking, then he should only recite the omitted phrase and continue from the point where he had stopped. However, if he recites the omitted phrase and continues from that point (repeating the phrases after

---

[216] فتاوى محمودية ١٢/١٩٠

the omitted phrase which he had already called out), it will be better, so that the entire azaan is called out according to the sunnah sequence. However, if he remembers after completing the azaan and he had spoken then he should repeat the azaan from the beginning.[217]

6. **Q:** Can the muazzin walk from one saff to the saff in front of him while calling out the iqaamah?

   A: It is makrooh for the muazzin to walk while calling out the iqaamah.[218]

7. **Q:** If one hears multiple azaans from different masaajid, does one have to reply separately to each azaan and recite the dua after azaan separately for each azaan? Kindly explain the ruling when one is in the musjid and when one is out of the musjid.

   A: If you are in the musjid at the time of azaan and azaan is called out from different masaajid at the same time, then you

---

[217] ولو قدم فيهما مؤخرا أعاد ما قدم فقط

قال العلامة ابن عابدين رحمه الله (قوله: أعاد ما قدم فقط) كما لو قدم الفلاح على الصلاة يعيده فقط أي ولا يستأنف الأذان من أوله (رد المحتار ٣٨٩/١)

(قول الشارح أعاد ما قدم فقط) أي أجزأه ذلك لكن الاستئناف أفضل حموي (تقريرات الرافعي ٤٦/١)

ويرتب بين كلمات الأذان والإقامة كما شرع كذا في محيط السرخسي وإذا قدم في أذانه أو في إقامته بعض الكلمات على بعض نحو أن يقول أشهد أن محمدا رسول الله قبل قوله أشهد أن لا إله إلا الله فالأفضل في هذا أن ما سبق على أوانه لا يعتد به حتى يعيده في أوانه وموضعه (الفتاوى الهندية ٥٦/١)

[218] كما كره مشيه في إقامته

قال العلامة ابن عابدين رحمه الله (قوله كما كره إلخ) ذكره في روضة الناطفي واختلفوا عند إتمامها أي عند قد قامت الصلاة فقيل يتمها ماشيا وقيل في مكانه إماما كان المؤذن أو غيره كما في البدائع وهو الأصح وقصر في السراج الخلاف على ما إذا كان إماما فلو يتمها في موضع البداءة بلا خلاف نهر (رد المحتار ٣٩٦/١)

should reply to the azaan of your musjid and recite the dua after the azaan.

If you are out of the musjid and the azaans of different masaajid are called out at the same time, then you may reply to the azaan of the musjid you are going to.

If the azaans of a few masaajid are called out at different times, then it is best to reply to each azaan separately and recite the dua after the azaan or at least reply to the first azaan that is called out.[219]

---

[219] ولو تكرر أجاب الأول

قال العلامة ابن عابدين رحمه الله (قوله ولو تكرر) أي بأن أذن واحد بعد واحد أما لو سمعهم في آن واحد من جهات فسيأتي قوله (أجاب الأول) سواء كان مؤذن مسجده أو غيره بحر عن الفتح بحثا ويفيده ما في البحر أيضا عن التفاريق إذا كان في المسجد أكثر من مؤذن أذنوا واحدا بعد واحد فالحرمة للأول اه لكنه يحتمل أن يكون مبنيا على أن الإجابة بالقدم أو على أن تكراره في مسجد واحد يوجب أن يكون الثاني غير مسنون بخلاف ما إذا كان من محلات مختلفة تأمل ويظهر لي إجابة الكل بالقول لتعدد السبب وهو السماع كما اعتمده بعض الشافعية (رد المحتار ١ / ٣٩٧)

ويدعو عند فراغه بالوسيلة لرسول لله صلى الله عليه وسلم (ولو كان في المسجد حين سمعه ليس عليه الإجابة ولو كان خارجه أجاب) بالمشيء إليه (بالقدم ولو أجاب باللسان لا به لا يكون مجيبا) وهذا (بناء على أن الإجابة المطلوبة بقدمه لا بلسانه) كما هو قول الحلواني وعليه (فيقطع قراءة القرآن لو) كان يقرأ (بمنزله ويجيب) لو أذان مسجده كما يأتي (ولو بمسجد لا) لأنه أجاب بالحضور وهذا متفرع على قول الحلواني وأما عندنا فيقطع ويجيب بلسانه مطلقا والظاهر وجوبها باللسان لظاهر الأمر في حديث إذا سمعتم المؤذن فقولوا مثل ما يقول كما بسط في البحر وأقره المصنف وقواه في النهر ناقلا عن المحيط وغيره بأنه على الأول لا يرد السلام ولا يسلم ولا يقرأ بل يقطعها ويجيب ولا يشتغل بغير الإجابة قال وينبغي أن لا يجيب بلسانه اتفاقا في الأذان بين يدي الخطيب وأن يجيب بقدمه اتفاقا في الأذان الأول يوم الجمعة لوجوب السعي بالنص

وفي التاترخانية إنما يجيب أذان مسجده وسئل ظهير الدين عمن سمعه في آن من جهات ماذا يجب عليه قال إجابة أذان مسجده بالفعل

قال العلامة ابن عابدين رحمه الله (قوله وهذا) راجع إلى قوله ولو كان في المسجد الخ ح قوله (المطلوبة) أي طلب إيجاب كما قدمه قوله (لا بلسانه) أي لأن الإجابة به مندوبة على هذا القول كما مر قوله (فيقطع قراءة القرآن) الظاهر أن المراد المسارعة للإجابة وعدم القعود لأجل القراءة لإخلال القعود بالسعي الواجب وإلا فلا مانع من القراءة ماشيا إلا أن يراد قطعها ندبا للإجابة باللسان أيضا لكن لا يناسبه التفريع ولا قوله ولو بمسجد لا لما علمت من أن الحلواني قائل بندبها باللسان فافهم قوله (ويجيب) أي بالقدم قوله (ولو أذان مسجده كما يأتي) أي عن التاترخانية وهذا ساقط من بعض النسخ قوله (ولو بمسجد لا) أي لا يجيب قطعها بالمعنى الذي ذكرناه آنفا فلا ينافي ما قدمه من أن إجابة اللسان مندوبة عند الحلواني فافهم قوله (وهذا متفرع على قول الحلواني) تكرار محض مع قوله وعليه فيقطع الخ ط قوله (والظاهر وجوبها باللسان الخ) كذا قاله في فتح القدير معللا بأنه لم تظهر قرينة تصرف الأمر عن الوجوب ونازعه في شرح المنية بما في آخر الحديث من قوله عليه الصلاة

والسلام ثم صلوا علي من صلى علي الخ لأن مثله من الترغيبات في الثواب يستعمل في المستحب غالبا اه أقول فيه نظر لأن ما ذكر إنما هو للصلاة وسؤال الوسيلة لإجابة المدعي وجوبها والقرآن في النظم لا يوجد القرآن في الحكم كما تقرر في الأصول نعم أخرج الإمام أبو جعفر الطحاوي في كتابه شرح الآثار بسنده إلى عبد الله رضي الله عنه قال كنا مع النبي صلى الله عليه وسلم في بعض أسفاره فسمع مناديا وهو يقول الله أكبر الله أكبر فقال صلى الله عليه وسلم على الفطرة فقال أشهد أن لا إله إلا الله فقال صلى الله عليه وسلم خرج من النار فابتدرناه فإذا صاحب ماشية أدركته الصلاة فنادى بها قال أبو جعفر فهذا رسول الله صلى الله عليه وسلم قال غير ما قال المنادي فدل أن الأمر للاستحباب والندب كأمره بالدعاء في أدبار الصلوات ونحوه اه فهذه قرينة صارفة للأمر عن الوجوب وبه تأيد ما صرح به جماعة من أصحابنا من عدم وجوب الإجابة باللسان وأنها مستحبة وهذا ظاهر في ترجيح قول الحلواني وعليه مشى في الخانية والفيض ويدل عليه قوله صلى الله عليه وسلم إذا سمعت النداء فأجب داعي الله وفي رواية فأجب وعليك السكينة ويكفي في ترجيحه الأدلة على وجوب الجماعة فإنك علمت أن قول الحلواني مبني على أن الإجابة لقصد الجماعة والذي ينبغي تحريره في هذا المحل أن الإجابة باللسان مستحبة وأن الإجابة بالقدم واجبة إن لزم من تركها تفويت الجماعة وإلا بأن أمكنه إقامتها بجماعة ثانية في المسجد أو بيته لا تجب بل تستحب مراعاة لأول الوقت والجماعة الكثيرة في المسجد بلا تكرار هذا ما ظهر لي ... قوله (إنما يجيب أذان مسجده) أي بالقدم وهو متفرع على قول الحلواني كما أشار إليه الشارح سابقا بقوله كما يأتي ثم قوله (قال إجابة أذان مسجده بالفعل) قال في الفتح وهذا ليس مما نحن فيه إذ مقصود السائل أي مؤذن يجيب باللسان استحبابا أو وجوبا والذي ينبغي إجابة الأول سواء كان مؤذن مسجده أو غيره فإن سمعهم معا أجاب معتبرا كون إجابته لمؤذن مسجده ولو لم يعتبر ذلك جاز وإنما فيه مخالفة الأولى اه ملخصا (رد المحتار ١ / ٣٩٨)

CHAPTER SIX

THE MUSJID

VIRTUES OF THE MUSJID

1. The masaajid have been declared as the most beloved of places to Allah تَبَارَكَوَتَعَالَى.

عن أبي هريرة أن رسول الله صلى الله عليه وسلم قال أحب البلاد إلى الله مساجدها
وأبغض البلاد إلى الله أسواقها (صحيح مسلم، الرقم: ٦٧١)

Hazrat Abu Hurairah رَضِيَاللهُعَنْهُ *reports that Hazrat Rasulullah* صَلَّىاللهُعَلَيْهِوَسَلَّمَ *said, "The most beloved of places to Allah* تَبَارَكَوَتَعَالَى *are the masaajid, and the most disliked of places to Allah* تَبَارَكَوَتَعَالَى *are the market places."*

2. If one builds a musjid for the pleasure of Allah تَبَارَكَوَتَعَالَى, then Allah تَبَارَكَوَتَعَالَى will build a palace for him in Jannah.

عن عبيد الله الخولاني يذكر أنه سمع عثمان بن عفان عند قول الناس فيه حين بنى
مسجد الرسول صلى الله عليه وسلم إنكم قد أكثرتم وإني سمعت رسول الله صلى الله
عليه وسلم يقول من بنى مسجدا لله تعالى قال بكير حسبت أنه قال يبتغي به وجه الله

بنى الله له بيتا في الجنة (صحيح مسلم، الرقم: ٥٣٣) وفي رواية أخرى بني له بيت أوسع منه في الجنة (مسند أحمد، الرقم: ٧٠٥٦)[220]

Ubaidullah Khawlaani رَحِمَهُٱللَّهُ reports that he heard Hazrat Uthmaan رَضِيَٱللَّهُعَنْهُ say, at the time when people objected to him (making vast changes when extending the musjid of Hazrat Rasulullah صَلَّىٱللَّهُعَلَيْهِوَسَلَّمَ, such as using teak wood and baked bricks), "Indeed you people have objected to my extension many times, whereas I heard Rasulullah صَلَّىٱللَّهُعَلَيْهِوَسَلَّمَ saying, 'Whoever builds a musjid for Allah تَبَارَكَوَتَعَالَى, seeking the pleasure of Allah تَبَارَكَوَتَعَالَى, then Allah تَبَارَكَوَتَعَالَى will build a palace for him in Jannah.'" According to another Hadith, the person who builds a musjid for the sake of Allah تَبَارَكَوَتَعَالَى will receive a palace in Jannah that is bigger and more spacious than the musjid which he built.

---

[220] قال المنذري في الترغيب (الرقم: ٤١٩): رواه أحمد بإسناد لين

لهذا الحديث شاهد من حديث عبد الله بن عمرو قال قال رسول الله صلى الله عليه وسلم من بنى لله مسجدا بنى الله له بيتا أوسع منه في الجنة رواه أحمد وفيه الحجاج بن أرطاة وهو متكلم فيه (مجمع الزوائد، الرقم: ١٩٣٥)

وله شاهد آخر من حديث أبي أمامة قال قال رسول الله صلى الله عليه وسلم من بنى لله مسجدا بنى الله له بيتا في الجنة أوسع منه رواه الطبراني في الكبير وفيه علي بن يزيد وهو ضعيف (مجمع الزوائد، الرقم: ١٩٤٦)

Virtues of the One who Goes to the Musjid to Perform Salaah

1. Performing wudhu at home and walking to the musjid for salaah is a means of one's sins being forgiven and one's rank being elevated.

عن أبي هريرة رضي الله عنه قال قال رسول الله صلى الله عليه وسلم من تطهر في بيته ثم مشى إلى بيت من بيوت الله ليقضي فريضة من فرائض الله كانت خطواته إحداهما تحط خطيئة والأخرى ترفع درجة (صحيح مسلم، الرقم: ٦٦٦)

Hazrat Abu Hurairah رَضِىَاللهُعَنْهُ *reports that Hazrat Rasulullah* صَلَّىاللهُعَلَيْهِوَسَلَّمَ *said, "Whoever makes wudhu at home and thereafter walks towards a house from the houses of Allah* تَبَارَكَوَتَعَالَى *in order to complete the obligation of Allah* تَبَارَكَوَتَعَالَى*, then for one step he takes, a sin is forgiven, and for the next step he takes, he will be elevated one rank higher."*

2. Those who come to the musjid are the guests of Allah تَبَارَكَوَتَعَالَى.

عن عمرو بن ميمون عن عمر رضي الله عنه قال المساجد بيوت الله في الأرض وحق على المزور أن يكرم زائره (المصنف لابن أبي شيبة، الرقم: ٣٥٧٥٨)

Hazrat Amr bin Maimoon رَحِمَهُاللهُ *reports that Hazrat Umar* رَضِىَاللهُعَنْهُ *said, "The masaajid are the houses of Allah* تَبَارَكَوَتَعَالَى *on the earth, and the host takes responsibility to honour the one who visits Him."*

3. Those who frequent the musjid have been given the title of being from the 'household' of Allah تَبَارَكَ وَتَعَالَى and His special servants.

عن أنس بن مالك رضي الله عنه قال سمعت رسول الله صلى الله عليه وسلم يقول إن عمار بيوت الله هم أهل الله عز وجل (مجمع الزوائد، الرقم: ٢٠٣٠)[221]

Hazrat Anas رَضِيَٱللَّهُعَنْهُ *reports that Hazrat Rasulullah* صَلَّىٱللَّهُعَلَيْهِوَسَلَّمَ *said, "It is only those who frequent the masaajid who are the household (special servants) of Allah* تَبَارَكَ وَتَعَالَى.*"*

4. Frequenting the musjid is a means of safety for one's imaan and Deen.

عن معاذ بن جبل رضي الله عنه أن رسول الله صلى الله عليه وسلم قال إن الشيطان ذئب الإنسان كذئب الغنم يأخذ الشاة القاصية والناحية فإياكم والشعاب وعليكم بالجماعة والعامة والمسجد (الترغيب والترهيب، الرقم: ٤٩٩)[222]

Hazrat Mu'aaz bin Jabal رَضِيَٱللَّهُعَنْهُ *reports that Hazrat Rasulullah* صَلَّىٱللَّهُعَلَيْهِوَسَلَّمَ *said, "Indeed Shaitaan is the wolf of man (who hunts man), just like the wolf of goats which seizes the goat that is far off and separates from the flock. Refrain from living in isolation in the*

---

[221] قال الهيثمي: رواه الطبراني في الأوسط وأبو يعلى والبزار وفيه صالح المري وهو ضعيف

صالح ابن بشير ابن وادع المري بضم الميم وتشديد الراء أبو بشر البصري القاص الزاهد ضعيف من السابعة مات سنة اثنتين وسبعين وقيل بعدها (تقريب التهذيب ص ٢٧١)

عن أبي الدرداء رضي الله عنه قال سمعت رسول الله صلى الله عليه وسلم يقول المسجد بيت كل تقي وتكفل الله لمن كان المسجد بيته بالروح والرحمة والجواز على الصراط إلى رضوان الله إلى الجنة (الترغيب والترهيب، الرقم: ٥٠١)

قال الهيثمي: رواه الطبراني في الكبير والأوسط والبزار وقال إسناده حسن وهو كما قال رحمه الله تعالى

[222] قال المنذري: رواه أحمد من رواية العلاء بن زياد عن معاذ ولم يسمع منه

valleys (or refrain from isolated opinions) and hold firmly to the Ahlus Sunnah wal Jamaa'ah and remaining with the majority of the Ummah and being connected to the musjid."

5. Frequenting the musjid is a sign of imaan.

عن أبي سعيد رضي الله عنه قال قال رسول الله صلى الله عليه وسلم إذا رأيتم الرجل يعتاد المسجد فاشهدوا له بالإيمان قال الله تعالى إنما يعمر مساجد الله من آمن بالله واليوم الآخر (سنن الترمذي، الرقم: ٣٠٩٣)[223]

Hazrat Abu Sa'eed Khudri رَضِيَ اللّٰهُ عَنْهُ reports that Hazrat Rasulullah صَلَّى اللّٰهُ عَلَيْهِ وَسَلَّمَ said, "When you see that a man regularly frequents the musjid then bear witness to his imaan. Allah تَبَارَكَ وَتَعَالَى mentions in the Quraan, 'The masaajid of Allah تَبَارَكَ وَتَعَالَى are only frequented by those who have imaan in Allah تَبَارَكَ وَتَعَالَى and the Last Day.'"

6. Those who walk to the musjid in darkness have been given the glad tidings of receiving complete noor on the Day of Qiyaamah.

عن بريدة الأسلمي عن النبي صلى الله عليه وسلم قال بشر المشائين في الظلم إلى المساجد بالنور التام يوم القيامة (سنن الترمذي، الرقم: ٢٢٣)[224]

Hazrat Buraidah Aslami رَضِيَ اللّٰهُ عَنْهُ reports that Hazrat Rasulullah صَلَّى اللّٰهُ عَلَيْهِ وَسَلَّمَ said, "Give glad tidings to those who walk in darkness to

---

[223] قال أبو عيسى: هذا حديث حسن غريب

[224] قال أبو عيسى: هذا حديث غريب

the masaajid of them receiving complete noor on the Day of Qiyaamah."

7. Every time a person proceeds to the musjid in the morning or evening, Allah تَبَارَكَوَتَعَالَى prepares his abode for him in Jannah.

عن أبي هريرة عن النبي صلى الله عليه وسلم قال من غدا إلى المسجد وراح أعد الله له نزله من الجنة كلما غدا أو راح (صحيح البخاري، الرقم: ٦٦٢)

Hazrat Abu Hurairah رَضِيَاللَّهُعَنْهُ reports that Hazrat Rasulullah صَلَّىاللَّهُعَلَيْهِوَسَلَّمَ said, "The one who goes to the musjid in the morning and evening, then every time he proceeds to the musjid, Allah تَبَارَكَوَتَعَالَى prepares for him his abode in Jannah."

SUNNATS OF THE MUSJID

1. Dress appropriately when coming to the musjid.[225]

يٰبَنِىٓ اٰدَمَ خُذُوْا زِيْنَتَكُمْ عِنْدَ كُلِّ مَسْجِدٍ

Allah تَبَارَكَوَتَعَالَى *says, "O children of Aadam* عَلَيْهِ ٱلسَّلَام*, take your adornment at the time of performing salaah in the musjid."*[226]

2. Remove any foul odour from your body, clothing or mouth before entering the musjid e.g. after eating onions or something with a foul odour, standing near a fire, etc.[227]

---

[225] (و) كره (كفه) أي رفعه ولو لتراب كمشمر كم أو ذيل (وعبثه به) أي بثوبه (وبجسده) للنهي إلا لحاجة ولا بأس به خارج صلاة (وصلاته في ثياب بذلة) يلبسها في بيته (ومهنة) أي خدمة إن له غيرها وإلا لا

قال العلامة ابن عابدين رحمه الله ... قال في البحر وفسرها في شرح الوقاية بما يلبسه ولا يذهب به إلى الأكابر والظاهر أن الكراهة تنزيهية (رد المحتار ٦٤٠/١)

عن نافع أن ابن عمر رضي الله عنهما كساه وهو غلام فدخل المسجد يصلي متوشحا فقال أليس لك ثوبان قال بلى قال أرأيت لو استعنت بك وراء الدار أكنت لابسهما قال نعم قال فالله أحق أن تزين له أم الناس قال نافع بل الله فأخبره عن رسول الله صلى الله عليه وسلم أو عن عمر رضي الله عنه قال نافع قد استيقنت أنه عن أحدهما وما أراه إلا عن رسول الله صلى الله عليه وسلم قال لا يشتمل أحدكم في الصلاة اشتمال اليهود من كان له ثوبان فليتزر وليرتد ومن لم يكن له ثوبان فليتزر ثم ليصل (شرح معاني الآثار، الرقم: ٢٢١٤) قال العيني في نخب الافكار (٤ / ٢) رجال السند كلهم ثقات

[226] سورة الأعراف: ٣١

[227] ويحرم فيه السؤال ويكره الإعطاء مطلقا وقيل إن تخطى وإنشاد ضالة أو شعر إلا ما فيه ذكر ورفع صوت بذكر إلا للمتفقهة والوضوء فيما أعد لذلك وغرس الأشجار إلا لنفع كتقليل نز وتكون للمسجد وأكل ونوم إلا لمعتكف ونوم وأكل نحو ثوم ويمنع منه

قال العلامة ابن عابدين رحمه الله (قوله وأكل نحو ثوم) أي كبصل ونحوه مما له رائحة كريهة للحديث الصحيح في النهي عن قربان آكل الثوم والبصل المسجد قال الإمام العيني في شرحه على صحيح البخاري قلت علة النهي أذى الملائكة وأذى المسلمين ولا يختص بمسجده عليه الصلاة والسلام بل الكل سواء لرواية مساجدنا بالجمع خلافا لمن شذ ويلحق بما نص عليه في الحديث كل ما له رائحة كريهة مأكولا أو غيره وإنما خص الثوم هنا بالذكر وفي غيره أيضا بالبصل والكراث لكثرة أكلهم لها وكذلك ألحق بعضهم بذلك من جرح له رائحة بخر أو به جرح له رائحة وكذلك القصاب والسماك والمجذوم والأبرص أولى بالإلحاق وقال سحنون لا أرى الجمعة عليهما واحتج بالحديث وألحق بالحديث كل من آذى الناس بلسانه وبه أفتى ابن عمر وهو أصل في نفي كل من يتأذى به ولا يبعد أن يعذر المعذور بأكل ما له ريح كريهة لما في صحيح ابن حبان عن

عن جابر رضي الله عنه قال قال رسول الله صلى الله عليه وسلم من أكل من هذه الشجرة المنتنة فلا يقربن مسجدنا فإن الملائكة تتأذى مما يتأذى منه الإنس (صحيح مسلم، الرقم: ٥٦٤)

Hazrat Jaabir ﵁ reports that Hazrat Rasulullah ﷺ said, "The one who eats from this foul-smelling tree (garlic or onions) should not come close to our musjid, for the malaa'ikah (angels) are inconvenienced through the bad odour of those things through which humans are inconvenienced."

3. Apply itr before coming to the musjid if you are able to.[228]

عن أبي سعيد الخدري رضي الله عنه أن رسول الله صلى الله عليه وسلم قال غسل يوم الجمعة على كل محتلم وسواك ويمس من الطيب ما قدر عليه (صحيح مسلم، الرقم: ٨٤٧)

Hazrat Abu Sa'eed Khudri ﵁ reports that Hazrat Rasulullah ﷺ said, "Every baaligh person should perform ghusl on the Day of Jumuah, make miswaak and apply any itr that he is able to."

4. Proceed to the musjid calmly and in a dignified manner. Do not come to the musjid running.[229]

المغيرة بن شعبة قال انتهيت إلى رسول الله صلى الله عليه وسلم فوجد مني ريح الثوم فقال من أكل الثوم فأخذت يده فأدخلتها فوجد صدري معصوبا فقال إن لك عذرا (رد المحتار ٦٦١/١)

[228] وفي المحيط وغيره ويستحب لمن حضر الجمعة أن يدهن ويمس طيبا إن وجده (البحر الرائق ١٦٩/٢)

[229] وسرعة المشي والعدو إلى المسجد لا تحب عندنا وعند عامة الفقهاء واختلف في استحبابه والأصح أن يمشي على السكينة والوقار كذا في القنية (الفتاوى الهندية ١٤٩/١)

عن أبي هريرة رضي الله عنه قال سمعت رسول الله صلى الله عليه وسلم يقول إذا أقيمت الصلاة فلا تأتوها تسعون وأتوها تمشون عليكم السكينة فما أدركتم فصلوا وما فاتكم فأتموا (صحيح البخاري، الرقم: ٩٠٨)

Hazrat Abu Hurairah ﵁ *once mentioned, "I heard Rasulullah* ﷺ *say, 'When the iqaamah is called out for salaah, then do not proceed towards the salaah whilst you are running. Rather, come walking with calmness and tranquillity. Whatever portion of the salaah you obtain with the imaam, then perform it; and whatever portion you missed, then complete it (after the imaam completes the salaah).'"*

5. It is better for one to be in the state of wudhu when entering the musjid.[230]

عن أبي هريرة رضي الله عنه أن رسول الله صلى الله عليه وسلم قال لا يزال العبد في صلاة ما كان في مصلاه ينتظر الصلاة وتقول الملائكة اللهم اغفر له اللهم ارحمه حتى ينصرف أو يحدث قلت ما يحدث قال يفسو أو يضرط (صحيح مسلم، الرقم: ٦٤٩)

Hazrat Abu Hurairah ﵁ *reports that Hazrat Rasulullah* ﷺ *said, "As long as one remains on his musalla awaiting salaah, he receives the reward of one who is in salaah. The malaa'ikah (angels) continue to make dua for him saying, 'O Allah* ﵎*, forgive him! O Allah* ﵎*, have mercy on him!' He*

---

[230] قال العلامة ابن عابدين رحمه الله تتمة ذكر في الدرر عن التاترخانية أنه يكره دخول المحدث مسجدا من المساجد وطوافه بالكعبة اه وفي القهستاني ولا يدخله من على بدنه نجاسة ثم قال وفي الخزانة وإذا فسا في المسجد لم ير بعضهم به بأسا وقال بعضهم إذا احتاج إليه يخرجه منه وهو الأصح اه (رد المحتار ١/١٧٢)

continues receiving reward until he leaves the musjid or hadath occurs while he is in the musjid." A Sahaabi رَضِيَ ٱللَّهُ عَنْهُ asked, "How does hadath occur?" Hazrat Rasulullah صَلَّى ٱللَّهُ عَلَيْهِ وَسَلَّمَ replied, "Through passing wind (breaking his wudhu)."

6. Recite the masnoon duas when proceeding to the musjid. Some of the masnoon duas are:

Dua One:

The one who recites the following dua when leaving for the musjid acquires the special mercy of Allah تَبَارَكَ وَتَعَالَى, and seventy thousand malaa'ikah (angels) make dua for his forgiveness.[231]

اَللّٰهُمَّ إِنِّيْ أَسْأَلُكَ بِحَقِّ السَّائِلِيْنَ عَلَيْكَ وَأَسْأَلُكَ بِحَقِّ مَمْشَايَ هٰذَا فَإِنِّيْ لَمْ أَخْرُجْ أَشَرًا وَلَا بَطَرًا وَلَا رِيَاءً وَلَا سُمْعَةً وَخَرَجْتُ اِتِّقَاءَ سَخَطِكَ وَابْتِغَاءَ مَرْضَاتِكَ فَأَسْأَلُكَ أَنْ تُعِيْذَنِيْ مِنَ النَّارِ وَأَنْ تَغْفِرَ لِيْ ذُنُوْبِيْ إِنَّهُ لَا يَغْفِرُ الذُّنُوْبَ إِلَّا أَنْتَ

O Allah تَبَارَكَ وَتَعَالَى! I beg You, through the intermediary of those who turn to You in dua, and I beg You, through the intermediary of this walking of mine – for indeed I have neither come out due to pride,

---

[231] عن أبي سعيد الخدري قال قال رسول الله صلى الله عليه وسلم من خرج من بيته إلى الصلاة فقال اللهم إني أسألك بحق السائلين عليك وأسألك بحق ممشاي هذا فإني لم أخرج أشرا ولا بطرا ولا رياء ولا سمعة وخرجت اتقاء سخطك وابتغاء مرضاتك فأسألك أن تعيذني من النار وأن تغفر لي ذنوبي إنه لا يغفر الذنوب إلا أنت أقبل الله عليه بوجهه واستغفر له سبعون ألف ملك (سنن ابن ماجة، الرقم: ٧٧٨)

قال الحافظ في نتائج الأفكار (٢٧٢/١): هذا حديث حسن أخرجه أحمد عن يزيد بن هارون عن فضيل بن مرزوق وأخرجه ابن ماجه عن محمد بن يزيد بن إبراهيم التستري عن الفضل بن موفق وأخرجه ابن خزيمة في كتاب التوحيد من رواية محمد بن فضيل بن غزوان ومن رواية أبي خالد الأحمر وأخرجه أبو نعيم الأصبهاني من رواية أبي نعيم الكوفي كلهم عن فضيل بن مرزوق وقد رويناه في كتاب الصلاة لأبي نعيم وقال في روايته عن فضيل عن عطية قال حدثني أبو سعيد فذكره لكن لم يرفعه وقد أمن بذلك تدليس عطية وعجبت للشيخ كيف اقتصر على سوق رواية بلال دون أبي سعيد وعلى عزو رواية أبي سعيد لابن السني دون ابن ماجه وغيره والله الموفق

nor boastfulness, nor to show off, nor to impress people. I have come out fearing Your anger and seeking Your pleasure. Thus, I beg You to save me from the fire (of Jahannum) and to forgive my sins, indeed only You can forgive sins.

Note: In the narration of Musnad Ahmad, it is also mentioned that seventy thousand malaa'ikah (angels) make dua for his forgiveness and he receives the special mercy of Allah تَبَارَكَ وَتَعَالَى until he completes his salaah.[232]

Dua Two:

اَللّٰهُمَّ اجْعَلْ فِيْ قَلْبِيْ نُوْرًا وَفِيْ لِسَانِيْ نُوْرًا وَاجْعَلْ فِيْ سَمْعِيْ نُوْرًا وَاجْعَلْ فِيْ بَصَرِيْ نُوْرًا وَاجْعَلْ مِنْ خَلْفِيْ نُوْرًا وَمِنْ أَمَامِيْ نُوْرًا وَاجْعَلْ مِنْ فَوْقِيْ نُوْرًا وَمِنْ تَحْتِيْ نُوْرًا اَللّٰهُمَّ أَعْطِنِيْ نُوْرًا[233]

O Allah تَبَارَكَ وَتَعَالَى! Instil in my heart noor, and in my tongue noor, and instil in my hearing noor, and instil in my vision noor, and place behind me noor, and before me noor, and place above me noor, and below me noor. O Allah تَبَارَكَ وَتَعَالَى! Bless me with noor.

---

232 عن أبي سعيد الخدري فقلت لفضيل رفعه قال أحسبه قال رفعه قد رفعه قال من قال حين يخرج إلى الصلاة اللهم إني أسألك بحق السائلين عليك وبحق ممشاي فإني لم أخرج أشرا ولا بطرا ولا رياء ولا سمعة خرجت اتقاء سخطك وابتغاء مرضاتك أسألك أن تنقذني من النار وأن تغفر لي ذنوبي إنه لا يغفر الذنوب إلا أنت وكل الله به سبعين ألف ملك يستغفرون له وأقبل الله عليه بوجهه حتى يفرغ من صلاته (مسند أحمد، الرقم: ١١١٥٦)

233 عن عبد الله بن عباس أنه رقد عند رسول الله صلى الله عليه وسلم فاستيقظ فتسوك وتوضأ وهو يقول إن في خلق السماوات والأرض واختلاف الليل والنهار لآيات لأولي الألباب فقرأ هؤلاء الآيات حتى ختم السورة ثم قام فصلى ركعتين فأطال فيهما القيام والركوع والسجود ثم انصرف فنام حتى نفخ ثم فعل ذلك ثلاث مرات ست ركعات كل ذلك يستاك ويتوضأ ويقرأ هؤلاء الآيات ثم أوتر بثلاث ثم أذن المؤذن فخرج إلى الصلاة وهو يقول اللهم اجعل في قلبي نورا وفي لساني نورا واجعل في سمعي نورا واجعل في بصري نورا واجعل من خلفي نورا ومن أمامي نورا واجعل من فوقي نورا ومن تحتي نورا اللهم أعطني نورا (صحيح مسلم، الرقم: ٧٦٣)

7. Enter the musjid with the right foot.[234]

عن أنس بن مالك رضي الله عنه أنه كان يقول من السنة إذا دخلت المسجد أن تبدأ برجلك اليمنى وإذا خرجت أن تبدأ برجلك اليسرى (المستدرك على الصحيحين للحاكم، الرقم: ٧٩١)[235]

It is reported that Hazrat Anas رَضِيَٱللَّهُعَنْهُ said, "It is from the sunnah that when you enter the musjid, you should enter with your right foot, and when you exit from the musjid, you should exit with your left foot."

8. Recite the masnoon duas when entering the musjid. Some of the masnoon duas are as follows:[See 234]

Dua One

بِسْمِ اللهِ وَالصَّلاَةُ وَالسَّلاَمُ عَلَى رَسُوْلِ اللهِ اَللّٰهُمَّ افْتَحْ لِيْ أَبْوَابَ رَحْمَتِكَ[236]

(I enter) with the name of Allah تَبَارَكَوَتَعَالَى. May peace and salutations be upon Hazrat Rasulullah صَلَّىٱللَّهُعَلَيْهِوَسَلَّمَ. O Allah تَبَارَكَوَتَعَالَى, open for me the doors of Your mercy.

---

[234] ويقدم رجله اليمنى في دخوله ويقول بسم الله والحمد لله والصلاة والسلام على رسول الله اللهم افتح لي أبواب رحمتك (الفتاوى الهندية ١/٢٢٥)

[235] هذا حديث صحيح على شرط مسلم فقد احتج بشداد بن سعيد أبي طلحة الراسبي ولم يخرجاه

قال الذهبي في التلخيص: على شرط مسلم

[236] عن أبي حميد أو أبي أسيد الأنصاري رضي الله عنه قال قال رسول الله صلى الله عليه وسلم إذا دخل أحدكم المسجد فليسلم على النبي صلى الله عليه وسلم ثم ليقل اللهم افتح لي أبواب رحمتك فإذا خرج فليقل اللهم إني أسألك من فضلك (سنن أبي داود، الرقم: ٤٦٥)

Dua Two

اَللّٰهُمَّ افْتَحْ لَنَا أَبْوَابَ رَحْمَتِكَ وَسَهِّلْ لَنَا أَبْوَابَ رِزْقِكَ[237]

O Allah تَبَارَكَوَتَعَالَى*, open for us the doors of Your mercy and make easy*
for us the avenues of Your sustenance.

Dua Three

بِسْمِ اللهِ وَالصَّلَاةُ وَالسَّلَامُ عَلَى رَسُوْلِ اللهِ رَبِّ اغْفِرْ لِيْ ذُنُوْبِيْ وَافْتَحْ لِيْ أَبْوَابَ
رَحْمَتِكَ[238]

(I enter) with the name of Allah تَبَارَكَوَتَعَالَى*. May peace and salutations*
be upon Hazrat Rasulullah صَلَّىَاللَّهُعَلَيْهِوَسَلَّمَ*. O my Rabb, forgive my sins*
and open for me the doors of Your mercy.

Dua Four

أَعُوْذُ بِاللهِ الْعَظِيْمِ وَبِوَجْهِهِ الْكَرِيْمِ وَسُلْطَانِهِ الْقَدِيْمِ مِنَ الشَّيْطَانِ الرَّجِيْمِ

I seek protection in Allah تَبَارَكَوَتَعَالَى*, the Most Great, and (I seek*
protection) in His noble countenance and in His eternal might and
power from the accursed Shaitaan.

---

[237] عن أبي حميد الساعدي أن النبي صلى الله عليه وسلم كان يقول إذا دخل المسجد اللهم افتح لنا أبواب رحمتك وسهل لنا أبواب رزقك (مستخرج أبي عوانة، الرقم: ١٢٣٦)

عن المطلب بن عبد الله بن حنطب قال كان رسول الله صلى الله عليه وسلم إذا دخل المسجد قال بسم الله اللهم افتح لي أبواب رحمتك وسهل علي أبواب رزقك (مصنف عبد الرزاق، الرقم: ١٦٦٦)

والرواة كلهم ثقات وعبد العزيز يحتمل أن يكون هو الدراوردي ويحتمل أن يكون ابن الماجشون فكلاهما يروي عن ربيعة ويروي عنهما الأويسي وجزم الحافظ في نتائج الأفكار بأنه الدراوردي

[238] عن فاطمة رضي الله عنها قالت كان رسول الله صلى الله عليه وسلم إذا دخل المسجد صلى على محمد وسلم وقال رب اغفر لي ذنوبي وافتح لي أبواب رحمتك وإذا خرج صلى على محمد وسلم وقال رب اغفر لي ذنوبي وافتح لي أبواب فضلك (سنن الترمذي، الرقم: ٣١٤)

Through reciting the above dua, one will receive divine protection from Shaitaan for the entire day.

عن عبد الله بن عمرو بن العاص رضي الله عنهما قال كان رسول الله صلى الله عليه وسلم يقول إذا دخل المسجد قال أعوذ بالله العظيم وبوجهه الكريم وسلطانه القديم من الشيطان الرجيم قال فإذا قال ذلك قال الشيطان حفظ مني سائر اليوم (سنن أبي داود، الرقم: ٤٦٦)[239]

Hazrat Abdullah bin Amr bin Aas ﷺ reports that when Hazrat Rasulullah ﷺ would enter the musjid, he would recite the following dua:

أَعُوْذُ بِاللهِ الْعَظِيْمِ وَبِوَجْهِهِ الْكَرِيْمِ وَسُلْطَانِهِ الْقَدِيْمِ مِنَ الشَّيْطَانِ الرَّجِيْمِ

Hazrat Rasulullah ﷺ said that when a person recites this dua, Shaitaan says, "He has gained divine protection from me for the entire day."

9. Make the intention of nafl i'tikaaf for as long as you will remain in the musjid.[240]

10. Upon entering the musjid, make salaam to those in the musjid, provided they are not engaged in any ibaadah.

---

[239] هذا الحديث سكت عنه أبو داود والمنذري (مختصر سنن أبي داود ١٩٣/١)

[240] باب الإعتكاف ... (وأقله نفلا ساعة) من ليل أو نهار عند محمد وهو ظاهر الرواية عن الإمام لبناء النفل على المسامحة وبه يفتى والساعة في عرف الفقهاء جزء من الزمان لا جزء من أربعة وعشرين كما يقوله المنجمون كذا في غرر الأذكار وغيره (الدر المختار ٤٤٣/٢)

However, if people are engaged in salaah, then do not make salaam.[241]

11. Perform two rakaats of Tahiyyatul Musjid upon entering, as long as it is not the makrooh time for performing salaah.[242]

عن أبي قتادة رضي الله عنه أن رسول الله صلى الله عليه وسلم قال إذا دخل أحدكم المسجد فليركع ركعتين قبل أن يجلس (صحيح البخاري، الرقم: ٤٤٤)

Hazrat Abu Qataadah رَضِيَٱللَّهُعَنْهُ *reports that Hazrat Rasulullah* صَلَّىٱللَّهُعَلَيْهِوَسَلَّمَ *said, "When any one of you enters the musjid, he should perform two rakaats of salaah before he sits."*

12. Do not carry out any business transaction in the musjid.[243]

عن عمرو بن شعيب عن أبيه عن جده رضي الله عنهما قال نهى رسول الله صلى الله عليه وسلم عن تناشد الأشعار في المسجد وعن البيع والاشتراء فيه وأن يتحلق الناس يوم الجمعة قبل الصلاة في المسجد (سنن الترمذي، الرقم: ٣٢٢)[244]

Hazrat Abdullah bin Amr رَضِيَٱللَّهُعَنْهُ *reports, "Rasulullah* صَلَّىٱللَّهُعَلَيْهِوَسَلَّمَ *prohibited the reciting of poetry in the musjid, buying and selling in the musjid, and people sitting in circles in the musjid on the Day of Jumuah before the Jumuah Salaah (as sitting in this manner will not allow them to focus towards the one delivering the khutbah)."*

---

[241] ذكر الفقيه رحمه الله تعالى في التنبيه حرمة المسجد خمسة عشر أولها أن يسلم وقت الدخول إذا كان القوم جلوسا غير مشغولين بدرس ولا بذكر فإن لم يكن فيه أحد أو كانوا في الصلاة فيقول السلام علينا من ربنا وعلى عباد الله الصالحين (الفتاوى الهندية ٣٢١/٥)

[242] ذكر الفقيه رحمه الله تعالى في التنبيه حرمة المسجد خمسة عشر ... والثاني أن يصلي ركعتين قبل أن يجلس (الفتاوى الهندية ٣٢١/٥)

[243] ذكر الفقيه رحمه الله تعالى في التنبيه حرمة المسجد خمسة عشر ... والثالث أن لا يشتري ولا يبيع (الفتاوى الهندية ٣٢١/٥)

[244] قال أبو عيسى: حديث عبد الله بن عمرو بن العاص حديث حسن

13. Do not make any announcement for lost items in the
   musjid.[245]

عن أبي هريرة رضي الله عنه قال قال رسول الله صلى الله عليه وسلم من سمع رجلا
ينشد ضالة في المسجد فليقل لا ردها الله عليك فإن المساجد لم تبن لهذا (صحيح
مسلم، الرقم: ٥٦٨)

Hazrat Abu Hurairah رَضِىَٱللَّهُعَنْهُ *reports that Hazrat Rasulullah*
صَلَّىٱللَّهُعَلَيْهِوَسَلَّمَ *said, "Whoever hears a person making an*
announcement for a lost item in the musjid, then he should say to
him, 'May Allah تَبَارَكَوَتَعَالَى *not return your lost item to you.' for*
indeed the masaajid were not built for this purpose."

14. Do not raise your voice or make a noise in the musjid and in
   the area surrounding the musjid.[246]

عن السائب بن يزيد رضي الله عنه قال كنت نائما في المسجد فحصبني رجل فنظرت
فإذا عمر بن الخطاب رضي الله عنه فقال اذهب فأتني بهذين فجئته بهما فقال ممن
أنتما أو من أين أنتما قالا من أهل الطائف قال لو كنتما من أهل المدينة لأوجعتكما

---

²⁴⁵ ويكره ... وإنشاد ضالة

قال العلامة ابن عابدين رحمه الله (قوله وإنشاد ضالة) هي الشيء الضائع وإنشادها السؤال عنها وفي الحديث إذا رأيتم من ينشد ضالة في
المسجد فقولوا لا ردها الله عليك (رد المحتار ١/٦٦٠)

²⁴⁶ ذكر الفقيه رحمه الله تعالى في التنبيه حرمة المسجد خمسة عشر ... والسادس أن لا يرفع فيه الصوت من غير ذكر الله تعالى (الفتاوى
الهندية ٥/٣٢١)

ترفعان أصواتكما في مسجد رسول الله صلى الله عليه وسلم (صحيح البخاري، الرقم: ٤٧٠)[247]

Hazrat Saaib bin Yazeed رَضِيَٱللَّهُعَنْهُ *reports, "On one occasion, I was asleep in the musjid when someone threw some pebbles on me (in order to awaken me). I looked and saw that it was Umar* رَضِيَٱللَّهُعَنْهُ*. He said to me, 'Go and bring these two people to me.' I brought them before him, and he asked them, 'Where are you two people from?' They replied that they were from Taaif. Hazrat Umar* رَضِيَٱللَّهُعَنْهُ *said, 'Had you been from the people of Madinah Munawwarah, I would have punished you severely! You are raising your voices in the musjid of Rasulullah* صَلَّىٱللَّهُعَلَيْهِوَسَلَّمَ*!'"*

عن أبي هريرة رضي الله عنه قال قال رسول الله صلى الله عليه وسلم إذا اتخذ الفيء دولا والأمانة مغنما والزكاة مغرما وتعلم لغير الدين وأطاع الرجل امرأته وعق أمه وأدنى صديقه وأقصى أباه وظهرت الأصوات في المساجد وساد القبيلة فاسقهم وكان زعيم القوم أرذلهم وأكرم الرجل مخافة شره وظهرت القينات والمعازف وشربت الخمور ولعن آخر هذه الأمة أولها فارتقبوا عند ذلك ريحا حمراء وزلزلة وخسفا ومسخا وقذفا وآيات تتابع كنظام قطع سلكه فتتابع (سنن الترمذي، الرقم: ٢٢١١)[248]

---

[247] قال الحافظ في الفتح (١/٥٦٦): قوله كنت قائما في المسجد كذا في الأصول بالقاف وفي رواية نائما بالنون ويؤيده رواية حاتم عن الجعيد بلفظ كنت مضطجعا

[248] قال أبو عيسى: وفي الباب عن علي وهذا حديث غريب

وعن علي رضي الله عنه عن النبي صلى الله عليه وسلم قال إذا فعلت أمتي خمس عشرة خصلة فقد حل بها البلاء قيل وما هي يا رسول الله قال إذا كان المغنم دولا وإذا كانت الأمانة مغنما والزكاة مغرما وأطاع الرجل زوجته وعق أمه وبر صديقه وجفا أباه وارتفعت الأصوات في المساجد وكان زعيم القوم أرذلهم وأكرم الرجل مخافة شره وشربت الخمر ولبس الحرير واتخذت القينات والمعازف ولعن آخر هذه الأمة أولها فليرتقبوا عند

Hazrat Abu Hurairah رَضِيَٱللَّهُعَنْهُ reports that *Hazrat Rasulullah* صَلَّىٱللَّهُعَلَيْهِوَسَلَّمَ said, "When spoils of war will be taken as people's personal wealth to be circulated among them, when a trust will be regarded as booty (i.e. as public property), when zakaat will be viewed as a tax, when the knowledge of Deen will be acquired for motives besides that of Deen, when a man will obey his wife and disobey his mother, and keep his friend close to him and distance his father from him, and voices will be raised in the masaajid, and the open sinner of a tribe will become their leader, and the lowest person of a people will become their representative, and a man will be honoured out of fear of his evil, and singing girls and musical instruments will become rife, and wine will be consumed (openly), and the latter people of this Ummah will curse the former people of this Ummah, (when these signs manifest) then the people should await hurricanes, earthquakes, people sinking into the earth, disfiguring of faces, stones raining from the sky and other similar signs that will follow in quick succession, just as the pearls in a string fall in quick succession when the string is cut."

15. Ensure that you switch off your cellphone when entering the musjid so that it does not cause a disturbance to those engaged in performing salaah and other ibaadaat.[See 246]

ذلك ريحا حمراء أو خسفا أو مسخا رواه الترمذي وقال لا نعلم أحدا روى هذا الحديث عن يحيى بن سعيد الأنصاري غير الفرج بن فضالة (سنن الترمذي، الرقم: ٢٢١٠)

16. Do not take photos or make videos while in the musjid. Taking photos or making videos of animate objects is haraam in Islam, and doing so in the musjid is an even greater sin.[249]

عن عبد الله رضي الله عنه قال سمعت النبي صلى الله عليه وسلم يقول إن أشد الناس عذابا عند الله يوم القيامة المصورون (صحيح البخاري، الرقم: ٥٩٥٠)

Hazrat Abdullah bin Mas'ood رَضِيَٱللَّهُعَنْهُ *reports that Hazrat Rasulullah* صَلَّىٱللَّهُعَلَيْهِوَسَلَّمَ *said, "Indeed the people who will be punished the most severely by Allah* تَبَارَكَوَتَعَالَى *on the Day of Qiyaamah will be those involved in picture making."*

17. Do not engage in worldly talk, nor discuss worldly affairs in the musjid.[250]

عن الحسن رحمه الله مرسلا قال قال رسول الله صلى الله عليه وسلم يأتي على الناس زمان يكون حديثهم في مساجدهم في أمر دنياهم فلا تجالسوهم فليس لله فيهم حاجة (شعب الإيمان، الرقم: ٢٧٠١)[251]

---

[249] (ولبس ثوب فيه تماثيل) ذي روح

قال العلامة ابن عابدين رحمه الله (قوله ولبس ثوب فيه تماثيل) عدل عن قول غيره تصاوير لما في المغرب الصورة عام في ذي الروح وغيره والتمثال خاص بمثال ذي الروح ويأتي أن غير ذي الروح لا يكره قال القهستاني وفيه إشعار بأنه لا تكره صورة الرأس وفيه خلاف كما في اتخاذها كذا في المحيط قال في البحر وفي الخلاصة وتكره التصاوير على الثوب صلى فيه أو لا انتهى وهذه الكراهة تحريمية وظاهر كلام النووي في شرح مسلم الإجماع على تحريم تصوير الحيوان وقال وسواء صنعه لما يمتهن أو لغيره فصنعته حرام بكل حال لأن فيه مضاهاة لخلق الله تعالى وسواء كان في ثوب أو بساط أو درهم أو إناء أو حائط وغيرها اه فينبغي أن يكون حراما لا مكروها إن ثبت الإجماع أو قطعية الدليل بتواتره اه كلام البحر ملخصا وظاهر قوله فينبغي الاعتراض على الخلاصة في تسميته مكروها (رد المحتار ٦٤٧/١)

[250] ذكر الفقيه رحمه الله تعالى في التنبيه حرمة المسجد خمسة عشر ... السابع أن لا يتكلم فيه من أحاديث الدنيا (الفتاوى الهندية ٣٢١/٥)

[251] عن الحسن بن أبي الحسن عن أنس بن مالك رضي الله عنه قال قال رسول الله صلى الله عليه وسلم يأتي على الناس زمان يتحلقون في مساجدهم وليس همهم إلا الدنيا ليس لله فيهم حاجة فلا تجالسوهم هذا حديث صحيح الإسناد ولم يخرجاه (المستدرك على الصحيحين للحاكم، الرقم: ٧٩١٦)

Hazrat Hasan رَحِمَهُٱللَّٰهُ *reports that Hazrat Rasulullah* صَلَّىٱللَّٰهُعَلَيْهِوَسَلَّمَ *said, "A time is soon to dawn upon the Ummah when people will discuss worldly affairs in the musjid. Do not sit with such people, for Allah* تَبَارَكَوَتَعَالَ *has no need for them."*

18. Do not quarrel or argue with anyone in the musjid as this violates the sanctity of the musjid.[252]

19. Do not use the musjid as a thoroughfare (to pass through to the other side).[253]

عن ابن عمر رضي الله عنهما عن رسول الله صلى الله عليه وسلم قال خصال لا تنبغي في المسجد لا يتخذ طريقا ولا يشهر فيه سلاح (سنن ابن ماجة، الرقم: ٧٤٨)[254]

Hazrat Ibnu Umar رَضِىَٱللَّٰهُعَنْهُ *reports that Hazrat Rasulullah* صَلَّىٱللَّٰهُعَلَيْهِوَسَلَّمَ *said, "The following actions should not be carried out in the musjid; it (the musjid) should not be used as a thoroughfare, nor should weapons be drawn in the musjid ..."*

20. It is disrespectful to unnecessarily climb onto the roof of the musjid.[255]

قال الذهبي في التلخيص: صحيح

[252] ذكر الفقيه رحمه الله تعالى في التنبيه حرمة المسجد خمسة عشر ... والتاسع أن لا ينازع في المكان (الفتاوى الهندية ٥/٣٢١) قال العلامة ابن عابدين رحمه الله (قوله ويحرم الخ) لما أخرجه المنذري مرفوعا جنبوا مساجدكم صبيانكم ومجانينكم وبيعكم وشراءكم ورفع أصواتكم وسل سيوفكم وإقامة حدودكم وجمروها في الجمع وجعلوا على أبوابها لمطاهر بحر (رد المحتار ٦٥٦/١)

[253] ويكره التوضؤ في المسجد كالبزق والمخط لما فيه من الاستخفاف وكذا يكره أن يتخذ طريقا (البحر الرائق ٢٧١/٥)

[254] رواه ابن ماجه وروى منه الطبراني في الكبير ولا تتخذوا المساجد طرقا إلا لذكر أو صلاة وإسناد الطبراني لا بأس به (الترغيب والترهيب، ٢٧٩/١)

عن ابن عمر رضي الله عنهما أن رسول الله صلى الله عليه وسلم نهى أن يصلى في

سبعة مواطن ... وفوق ظهر بيت الله (سنن الترمذي، الرقم: ٣٤٦)[256]

Hazrat Ibnu Umar ﵄ reports that Hazrat Rasulullah
ﷺ prohibited performing salaah in seven places; (from
which is) on the roof of the house of Allah ﵎.

21. Do not force yourself into the front saff if there is insufficient space, thereby causing inconvenience to others.[257]

عن عبد الله بن بسر رضي الله عنه قال جاء رجل يتخطى رقاب الناس يوم الجمعة

والنبي صلى الله عليه وسلم يخطب فقال له النبي صلى الله عليه وسلم اجلس فقد

آذيت (سنن أبي داود، الرقم: ١١٢٠)[258]

Hazrat Abdullah bin Busr ﵁ reports that on one occasion, a
person entered the musjid on the Day of Jumuah while Hazrat
Rasulullah ﷺ was delivering the khutbah. The man began

---

[255] الصعود على سطح كل مسجد مكروه (الفتاوى الهندية ٣٢٢/٥)

[256] حديث روي أنه صلى الله عليه وسلم نهى عن الصلاة فوق الكعبة الترمذي عن ابن عمر في حديث أوله نهى أن يصلى في مواطن في المزبلة والمجزرة والمقبرة وقارعة الطريق وفي الحمام ومعاطن الإبل وفوق ظهر بيت الله ورواه ابن ماجه من طريق ابن عمر وفي سند الترمذي زيد بن حبيرة وهو ضعيف جدا وفي سند ابن ماجه عبد الله بن صالح وعبد الله بن عمر العمري المذكور في سنده ضعيف أيضا ووقع في بعض النسخ بسقوط عبد الله بن عمر بين الليث ونافع فصار ظاهره الصحة وقال ابن أبي حاتم في العلل عن أبيه هما جميعا واهيان وصححه ابن السكن وإمام الحرمين وذكر المصنف هذا الحديث في أثناء شروط الصلاة وذكر فيه بطن الوادي بدل المقبرة وهي زيادة باطلة لا تعرف (التلخيص الحبير، الرقم: ٣٢٠)

لهذا الحديث شاهد ضعيف من حديث عمر بن الخطاب أن رسول الله صلى الله عليه وسلم قال سبع مواطن لا تجوز فيها الصلاة ظاهر بيت الله والمقبرة والمزبلة والمجزرة والحمام وعطن الإبل ومحجة الطريق (سنن ابن ماجة، الرقم: ٧٤٧)

[257] ذكر الفقيه رحمه الله تعالى في التنبيه حرمة المسجد خمسة عشر ... والثامن أن لا يخطي رقاب الناس (الفتاوى الهندية ٣٢١/٥)

[258] قال المنذري في الترغيب والترهيب (٥٦٥/١): عن عبد الله بن بسر رضي الله عنهما قال جاء رجل يتخطى رقاب الناس يوم الجمعة والنبي صلى الله عليه وسلم يخطب فقال النبي صلى الله عليه وسلم اجلس فقد آذيت وآنيت. رواه أحمد وأبو داود والنسائي وابن خزيمة وابن حبان في صحيحيهما وليس عند أبي داود والنسائي وآنيت وعند ابن خزيمة فقد آذيت وأوذيت ورواه ابن ماجه من حديث جابر بن عبد الله

climbing over the shoulders of people (trying to reach the front saff). Hazrat Rasulullah ﷺ (reproached him) saying, "Sit down, for certainly you have caused inconvenience (to the people)."

عن سهل بن معاذ بن أنس الجهني عن أبيه رضي الله عنه قال قال رسول الله صلى الله عليه وسلم من تخطى رقاب الناس يوم الجمعة اتخذ جسرا إلى جهنم (سنن الترمذي، الرقم: ٥١٣)[259]

Hazrat Mu'aaz bin Anas رضي الله عنه reports that Hazrat Rasulullah ﷺ said, "The one who climbs over the shoulders of people on the Day of Jumuah has made a bridge for himself to Jahannum."

22. You should not perform salaah in such a place in the musjid that obstructs the free movement of the musallis e.g. performing salaah at the entrance, thereby preventing others from passing.[260]

عن ابن عمر رضي الله عنهما أن رسول الله صلى الله عليه وسلم نهي أن يصلى في سبعة مواطن ... وقارعة الطريق ... (سنن الترمذي، الرقم: ٣٤٦)

Hazrat Ibnu Umar رضي الله عنهما reports that Hazrat Rasulullah ﷺ prohibited performing salaah in seven places; (and from them is) on the pathway.[See 256]

---

[259] قال المنذري في الترغيب والترهيب (٥٦٥/١): رواه ابن ماجه والترمذي وقال حديث غريب والعمل عليه عند أهل العلم

[260] وقيدوا بقولهم ولم يواجه الطريق لأن الصلاة في الطريق أي في طريق العامة مكروهة وعلله في المحيط بما يفيد أنها كراهة تحريم بقوله لأن فيه منع الناس عن المرور والطريق حق الناس أعد للمرور فيه فلا يجوز شغله بما ليس له حق الشغل (البحر الرائق ٢٠/٢)

23. If you are in a musjid-e-kabeer (334,451 m² or larger), then it will be permissible for you to pass in front of those performing salaah, provided you avoid walking on their place of sajdah (i.e. there should be the amount of one saff or more between you and those performing salaah).[261]

24. If you are in a musjid-e-sagheer (a musjid which is smaller than 334,451 m²) then it is not permissible for you to pass in front of those performing salaah. However, if a sutrah is placed in front of those performing salaah, then passing in front of them will be permissible.[See 261]

عن أبي جهيم رضي الله عنه قال قال رسول الله صلى الله عليه وسلم لو يعلم المار بين يدي المصلي ماذا عليه لكان أن يقف أربعين خيرا له من أن يمر بين يديه قال أبو النضر لا أدري أقال أربعين يوما أو شهرا أو سنة (صحيح البخاري، الرقم: ٥١٠)

---

[261] (ولا يفسدها نظره إلى مكتوب وفهمه) ولو مستفهما وإن كره (ومرور مار في الصحراء أو في مسجد كبير بموضع سجوده) في الأصح (أو) مروره (بين يديه) إلى حائط القبلة (في) بيت و (مسجد) صغير فإنه كبقعة واحدة (مطلقا) (أو) مروره (أسفل من الدكان أمام المصلي لو كان يصلي عليها) أي الدكان (بشرط محاذاة بعض أعضاء المار بعض أعضائه وكذا سطح وسرير وكل مرتفع) دون قامة المار وقيل دون السترة كما في غرر الأذكار (وإن أثم المار) لحديث البزار لو يعلم المار ماذا عليه من الوزر لوقف أربعين خريفا (في ذلك) المرور لو بلا حائل ولو ستارة ترتفع إذا سجد وتعود إذا قام

قال العلامة ابن عابدين رحمه الله (قوله بموضع سجوده) أي من موضع قدمه إلى موضع سجوده كما في الدرر وهذا مع القيود التي بعده إنما هو للإثم وإلا فالفساد منتف مطلقا قوله (في الأصح) هو ما اختاره شمس الأئمة وقاضيخان وصاحب الهداية واستحسنه في المحيط وصححه الزيلعي ومقابله ما صححه التمرتاشي وصاحب البدائع واختاره فخر الإسلام ورجحه في النهاية والفتح أنه قدر ما يقع بصره على المار لو صلى بخشوع أي راميا ببصره إلى موضع سجوده وأرجع في العناية الأول إلى الثاني بحمل موضع السجود على القريب منه وخالفه في البحر وصحح الأول وكتبت فيما علقته عليه عن التجنيس ما يدل على ما في العناية فراجعه قوله (إلى حائط القبلة) أي من موضع قدميه إلى الحائط إن لم يكن له سترة فلو كانت لا يضر المرور وراءها على ما يأتي بيانه قوله (في بيت) ظاهره ولو كبيرا وفي القهستاني وينبغي أن يدخل فيه أي في حكم المسجد الصغير الدار والبيت قوله (ومسجد صغير) هو أقل من ستين ذراعا وقيل من أربعين وهو المختار كما أشار إليه في الجواهر قسمهاني قوله (فإنه كبقعة واحدة) أي من حيث إنه لم يجعل الفاصل فيه بقدر صفين مانعا من الاقتداء تنزيلا لمكان واحد بخلاف المسجد الكبير فإنه جعل فيه مانعا فكذا جعل هنا جميع ما بين يدي المصلي إلى حائط القبلة مكانا واحدا بخلاف المسجد الكبير والصحراء فإنه لو جعل كذلك لزم الحرج على المارة فاقتصر على موضع السجود هذا ما ظهر لي في تقرير هذا المحل (رد المحتار ٦٣٤/١)

Hazrat Abu Juhaim رَضِيَ ٱللَّهُ عَنْهُ *reports that Hazrat Rasulullah* صَلَّى ٱللَّهُ عَلَيْهِ وَسَلَّمَ *said, "If the one crossing in front of a musalli only knew the severity of his action, then waiting for forty would have been better for him than crossing in front of him (i.e. the person performing salaah)." Abu Nadhr says, "I do not know whether he intended forty days, forty months or forty years." (In other Ahaadith, mention is made of forty years.)*

25. It is not permissible to remove any item from the musjid that has been given as waqf for the musjid.[262]

26. Every musalli has an equal right in the use of the musjid and its items. Hence, it is not permissible for one to reserve any place or item of the musjid for himself.[263]

---

[262] وفي الدرر وقف مصحفا على أهل مسجد للقراءة إن يحصون جاز وإن وقف على المسجد جاز ويقرأ فيه ولا يكون محصورا على هذا المسجد وبه عرف حكم نقل كتب الأوقاف من محالها للانتفاع بها والفقهاء مبتلون بذلك فإن وقفها على مستحقي وقفه لم يجز نقلها وإن على طلبة العلم وجعل مقرها في خزانته التي في مكان كذا ففي جواز النقل تردد نهر

قال العلامة ابن عابدين رحمه الله (قوله ولا يكون محصورا على هذا المسجد) هذا ذكر في الخلاصة بقوله وفي موضع آخر ولا يكون الخ أي وذكر في كتاب آخر فهو قول آخر مقابل لقوله ويقرأ فيه فإن ظاهره أنه يكون مقصورا على ذلك المسجد وهذا هو الظاهر حيث كان الواقف عين ذلك المسجد فلما فعله صاحب الدر حيث نقل العبارة عن الخلاصة وأسقط منها قوله وفي موضع آخر غير مناسب لإيهامه أنه من تتمة ما قبله إلا أن يكون قد فهم أن قوله ويقرأ فيه محمول على الأولوية فيكون ما في موضع آخر غير مخالف له تأمل لكن في القنية سبل مصحفا في مسجد بعينه للقراءة ليس له بعد ذلك أن يدفعه إلى آخر من غير أهل تلك المحلة للقراءة قال في النهر وهذا يوافق القول الأول لا ما ذكر في موضع آخر اه فهذا يفيد أنهما قولان متغايران خلافا لما فهمه في الدرر وتبعه الشارح قوله (وبه عرف حكم الخ) الحكم هو ما بينه بعد قوله فإن وقفها الخ قوله (لم يجز نقلها) ولا سيما إذا كان الناقل ليس منهم نهر ومفاده أنه عين مكانها بأن بنى مدرسة وعين وضع الكتب فيها لانتفاع سكانها (رد المحتار ٤/٣٦٥)

[263] ولا يتعين مكان مخصوص لأحد حتى لو كان للمدرس موضع من المسجد يدرس فيه فسبقه غيره إليه ليس له إزعاجه وإقامته منه (البحر الرائق ٢/٣٦)

عن عبد الرحمن بن شبل رضي الله عنه قال نهى رسول الله صلى الله عليه وسلم عن نقرة الغراب وافتراش السبع وأن يوطن الرجل المكان في المسجد كما يوطن البعير (سنن أبي داود، الرقم: ٨٦٢)[264]

Hazrat Abdur Rahmaan bin Shibl رَضِيَٱللَّهُعَنْهُ *reports, "Rasulullah* صَلَّىٱللَّهُعَلَيْهِوَسَلَّمَ *prohibited (making sajdah like) the pecking of a crow (i.e. making sajdah extremely swiftly), and spreading one's forearms on the ground (during sajdah) in the manner a predatory animal sits down, and reserving a place for oneself (in the musjid) as a camel reserves a place for itself."*

27. It is not permissible to make a person move from his place in the musjid so that someone else can sit in his place.[265]

عن ابن عمر رضي الله عنهما عن النبي صلى الله عليه وسلم أنه نهى أن يقام الرجل من مجلسه ويجلس فيه آخر ولكن تفسحوا وتوسعوا (صحيح البخاري، الرقم: ٦٢٧٠)

Hazrat Ibnu Umar رَضِيَٱللَّهُعَنْهُمَا *reports that Hazrat Rasulullah* صَلَّىٱللَّهُعَلَيْهِوَسَلَّمَ *had prohibited that a man be made to move from his place (in the musjid) and another man sit in his place. Rather, the people should make place (for those who arrive if it is possible to make place for them).*

---

[264] سكت عنه ثم المنذري بعده (مختصر سنن أبي داود، ١/٢٩٩)

قال المنذري في الترغيب والترهيب (الرقم: ٧٤٧): رواه أحمد وأبو داود والنسائي وابن ماجه وابن خزيمة وابن حبان في صحيحيهما

[265] ويكره ... وتخصيص مكان لنفسه وليس له إزعاج غيره منه ولو مدرسا

قال العلامة ابن عابدين رحمه الله (قوله وليس له إلخ) قال في القنية له في المسجد موضع معين يواظب عليه وقد شغله غيره قال الأوزاعي له أن يزعجه وليس له ذلك عندنا اه أي لأن المسجد ليس ملكا لأحد بحر عن النهاية قلت وينبغي تقييده بما إذا لم يقم عنه على نية العود بلا مهلة كما لو قام للوضوء مثلا ولا سيما إذا وضع فيه ثوبه لتحقق سبق يده تأمل (رد المحتار ١/٦٦٢)

28. Do not crack your knuckles while in the musjid. Similarly, do not intertwine your fingers while seated in the musjid.[266]

عن مولى لأبي سعيد الخدري قال بينا أنا مع أبي سعيد رضي الله عنه وهو مع رسول الله صلى الله عليه وسلم إذ دخلنا المسجد فإذا رجل جالس في وسط المسجد محتبيا مشبكا أصابعه بعضها في بعض فأشار إليه رسول الله صلى الله عليه وسلم فلم يفطن الرجل لإشارة رسول الله صلى الله عليه وسلم فالتفت إلى أبي سعيد فقال إذا كان أحدكم في المسجد فلا يشبكن فإن التشبيك من الشيطان وإن أحدكم لا يزال في صلاة ما كان في المسجد حتى يخرج منه (مجمع الزوائد، الرقم: ٢٠٤٧ ، الترغيب والترهيب، الرقم: ٤٥٠)

The freed slave of Hazrat Abu Sa'eed Khudri ﷺ reports, "On one occasion, while I was with Abu Sa'eed ﷺ and he was with Rasulullah ﷺ, we entered the musjid and saw a man seated in the centre of the musjid. This man was sitting on his buttocks in the manner that his knees were raised, and his arms were wrapped around his knees, with the fingers of both his hands intertwined. Rasulullah ﷺ gestured towards this man (to draw his attention), but the man did not notice the gesture of Rasulullah ﷺ. Rasulullah ﷺ thus turned towards Abu Sa'eed ﷺ and said, 'When any one of you is in the musjid, then he should not intertwine his fingers, as intertwining the fingers is from Shaitaan. As long as you remain in the musjid waiting for salaah, you will receive the reward of salaah, as though

---

[266] ذكر الفقيه رحمه الله تعالى في التنبيه حرمة المسجد خمسة عشر ... والثالث عشر أن لا يفرقع أصابعه فيه (الفتاوى الهندية ٣٢١/٥)

you are in salaah, until you leave the musjid (hence, when intertwining the fingers during salaah is against the etiquette of salaah, then one should also not intertwine the fingers when waiting for salaah)."'

29. Do not mess or soil the musjid e.g. by spitting in the musjid or blowing one's nose and allowing the dirt to fall onto the ground.[267]

عن أبي ذر رضي الله عنه قال قال رسول الله صلى الله عليه وسلم عرضت علي أعمال أمتي حسنها وسيئها فوجدت في محاسن أعمالها الأذى يماط عن الطريق ووجدت في مساوئ أعمالها النخاعة تكون في المسجد لا تدفن (صحيح مسلم، الرقم: ٥٥٣)

Hazrat Abu Zar رَضِيَٱللَّهُعَنْهُ reports that Hazrat Rasulullah صَلَّىٱللَّهُعَلَيْهِوَسَلَّمَ said, "The good deeds and evil deeds of my Ummah were presented before me. I found that among the good deeds is for one to remove a harmful object from the pathway, and I found that among the evil deeds is (for one to leave) the dirt of one's nose (which had fallen to the floor) in the musjid without burying it."

عن أنس رضي الله عنه قال قال رسول الله صلى الله عليه وسلم البزاق في المسجد خطيئة وكفارتها دفنها (صحيح البخاري، الرقم: ٤١٥)

Hazrat Anas ﷺ *reports that Hazrat Rasulullah* ﷺ *said, "To spit in the musjid is a sin, and its compensation is to bury it (with sand)." (This was at the time when the salaah in the musjid used to be performed on the bare ground.)*

30. Do not distribute parcels, hampers and other goods in the musjid. Similarly, do not make the musjid a drop off point for collecting parcels.[268]

31. Remain calm and dignified while in the musjid and do not be unmindful of the sanctity of the musjid. Some people, whilst waiting for the salaah to commence, fidget with their clothing or play with their cell phones. This is against the honour and respect of the musjid.[269]

32. Assist in keeping the musjid clean and tidy.[270]

---

[268] (وكره إحضار المبيع والصمت والتكلم إلا بخير) أما إحضار المبيع وهي السلع للبيع فلأن المسجد محرز عن حقوق العباد وفيه شغله بما جعله كالدكان ... وأما إذا أراد أن يتخذ ذلك متجرا يكره له ذلك وهذا صحيح لأنه منقطع إلى الله تعالى فلا ينبغي له أن يشتغل فيه بأمور الدنيا ولهذا تكره الخياطة والخرز فيه (تبيين الحقائق ٣٥١/)

ولا يشغل المسجد بالمتاع إلا للخوف في الفتنة العامة (الأشباه والنظائر ٥٢٨/١)

[269] وَمَنْ يُّعَظِّمْ شَعَآئِرَ اللّٰهِ فَاِنَّهَا مِنْ تَقْوَى الْقُلُوْبِ (سورة الحج: ٣٢)

وَ مَنْ اَظْلَمُ مِمَّنْ مَّنَعَ مَسَاجِدَ اللّٰهِ اَنْ يُّذْكَرَ فِيْهَا اسْمُهٗ وَ سَعٰى فِيْ خَرَابِهَا ۚ اُولٰٓئِكَ مَا كَانَ لَهُمْ اَنْ يَّدْخُلُوْهَاۤ اِلَّا خَآئِفِيْنَ ۚ لَهُمْ فِى الدُّنْيَا خِزْيٌ وَّ لَهُمْ فِى الْاٰخِرَةِ عَذَابٌ عَظِيْمٌ (سورة البقرة: ١١٤)

[270] ذكر الفقيه رحمه الله تعالى في التنبيه حرمة المسجد خمسة عشر ... والرابع عشر أن ينزهه عن النجاسات والصبيان والمجانين وإقامة الحدود (الفتاوى الهندية ٣٢١/٥)

عن أبي قرصافة رضي الله عنه أنه سمع النبي صلى الله عليه وسلم يقول ابنوا المساجد وأخرجوا القمامة منها فمن بنى لله مسجدا بنى الله له بيتا في الجنة فقال رجل يا رسول الله وهذه المساجد التي تبنى في الطريق قال نعم وإخراج القمامة منها مهور الحور العين (الترغيب والترهيب، الرقم: ٤٢٨ ، مجمع الزوائد، الرقم: ١٩٤٩)

قال الهيثمي في مجمع الزوائد (الرقم: ١٩٤٩): رواه الطبراني في الكبير وفي إسناده مجاهيل

قال المنذري في الترغيب والترهيب (الرقم: ٤٢٨): رواه الطبراني في الكبير

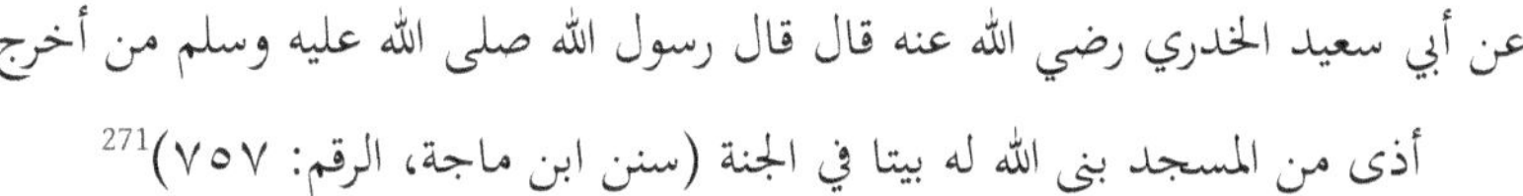

عن أبي سعيد الخدري رضي الله عنه قال قال رسول الله صلى الله عليه وسلم من أخرج
أذى من المسجد بنى الله له بيتا في الجنة (سنن ابن ماجة، الرقم: ٧٥٧)[271]

Hazrat Abu Sa'eed Khudri رَضِىَاللَّهُعَنْهُ reports that Hazrat Rasulullah صَلَّىَاللَّهُعَلَيْهِوَسَلَّمَ said, "Whoever removes some dirt from the musjid, Allah تَبَارَكَوَتَعَالَى will build for him a magnificent palace in Jannah."

33. Do not bring into the musjid infants, insane people or children who are underage and do not know the aadaab (etiquettes) of the musjid.[272]

34. While in the musjid, remain constantly engaged in the aa'maal of the musjid e.g. zikr of Allah تَبَارَكَوَتَعَالَى, tilaawah of the Quraan Majeed, salaah, etc.[273]

35. Apart from going to the musjid to perform salaah, if there is a program being held in the musjid, then one should make the intention of going to the musjid to acquire the knowledge of Deen. If one has the ability to teach Deen then one should

---

قال ابن عراق في تنزيه الشريعة (٢/٣٨٣): أخرجه الطبراني وصححه الضياء المقدسي في المختارة

[271] قال المنذري: رواه ابن ماجه وفي إسناده احتمال للتحسين (الترغيب والترهيب: الرقم ٤٣٠)

[272] ذكر الفقيه رحمه الله تعالى في التنبيه حرمة المسجد خمسة عشر ... والرابع عشر أن ينزهه عن النجاسات والصبيان والمجانين وإقامة الحدود (الفتاوى الهندية ٥/٣٢١)

[273] عن علي بن أبي طالب رضي الله عنه قال قال رسول الله صلى الله عليه وسلم يوشك أن يأتي على الناس زمان لا يبقى من الإسلام إلا اسمه ولا يبقى من القرآن إلا رسمه مساجدهم عامرة وهي خراب من الهدى (شعب الإيمان، الرقم: ١٧٦٣)

عن ابن مسعود رضي الله عنه قال قال رسول الله صلى الله عليه وسلم إن من أشراط الساعة أن يمر الرجل في طول المسجد وعرضه لا يصلي فيه ركعتين (المعجم الكبير للطبراني، الرقم: ٩٤٨٨) رواه الطبراني في الكبير ورجاله رجال الصحيح إلا أن سلمة بن كهيل وإن كان سمع من الصحابة لم أجد له رواية عن ابن مسعود (مجمع الزوائد، الرقم: ٢٠٣٩)

عن أنس بن مالك رضي الله عنه قال قال رسول الله صلى الله عليه وسلم ... إن هذه المساجد لا تصلح لشيء من هذا البول ولا القذر إنما هي لذكر الله عز وجل والصلاة وقراءة القرآن أو كما قال رسول الله صلى الله عليه وسلم (صحيح مسلم، الرقم: ٢٨٥)

make the intention of coming to the musjid to impart the knowledge of Deen to people if one finds the opportunity to do so.

عن أبي هريرة رضي الله عنه قال سمعت رسول الله صلى الله عليه وسلم يقول من جاء مسجدي هذا لم يأته إلا لخير يتعلمه أو يعلمه فهو بمنزلة المجاهد في سبيل الله ومن جاء لغير ذلك فهو بمنزلة الرجل ينظر إلى متاع غيره (سنن ابن ماجة، الرقم: ٢٢٧)[274]

Hazrat Abu Hurairah رَضِيَٱللَّهُعَنْهُ *mentions, "I heard Rasulullah* صَلَّىٱللَّهُعَلَيْهِوَسَلَّمَ *saying, "Whoever comes to this musjid of mine, and he does not come for any purpose besides learning some good or teaching some good, then he is like the one who is striving in the path of Allah* تَبَارَكَوَتَعَالَى, *and the one who comes to the musjid for any other purpose (besides the worship of Allah* تَبَارَكَوَتَعَالَى), *then he is like a man who looks at the merchandise of others (being sold, yet he does not earn anything)."*

عن أبي هريرة قال قال رسول الله صلى الله عليه وسلم من أتى المسجد لشيء فهو حظه (سنن أبي داود، الرقم: ٤٧٢)[275]

Hazrat Abu Hurairah رَضِيَٱللَّهُعَنْهُ *reports that Rasulullah* صَلَّىٱللَّهُعَلَيْهِوَسَلَّمَ *said, "Whoever comes to the musjid for some purpose, then that will be his share (i.e. he will be rewarded according to his intention)."*

---

[274] قال البوصيري في الزوائد (٨٣/١): إسناده صحيح على شرط مسلم

[275] قال المنذري: في إسناده عثمان بن أبي العاتكة الدمشقي وقد ضعفه غير واحد (مختصر سنن أبي داود ١٩٤/١)

قال الذهبي في ميزان الإعتدال (٥٣/٥): تحت ترجمة عثمان بن أبي العاتكة قال أحمد لا بأس به

36. Together with keeping the musjid clean, also keep the musjid fragranced by burning oudh, etc.

عن عائشة رضي الله عنها قالت أمر رسول الله صلى الله عليه وسلم ببناء المساجد في الدور وأن تنظف وتطيب وقال سفيان قوله ببناء المساجد في الدور يعني القبائل (سنن الترمذي، الرقم: ٥٩٤)[276]

Hazrat Aaishah ﷺ reports that Hazrat Rasulullah ﷺ commanded that masaajid be built in the different localities, and that the masaajid be kept clean and be fragranced."

عن ابن عمر رضي الله عنهما أن عمر بن الخطاب رضي الله عنه كان يجمر المسجد في كل جمعة (المصنف لابن أبي شيبة، الرقم: ٧٥٢٣)

Hazrat Abdullah bin Umar ﷺ reports that Hazrat Umar ﷺ would burn incense in the musjid on the Day of Jumuah.

37. If you are feeling sleepy in the musjid then change your place by moving and sitting in a different place in the musjid, provided it is not at the time when the khutbah is in progress. Through moving to another place, one's sleepiness will be removed.

عن ابن عمر رضي الله عنهما قال سمعت رسول الله صلى الله عليه وسلم يقول إذا نعس أحدكم وهو في المسجد فليتحول من مجلسه ذلك إلى غيره (سنن أبي داود، الرقم: ١١١٩)[277]

---

[276] قال المنذري: رواه أحمد والترمذي وقال حديث صحيح وأبو داود وابن ماجه وابن خزيمة في صحيحه ورواه الترمذي مسندا ومرسلا وقال في المرسل هذا أصح (الترغيب والترهيب، الرقم: ٤٣٢)

Hazrat Ibnu Umar رَضِىَٱللَّهُعَنْهُمَا *mentions, "I heard Rasulullah* صَلَّىٱللَّهُعَلَيْهِوَسَلَّمَ *saying, 'When any one of you feels sleepy while he is in the musjid then he should move from the place where he is sitting to another place.'"*

38. After the azaan has been called out, if you have not performed the salaah, then do not leave the musjid without a valid excuse.[278]

عن أبي الشعثاء قال كنا قعودا في المسجد مع أبي هريرة رضي الله عنه فأذن المؤذن فقام رجل من المسجد يمشي فأتبعه أبو هريرة رضي الله عنه بصره حتى خرج من المسجد فقال أبو هريرة رضي الله عنه أما هذا فقد عصى أبا القاسم صلى الله عليه وسلم (صحيح مسلم، الرقم: ٦٥٥)[279]

Abu Sha'thaa رَحِمَهُٱللَّهُ *mentions, "On one occasion, we were seated with Abu Hurairah* رَضِىَٱللَّهُعَنْهُ *in the musjid when the muazzin called out the azaan. After the azaan was called out, a man stood and began to walk (out of the musjid without an excuse, before performing the salaah). Abu Hurairah* رَضِىَٱللَّهُعَنْهُ *watched this person as he left the musjid and then remarked, 'As for this person, he has*

disobeyed Abul Qaasim صَلَّى ٱللَّهُ عَلَيْهِ وَسَلَّمَ' (as Hazrat Rasulullah صَلَّى ٱللَّهُ عَلَيْهِ وَسَلَّمَ has instructed that after the azaan is called out, no person should leave the musjid without performing the fardh salaah, unless he has a valid excuse)."

39. Leave the musjid with the left foot.[280]

40. Recite the masnoon dua upon leaving the musjid.[281]

Dua One:

بِسْمِ اللهِ وَالصَّلَاةُ وَالسَّلَاَمُ عَلَى رَسُوْلِ اللهِ اَللّٰهُمَّ إِنِّيْ أَسْأَلُكَ مِنْ فَضْلِكَ

In the name of Allah تَبَارَكَ وَتَعَالَى. May peace and salutations be upon Hazrat Rasulullah صَلَّى ٱللَّهُ عَلَيْهِ وَسَلَّمَ. O Allah تَبَارَكَ وَتَعَالَى, I ask You for Your bounties.[See 236]

Dua Two:

بِسْمِ اللهِ وَالصَّلَاةُ وَالسَّلَاَمُ عَلَى رَسُوْلِ اللهِ رَبِّ اغْفِرْ لِيْ ذُنُوْبِيْ وَافْتَحْ لِيْ أَبْوَابَ فَضْلِكَ

---

[280] ويقدم رجله اليسرى في الخروج كذا في التبيين (الفتاوى الهندية ٢٢٦/١)

عن أنس بن مالك أنه كان يقول من السنة أنه إذا دخلت المسجد أن تبدأ برجلك اليمنى وإذا خرجت أن تبدأ برجلك اليسرى (المستدرك للحاكم، الرقم: ٧٩١)

هذا حديث صحيح على شرط مسلم فقد احتج بشداد بن سعيد أبي طلحة الراسبي ولم يخرجاه قال الذهبي في التلخيص: على شرط مسلم

[281] وندب أن يقول عند دخوله المسجد اللهم افتح لي أبواب رحمتك وعند خروجه اللهم إني أسألك من فضلك لأمر النبي صلى الله عليه وسلم به

قال الطحطاوي رحمه الله (قوله وندب) أي بعد ذكر الصلاة على النبي صلى الله عليه وسلم كما دلت عليه الأحاديث قوله (اللهم افتح لي أبواب رحمتك) أي إحسانك وإنعامك بالإخلاص والقبول وغير ذلك قوله (اللهم إني أسألك من فضلك) مأخوذ من قوله تعالى فإذا قضيت الصلاة فانتشروا في الأرض وابتغوا من فضل الله (حاشية الطحطاوي على مراقي الفلاح ص ٥٩٥)

In the name of Allah تَبَارَكَ وَتَعَالَى*. May peace and salutations be upon Hazrat Rasulullah* صَلَّى ٱللَّهُ عَلَيْهِ وَسَلَّمَ*. O Allah* تَبَارَكَ وَتَعَالَى*, forgive for me my sins and open for me the doors of Your bounties.*[See 238]

Dua Three:

اَللّٰهُمَّ اعْصِمْنِيْ مِنَ الشَّيْطَانِ الرَّجِيْمِ [282]

O Allah تَبَارَكَ وَتَعَالَى*! Protect me from the accursed Shaitaan.*

41. Keep your heart attached to the musjid i.e. when leaving the musjid after one salaah, make the intention of coming to the musjid for the next salaah and await it with eagerness.[283]

عن أبي هريرة رضي الله عنه أن رسول الله صلى الله عليه وسلم قال ألا أدلكم على ما يمحو الله به الخطايا ويرفع به الدرجات قالوا بلى يا رسول الله قال إسباغ الوضوء على المكاره وكثرة الخطا إلى المساجد وانتظار الصلاة بعد الصلاة فذلكم الرباط (صحيح مسلم، الرقم: ٢٥١)

Hazrat Abu Hurairah رَضِيَ ٱللَّهُ عَنْهُ *reports that Hazrat Rasulullah* صَلَّى ٱللَّهُ عَلَيْهِ وَسَلَّمَ *once asked the Sahaabah* رَضِيَ ٱللَّهُ عَنْهُمْ*, "Should I not inform you of such actions through which Allah* تَبَارَكَ وَتَعَالَى *will erase your sins and raise your ranks?" The Sahaabah* رَضِيَ ٱللَّهُ عَنْهُمْ *replied,*

---

[282] عن أبي هريرة أن رسول الله صلى الله عليه وسلم قال إذا دخل أحدكم المسجد فليسلم على النبي صلى الله عليه وسلم وليقل اللهم افتح لي أبواب رحمتك وإذا خرج فليسلم على النبي صلى الله عليه وسلم وليقل اللهم اعصمني من الشيطان الرجيم (سنن ابن ماجة، الرقم: ٧٧٣)

قال العلامة البوصيري فى زوائد ابن ماجة (ص ٢٥٤): هذا إسناد صحيح رجاله ثقات

[283] عن أبي هريرة رضي الله عنه عن النبي صلى الله عليه وسلم قال: سبعة يظلهم الله تعالى في ظله يوم لا ظل إلا ظله إمام عدل وشاب نشأ في عبادة الله ورجل قلبه معلق في المساجد ورجلان تحابا في الله اجتمعا عليه وتفرقا عليه ورجل دعته امرأة ذات منصب وجمال فقال إني أخاف الله ورجل تصدق بصدقة فأخفاها حتى لا تعلم شماله ما تنفق يمينه ورجل ذكر الله خاليا ففاضت عيناه (صحيح البخاري، الرقم: ١٤٢٣)

"*Certainly inform us, O Rasul of Allah* صَلَّى ٱللَّهُ عَلَيْهِ وَسَلَّمَ!" *Hazrat Rasulullah* صَلَّى ٱللَّهُ عَلَيْهِ وَسَلَّمَ *said, "Performing a complete wudhu despite difficulties, taking abundant steps in walking towards the masaajid and awaiting the next salaah after one salaah is performed. These actions resemble the action of those who protect the Islamic frontiers against the enemies of Islam (i.e. through these actions, one protects himself from the nafs and Shaitaan, just as those guarding the frontiers protect the Muslims against the enemies of Islam)."*

42. Do not spend wealth from public funds for the adornment of the musjid. If one wishes, he may spend his own wealth to adorn the musjid, provided it is within the limits of Shari'ah.[284]

عن ابن عباس رضي الله عنهما قال قال رسول الله صلى الله عليه وسلم ما أمرت بتشييد المساجد قال ابن عباس لتزخرفنها كما زخرفت اليهود والنصارى (سنن أبي داود، الرقم: ٤٤٨)[285]

Hazrat Ibnu Abbaas رَضِيَ ٱللَّهُ عَنْهُمَا *reports that Hazrat Rasulullah* صَلَّى ٱللَّهُ عَلَيْهِ وَسَلَّمَ *said, "I was not commanded to raise the structures of the musjid (without any need and just for beautification purposes)." Hazrat Ibnu Abbaas* رَضِيَ ٱللَّهُ عَنْهُمَا *mentioned, "(A time will come when) you will most certainly adorn and beautify the*

---

[284] عن أنس رضي الله عنه أن النبي صلى الله عليه وسلم قال لا تقوم الساعة حتى يتباهى الناس في المساجد (سنن أبي داود، الرقم: ٤٤٩)

[285] هذا الحديث سكت عنه أبو داود والمنذري (مختصر سنن أبي داود ١٨٩/١)

masaajid (beyond the limits of Shari'ah) as the Jews and Christians adorned and beautified their places of worship."

CHAPTER SEVEN

MEN'S SALAAH

The lofty position which salaah holds in the life of a Muslim does not require any explanation. The fact that it will be the first aspect regarding which a person will be questioned on the Day of Qiyaamah is sufficient proof of its importance.

Hazrat Rasulullah ﷺ said:

إن أول ما يحاسب الناس به يوم القيامة من أعمالهم الصلاة قال يقول ربنا جل وعز لملائكته وهو أعلم انظروا في صلاة عبدي أتمها أم نقصها فإن كانت تامة كتبت له تامة وإن كان انتقص منها شيئا قال انظروا هل لعبدي من تطوع فإن كان له تطوع قال أتموا لعبدي فريضته من تطوعه ثم تؤخذ الأعمال على ذاكم (سنن أبي داود، الرقم: ٨٦٤)[286]

Indeed the first action for which people will be called to account for on the Day of Qiyaamah will be their salaah. Our Rabb تَبَارَكَ وَتَعَالَى will say to the malaa'ikah (angels), while Allah تَبَارَكَ وَتَعَالَى has complete knowledge over everything, "Look at the (fardh) salaah of my servant; has he

---

[286] هذا الحديث سكت عنه أبو داود والمنذري (مختصر سنن أبي داود، ٣٠٦/١)

performed it in a complete and perfect manner or has he performed it in a deficient manner?" If his salaah was performed in a complete and perfect manner, the complete reward will be recorded for him. If there was some deficiency in his salaah, Allah تَبَارَكَ وَتَعَالَى will say to the malaa'ikah (angels), "Compensate for the deficiency in his fardh salaah through his nafl salaah. Thereafter, other ibaadaat will follow the same pattern."

CORRECT TIME AND MANNER

Just as the performance of salaah is important, carrying it out in the preferred time and in the correct manner is equally important.

Hazrat Rasulullah ﷺ said, "When a person offers his salaah on its prescribed time with proper wudhu, fulfilling its qiyaam (standing posture), ruku and sajdah in the correct manner with the desired level of concentration and devotion, then the salaah rises up in a bright and beautiful form saying to him, 'May Allah تَبَارَكَ وَتَعَالَى safeguard you as you have safeguarded me.' (On the contrary,) if a person does not perform his salaah on its prescribed time, nor does he perform a proper wudhu or fulfil his ruku and sajdah in the correct manner and with the desired level of concentration, then the salaah rises up in an ugly and dark form and curses him saying, 'May Allah تَبَارَكَ وَتَعَالَى destroy you as you have destroyed me.' The salaah then rises to the point where Allah تَبَارَكَ وَتَعَالَى wishes, and thereafter it is folded like a dirty rag and flung on his face."[287]

---

²⁸⁷ عن أنس بن مالك قال قال رسول الله صلى الله عليه وسلم من صلى الصلوات لوقتها وأسبغ لها وضوءها وأتم لها قيامها وخشوعها وركوعها وسجودها خرجت وهي بيضاء مسفرة تقول حفظك الله كما حفظتني ومن صلى لغير وقتها ولم يسبغ لها وضوءها ولم يتم لها خشوعها ولا ركوعها ولا سجودها خرجت وهي سوداء مظلمة تقول ضيعك الله كما ضيعتني حتى إذا كانت حيث شاء الله لفت كما يلف الثوب الخلق ثم ضرب بها وجهه رواه الطبراني في الأوسط وفيه عباد بن كثير وقد أجمعوا على ضعفه قلت ويأتي حديث عبادة بنحو هذا في باب من لا يتم صلاته ويسيء ركوعها (مجمع الزوائد، الرقم: ١٦٧٧)

لهذا الحديث شاهد من حديث عبادة بن الصامت قال قال رسول الله صلى الله عليه وسلم إذا توضأ العبد فأحسن الوضوء ثم قام إلى الصلاة فأتم ركوعها وسجودها والقراءة فيها قالت حفظك الله كما حفظتني ثم أصعد بها إلى السماء ولها ضوء ونور وفتحت لها أبواب السماء وإذا لم يحسن العبد الوضوء ولم يتم الركوع والسجود والقراءة قالت ضيعك الله كما ضيعتني ثم أصعد بها إلى السماء وعليها ظلمة وغلقت أبواب السماء ثم تلف كما يلف الثوب الخلق ثم ضرب بها وجه صاحبها رواه الطبراني في الكبير والبزار بنحوه وفيه الأحوص بن حكيم وثقه ابن المديني والعجلي وضعفه جماعة وبقية رجاله موثقون (مجمع الزوائد، الرقم: ٢٧٣٤)

ADMONITION FOR THOSE WHO NEGLECT SALAAH WITH JAMAAT IN THE MUSJID

It was the burning desire of Rasulullah ﷺ that the men of the Ummah perform their Salaah with jamaat in the musjid. Rasulullah ﷺ used to be greatly hurt when he learnt of people performing their salaah at their homes that he said: "Had it not been for the women and children, I would have commanded a group of youth to gather firewood and set fire to the dwellings of those people who perform their salaah at their homes without any excuse"[288]

The Sahaabah ﷺ had once seen Rasulullah ﷺ weeping. On enquiring from him as to what caused him to weep, he said: "I was shown by Allah ﷻ that among the signs of Qiyaamah are that the people from my Ummah will discard their Salaah and follow their (evil) desires"[289]

---

[288] عن أبي هريرة أن رسول الله صلى الله عليه وسلم فقد ناسا في بعض الصلوات فقال لقد هممت أن آمر رجلا يصلي بالناس ثم أخالف إلى رجال يتخلفون عنها فآمر بهم فيحرقوا عليهم بحزم الحطب بيوتهم ولو علم أحدهم أنه يجد عظما سمينا لشهدها يعني صلاة العشاء (صحيح مسلم، الرقم: ٦٥١)

عن أبي هريرة قال قال رسول الله صلى الله عليه وسلم لولا ما في البيوت من النساء والذرية لأقمت صلاة العشاء وأمرت فتياني يحرقون ما في البيوت بالنار (مسند أحمد، الرقم: ٨٧٨٢)

[289] عن ابن عباس رضي الله عنهما قال لما حج النبي صلى الله عليه وسلم حجة الوداع أخذ بحلقتي باب الكعبة ثم أقبل بوجهه على الناس فقال يا أيها الناس قالوا لبيك يا رسول الله يفديك آباؤنا وأمهاتنا ثم بكى حتى علا انتحابه فقال يا أيها الناس إني أخبركم بأشراط القيامة إن من أشراط القيامة إماتة الصلوات واتباع الشهوات والميل مع الهوى وتعظيم رب المال (الإشاعة لأشراط الساعة ص ١٧١)

THE PRACTICE OF SAHAABAH رَضِيَ ٱللَّهُ عَنْهُمْ REGARDING CONGREGATIONAL SALAAH

Hazrat Abdullah bin Masood رَضِيَ ٱللَّهُ عَنْهُ is reported to have said: "Guard your five daily salaah through performing it at a place where the azaan is called out (i.e. the musjid). Verily performing these (fardh) salaah in the musjid is from the sunan-e-huda (the prescribed acts of worship in Deen). Allah تَبَارَكَ وَتَعَالَى has prescribed for His Nabi صَلَّى ٱللَّهُ عَلَيْهِ وَسَلَّمَ sunan-e-huda (such acts of worship which are complete guidance for you). During the mubaarak lifetime of Nabi صَلَّى ٱللَّهُ عَلَيْهِ وَسَلَّمَ none would omit the jamaat salaah in the musjid except an open munaafiq (an open hypocrite), to such an extent that even a sick person would not remain absent from the congregational salaah in the musjid. Rather, he would be taken to the musjid while being supported on the shoulders of two men. Each one of you (the Sahaabah رَضِيَ ٱللَّهُ عَنْهُمْ) has a specified place in his home reserved for performing nafl salaah, etc. However, if you begin performing your fardh salaah at home and leave attending the congregational prayer in the musjid, then you will be abandoning the emphasized sunnah of Nabi صَلَّى ٱللَّهُ عَلَيْهِ وَسَلَّمَ. As soon as you will abandon his mubaarak sunnah, you will certainly go astray."[290]

---

[290] عن عبد الله بن مسعود قال حافظوا على هؤلاء الصلوات الخمس حيث ينادى بهن فإنهن من سنن الهدى وإن الله شرع لنبيه صلى الله عليه وسلم سنن الهدى ولقد رأيتنا وما يتخلف عنها إلا منافق بين النفاق ولقد رأيتنا وإن الرجل ليهادى بين الرجلين حتى يقام في الصف وما منكم

It is reported that somebody asked Hazrat Abdullah bin Abbaas رَضِيَٱللَّهُعَنْهُمَا, "What is the condition of the person who observes nafl fasts during the day and offers nafl salaah the entire night, but neither goes to the musjid to perform salaah with jamaat nor attends the jumuah?" Hazrat Abdullah bin Abbaas رَضِيَٱللَّهُعَنْهُمَا replied, "He is doomed to Hell."[291]

من أحد إلا وله مسجد في بيته ولو صليتم في بيوتكم وتركتم مساجدكم تركتم سنة نبيكم صلى الله عليه وسلم ولو تركتم سنة نبيكم صلى الله عليه وسلم لكفرتم (سنن أبي داود، الرقم: ٥٥٠)

291 وسئل ابن عباس عن رجل يصوم النهار ويقوم الليل لا يشهد جمعة ولا جماعة فقال هو في النار (سنن الترمذي، الرقم: ٢١٨)

BEFORE SALAAH

1. Prepare for salaah well in advance, before the salaah time enters, and ensure that you are not only physically prepared but you are also mentally conscious that you are going to present yourself in the court of Almighty Allah تَبَارَكَ وَتَعَالَى.[292]

2. Ensure that you perform every salaah on its prescribed time with jamaat in the musjid.[293]

---

[292] إِنَّ الْمُنَافِقِينَ يُخَادِعُونَ اللَّهَ وَهُوَ خَادِعُهُمْ وَإِذَا قَامُوا إِلَى الصَّلَاةِ قَامُوا كُسَالَى يُرَاؤُونَ النَّاسَ وَلَا يَذْكُرُونَ اللَّهَ إِلَّا قَلِيلًا (سورة النساء: ١٤٢)

مُحَمَّدٌ رَسُولُ اللَّهِ وَالَّذِينَ مَعَهُ أَشِدَّاءُ عَلَى الْكُفَّارِ رُحَمَاءُ بَيْنَهُمْ تَرَاهُمْ رُكَّعًا سُجَّدًا يَبْتَغُونَ فَضْلًا مِنَ اللَّهِ وَرِضْوَانًا سِيمَاهُمْ فِي وُجُوهِهِمْ مِنْ أَثَرِ السُّجُودِ ذَلِكَ مَثَلُهُمْ فِي التَّوْرَاةِ وَمَثَلُهُمْ فِي الْإِنْجِيلِ كَزَرْعٍ أَخْرَجَ شَطْأَهُ فَآزَرَهُ فَاسْتَغْلَظَ فَاسْتَوَى عَلَى سُوقِهِ يُعْجِبُ الزُّرَّاعَ لِيَغِيظَ بِهِمُ الْكُفَّارَ وَعَدَ اللَّهُ الَّذِينَ آمَنُوا وَعَمِلُوا الصَّالِحَاتِ مِنْهُمْ مَغْفِرَةً وَأَجْرًا عَظِيمًا (سورة الفتح: ٢٩)

رِجَالٌ لَا تُلْهِيهِمْ تِجَارَةٌ وَلَا بَيْعٌ عَنْ ذِكْرِ اللَّهِ وَإِقَامِ الصَّلَاةِ وَإِيتَاءِ الزَّكَاةِ يَخَافُونَ يَوْمًا تَتَقَلَّبُ فِيهِ الْقُلُوبُ وَالْأَبْصَارُ (سورة النور: ٣٧)

(ومن آدابه ... تقديمه على الوقت لغير المعذور)

قال العلامة ابن عابدين رحمه الله (قوله تقديمه الخ) لأن فيه انتظار الصلاة ومنتظر الصلاة كمن هو في الحديث الصحيح وقطع طمع الشيطان عن تثبيطه عنها شرح المنية الكبير وفي الحلية وعندي أنه من آداب الصلاة لا الوضوء لأنه مقصود لفعل الصلاة اه (رد المحتار ١/١٢٤-١٢٥)

[293] عن عبد الله بن مسعود قال حافظوا على هؤلاء الصلوات الخمس حيث ينادى بهن فإنهن من سنن الهدى وإن الله شرع لنبيه صلى الله عليه وسلم سنن الهدى ولقد رأيتنا وما يتخلف عنها إلا منافق بين النفاق ولقد رأيتنا وإن الرجل ليهادى بين الرجلين حتى يقام في الصف وما منكم من أحد إلا وله مسجد في بيته ولو صليتم في بيوتكم وتركتم مساجدكم تركتم سنة نبيكم صلى الله عليه وسلم ولو تركتم سنة نبيكم صلى الله عليه وسلم لكفرتم (سنن أبي داود، الرقم: ٥٥٠)

رواه أبو داود وسكت عليه هو والمنذري (مختصر سنن أبي داود ١/٢١٤)

(أما) الأول فقد قال عامة مشايخنا إنها واجبة وذكر الكرخي أنها سنة (واحتج) بما روي عن النبي صلى الله عليه وسلم أنه قال صلاة الجماعة تفضل على صلاة الفرد بسبع وعشرين درجة وفي رواية بخمس وعشرين درجة جعل الجماعة لإحراز الفضيلة وذا آية السنن (وجه) قول العامة الكتاب والسنة وتوارث الأمة أما الكتاب فقوله تعالى واركعوا مع الراكعين أمر الله تعالى بالركوع مع الراكعين وذلك يكون في حال المشاركة في الركوع فكان أمرا بإقامة الصلاة بالجماعة ومطلق الأمر لوجوب العمل (وأما) السنة فما روي عن النبي صلى الله عليه وسلم أنه قال لقد هممت أن آمر رجلا يصلي بالناس فأنصرف إلى أقوام تخلفوا عن الصلاة فأحرق عليهم بيوتهم ومثل هذا الوعيد لا يلحق إلا بترك الواجب (وأما) توارث الأمة فلأن الأمة من لدن رسول الله صلى الله عليه وسلم إلى يومنا هذا واظبت عليها وعلى النكير على تاركها والمواظبة على هذا الوجه دليل الوجوب وليس هذا اختلافا في الحقيقة بل من حيث العبارة لأن السنة المؤكدة والواجب سواء خصوصا ما كان من شعائر الإسلام ألا ترى أن الكرخي سماها سنة ثم فسرها بالواجب فقال: الجماعة سنة لا يرخص لأحد التأخر عنها إلا لعذر وهو تفسير الواجب عند العامة (بدائع الصنائع ١/٦٦١)

عن أبي هريرة قال قال رسول الله صلى الله عليه وسلم لولا ما في البيوت من النساء والذرية لأقمت الصلاة صلاة العشاء وأمرت فتياني يحرقون ما في البيوت بالنار (مسند أحمد، الرقم: ٨٧٩٦)[294]

Hazrat Abu Hurairah رَضِيَٱللَّهُعَنْهُ reports that Hazrat Rasulullah صَلَّىٱللَّهُعَلَيْهِوَسَلَّمَ said, "Had it not been for the women and children in the homes, I would have performed the Esha Salaah and thereafter commanded a group of youth to set alight the homes (in the narration of Saheeh Muslim, "Set alight the homes of those people who perform their fardh salaah in their homes without any valid excuse")."

3. Try your level best to perform every salaah with takbeer-e-ula (join the salaah from the very first takbeer).[295]

---

[294] عن أبي هريرة أن رسول الله صلى الله عليه وسلم فقد ناسا في بعض الصلوات فقال لقد هممت أن آمر رجلا يصلي بالناس ثم أخالف إلى رجال يتخلفون عنها فآمر بهم فيحرقوا عليهم بحزم الحطب بيوتهم ولو علم أحدهم أنه يجد عظما سمينا لشهدها يعني صلاة العشاء (صحيح مسلم، الرقم: ٦٥١)

[295] قال أبو الدرداء قال رسول الله صلى الله عليه وسلم إن لكل شيء أنفة وإن أنفة الصلاة التكبيرة الأولى فحافظوا عليها قال أبو عبيد فحدثت به رجاء بن حيوة حدثتنيه أم الدرداء عن أبي الدرداء

قال الشيخ محمد عوامة: رواه المصنف في مسنده بهذا الاسناد ورواه من طريق المصنف أبو نعيم في الحلية وقال غريب من حديث رجاء لم يرو عنه إلا أبو فروة عن أبي عبيد ورواه من طريق أبي أسامة البزار كشف الأستار وقال لا نعلمه يروى مرفوعا إلا بهذا الإسناد كذا قال وذكره الهيثمي في مجمع الزوائد وقال رواه البزار والطبراني في الكبير بنحوه موقوفا وفيه رجل لم يسم ولا يضره كما ترى وأبو فروة ضعفه جماعة ووثقه بعضهم لكن البخاري قوى حديثه إذا لم يكن من رواية ابنه محمد عنه وهذا منها انظر التعليق على الكاشف للذهبي لذا قال البوصيري في إتحاف الخيرة عن طريق أم الدرداء هذا إسناد حسن (المصنف لابن أبي شيبة بتحقيق الشيخ محمد عوامة، الرقم: ٣١٣٧)

عن الوليد البجلي قال قال عبد الله عليكم بحد الصلاة التكبيرة الأولى (المصنف لابن أبي شيبة، الرقم: ٣١٣٥)

عن أنس بن مالك قال قال رسول الله صلى الله عليه وسلم من صلى لله أربعين يوما في جماعة يدرك التكبيرة الأولى كتبت له براءتان براءة من النار وبراءة من النفاق (سنن الترمذي، الرقم: ٢٤١)

أما فضيلة تكبيرة الافتتاح فتكلموا في وقت إدراكها والصحيح أن من أدرك الركعة الأولى فقد أدرك فضيلة تكبيرة الافتتاح كذا في الحصر في باب أبي يوسف (الفتاوى الهندية ١/٦٩)

4. Ensure that your body, clothing and the place in which you are performing salaah are clean.[296]

5. Before commencing salaah, ensure that your clothing is decent and loose-fitting. Refrain from wearing clothing which is not in keeping with the respect and sanctity of salaah, and clothing which has pictures or inscriptions upon it.[297]

6. Ensure that you perform salaah with a topi as it was the sunnah practice of Hazrat Rasulullah ﷺ and the Sahaabah رضي الله عنهم to perform salaah while wearing a topi.[298]

روي عن ابن عباس رضي الله عنهما أن رسول الله صلى الله عليه وسلم كان يلبس القلانس تحت العمائم ويلبس العمائم بغير القلانس (جمع الوسائل صـ ٢٠٧)[299]

Hazrat Abdullah bin Abbaas رضي الله عنها reports that Hazrat Rasulullah ﷺ used to wear a topi under the turban, and at times, he ﷺ used to wear the turban without the topi.

---

[296] تطهير النجاسة من بدن المصلي وثوبه والمكان الذي يصلي عليه واجب (الفتاوى الهندية ٥٨/١ ، حاشية الطحطاوي على مراقي الفلاح صـ ٢٠٧)

[297] (وكره ... صلاته ... في ثياب البذلة) وهي ما يلبس في البيت ولا يذهب بها الي الكبراء (شرح الوقاية ١٦٨/١ ، رد المحتار ٦٤٠/١)

(وعادم ساتر) لا يصف ما تحته ولا يضر التصاقه وتشكله

قال العلامة ابن عابدين رحمه الله قوله (لا يصف ما تحته) بأن لا يرى منه لون البشرة احترازا عن الرقيق ونحو الزجاج قوله (ولا يضر التصاقه) أي بالألية مثلا وقوله وتشكله من عطف المسبب على السبب وعبارة شرح المنية أما لو كان غليظا لا يرى منه لون البشرة إلا أنه التصق بالعضو وتشكل بشكله فصار شكل العضو مرئيا فينبغي أن لا يمنع جواز الصلاة لحصول الستر اه قال ط وانظر هل يحرم النظر إلى ذلك المتشكل مطلقا أو حيث وجدت الشهوة اه قلت سنتكلم على ذلك في كتاب الحظر والذي يظهر من كلامهم هناك هو الأول (رد المحتار ٤١٠/١)

[298] (وكره ... صلاته حاسرا رأسه للتكاسل أو للتهاون بها) ليس المراد بالتهاون الإهانة بالصلاة فإنها كفر بل المراد قلة رعايتها ومحافظة حدودها (لا للتذلل) (شرح الوقاية ١٦٨-١٦٧/١)

[299] لهذا الحديث شواهد

قال الحسن كان القوم يسجدون على العمامة والقلنسوة (صحيح البخاري ١/٥٦)[300]

Hazrat Hasan Basri رَحِمَهُ ٱللَّهُ says, "The Sahaabah رَضِىَ ٱللَّهُ عَنْهُمْ would make sajdah during salaah on their turbans and topis."

---

[300] عن الحسن أن أصحاب رسول الله صلى الله عليه وسلم كانوا يسجدون وأيديهم في ثيابهم ويسجد الرجل منهم على قلنسوته وعمامته وهكذا رواه عبد الرزاق موصولا عن هشام بن حسان عن الحسن ورواه ابن أبي شيبة أيضا من طريق هشام (فتح الباري ١/٥٨٨)

QIYAAM

1. When intending to perform salaah, stand and face the qiblah.[301]

2. Thereafter, make the intention of the salaah that you are performing and raise your hands until your thumbs are in line with the earlobes.[302]

3. When standing for salaah, stand with utmost respect. Face both feet towards the qiblah and keep a gap of approximately four fingers between them. When performing salaah in congregation, straighten the saffs (rows) and stand as close to each other as possible, without leaving any gaps in between. The feet should not be spread apart in such a manner that the toes of one person touch the toes of the next person.[303]

4. When raising the hands to the earlobes, ensure that the palms are facing the qiblah and the

---

301 شروط الصلاة وهي عندنا سبعة ... واستقبال القبلة (الفتاوى الهندية ١/٥٨ ، البحر الرائق ١/٢٨٣)

302 رفع يديه حذاء أذنيه حتى يحاذي بإبهاميه شحمتي أذنيه وبرؤوس الأصابع فروع أذنيه (الفتاوى الهندية ١/٧٣)

فالأول من شروط صحة التحريمة أن توجد مقارنة للنية حقيقية أو حكما (حاشية الطحطاوي على مراقي الفلاح ص ٢١٧)

303 وينبغي أن يكون بين قدميه أربع أصابع كذا في الخلاصة (الفتاوى الهندية ١/٧٣ ، رد المحتار ١/٤٤٤)

(ويصف) أي يصفهم الإمام بأن يأمرهم بذلك قال الشمني وينبغي أن يأمرهم بأن يتراصوا ويسدوا الخلل ويسووا مناكبهم (الدر المختار ١/٥٦٨)

ويكره أن يحرف أصابع يديه أو رجليه عن القبلة في السجود وغيره كذا في فتاوى قاضي خان (الفتاوى الهندية ١/١٠٨)

fingers are kept in their natural position (neither spread apart nor tightly closed).[304]

5. At the time of reciting the takbeer-e-tahreemah, ensure that your head is kept straight. You should neither bend your head forward nor backward at the time of reciting the takbeer-e-tahreemah.[305]

6. After raising your hands parallel to your earlobes, recite the takbeer (Allahu Akbar).[306]

7. Lower the hands while saying the takbeer and fold them below the navel.[307]

8. Place the right hand over the left hand.[See 307]

9. Form a ring with the thumb and small finger of the right hand around the left wrist and place the remaining three fingers on the forearm.[308]

---

[304] قال الفقيه أبو جعفر يستقبل ببطون كفيه القبلة (الفتاوى الهندية ٧٣/١ ، رد المحتار ٤٨٢/١)

وإذا رفع يديه لا يضم أصابعه كل الضم ولا يفرج كل التفريج بل يتركها على ما كانت عليه بين الضم والتفريج (الفتاوى الهندية ٧٣/١)

[305] ولا يطأطئ رأسه عند التكبير (الفتاوى الهندية ٧٣/١)

[306] (ورفع يديه) قبل التكبير وقيل معه

قال العلامة ابن عابدين رحمه الله (قبل التكبير وقيل معه) الأول نسبه في المجمع إلى أبي حنيفة ومحمد وفي غاية البيان إلى عامة علمائنا وفي المبسوط إلى أكثر مشايخنا وصححه في الهداية والثاني اختاره في الخانية والخلاصة والتحفة والبدائع والمحيط بأن يبدأ بالرفع عند بداءته التكبير ويختم به عند ختمه وعزاه البقالي إلى أصحابنا جميعا ورجحه في الحلية وثمة قول ثالث وهو أنه بعد التكبير والكل مروي عنه عليه الصلاة والسلام وما في الهداية أولى كما في البحر والنهر ولذا اعتمده الشارح فافهم (رد المحتار ٤٨٢/١)

[307] وضع يمينه على يساره تحت سرته (الفتاوى الهندية ٧٢/١)

[308] ويأخذ الرسغ بالخنصر والإبهام ويرسل الباقي على الذراع (الفتاوى الهندية ٧٣/١)

10. Your gaze should not wander in any direction. Instead, it should be focused on the place of sajdah.[309]

11. Once you have commenced your salaah, recite the thanaa silently:[310]

سُبْحَانَكَ اللّٰهُمَّ وَبِحَمْدِكَ وَتَبَارَكَ اسْمُكَ وَتَعَالٰى جَدُّكَ وَلَا اِلٰهَ غَيْرُكَ

Glory be to You O Allah تَبَارَكَوَتَعَالَى*! Praise be to You, blessed is Your name, very lofty is Your majesty, and there is no deity besides You.*

Note: The thanaa will be recited by the munfarid (the one performing salaah individually) as well as the imaam and muqtadi (the one following the imaam).[311]

12. Recite ta'awwuz and tasmiyah silently.[312]

Ta'awwuz is to recite:

أَعُوْذُ بِاللهِ مِنَ الشَّيْطَانِ الرَّجِيْم

I seek protection in Allah تَبَارَكَوَتَعَالَى *from the accursed Shaitaan.*

---

[309] نظر المصلي إلى موضع سجوده قائما (نور الإيضاح ص ٧٢)

[310] عن عائشة قالت كان رسول الله صلى الله عليه وسلم إذا استفتح الصلاة قال سبحانك اللهم وبحمدك وتبارك اسمك وتعالى جدك ولا إله غيرك (سنن أبي داود، الرقم: ٧٧٦)

[311] (ويستفتح كل مصل) سواء المقتدي وغيره ما لم يبدأ الإمام بالقراءة (حاشية الطحطاوي على مراقي الفلاح ص ٢٨١)

[312] (ثم يتعوذ) ... (سرا للقراءة) ... (فيأتي به المسبوق) ... (لا المقتدي) لأنه للقراءة ولا يقرأ المقتدي ... (ثم يسمي سرا) ... (ويسمي) كل من يقرأ في صلاته (في كل ركعة) (حاشية الطحطاوي على مراقي الفلاح ص ٢٨١-٢٨٢)

Tasmiyah is to recite:

بِسْمِ اللهِ الرَّحْمٰنِ الرَّحِيْم

In the name of Allah تَبَارَكَ وَتَعَالَى, the most kind, the most merciful.

13. After reciting thanaa, ta'awwuz and tasmiyah silently, commence the qiraat of Surah Faatihah followed by a surah or any portion of the Quraan Majeed.[313]

14. Upon the completion of Surah Faatihah, you should say "aameen" silently, regardless of whether you are performing salaah individually or performing salaah behind the imaam.[See 313]

15. If you are commencing a surah after reciting Surah Faatihah, then you should recite tasmiyah silently before commencing the surah.[314]

Note: The ta'awwuz and tasmiyah will only be recited by the munfarid and the imaam. The muqtadi will not recite the ta'awwuz and tasmiyah.[See 312] Instead, after reciting thanaa, the muqtadi will remain silent behind the imaam for the entire duration of qiyaam. It is makrooh-e-tahreemi for the

---

[313] (ثم قرأ الفاتحة وأمن الإمام والمأموم سرا ثم قرأ سورة أو) قرأ (ثلاث آيات) قصار أو آية طويلة وجوبا (حاشية الطحطاوي على مراقي الفلاح ص ٢٨٢)

[314] (لا) تسن (بين الفاتحة والسورة مطلقا) ولو سرية ولا تكره اتفاقا

قال العلامة ابن عابدين رحمه الله قوله (لا تسن) مقتضى كلام المتن أن لا يقال لا يسمي لكنه عدل عنه لإيهامه الكراهة بخلاف نفي السنية ثم إن هذا قولهما وصححه في البدائع وقال محمد تسن إن خافت لا إن جهر بحر ونسب ابن الضياء في شرح الغزنوية الأول إلى أبي يوسف فقط فقال وهذا قول أبي يوسف وذكر في المصفي أن الفتوى على قول أبي يوسف أنه يسمي في أول كل ركعة ويخفيها وذكر في المحيط المختار قول محمد وهو أن يسمي قبل الفاتحة وقبل كل سورة في كل ركعة (رد المحتار ٤٩٠/١)

muqtadi to recite any qiraat (whether Surah Faatihah or anything else) behind the imaam.[315]

16. If you are performing a three or four rakaat fardh salaah, then in the third and fourth rakaat you will only recite Surah Faatihah. You should not recite any surah after reciting Surah Faatihah.

In the third and fourth rakaat of the fardh salaah, Surah Faatihah will be recited by the imaam and munfarid (the one performing salaah alone). The muqtadi who is performing salaah behind the imaam will remain silent and not recite anything in all the rakaats.

17. If you are performing sunnah or nafl salaah, you will recite qiraat in all the rakaats, regardless of whether you are performing two rakaats or four rakaats.

---

[315] (ولا يقرأ المؤتم بل يستمع) حال جهر الإمام (وينصت) حال إسراره لقوله تعالى وإذا قرئ القرآن فاستمعوا له وأنصتوا وقال صلى الله عليه وسلم يكفيك قراءة الإمام جهر أم خافت واتفق الإمام الأعظم وأصحابه والإمام مالك والإمام أحمد بن حنبل على صحة صلاة المأموم من غير قراءته شيئا وقد بسطته بالأصل (و) قلنا (إن قرأ) المأموم الفاتحة وغيرها (كره) ذلك (تحريما) للنهي (مراقي الفلاح مع حاشية الطحطاوي صـ ٢٢٧)

RUKU AND QAWMAH

1. When you have completed the recitation of Surah Faatihah and the qiraat, repeat the takbeer, and without raising your hands, go into ruku.[316]

   Note: The takbeeraat-e-intiqaaliyyah (takbeer which is recited when moving from one posture to another) should be commenced as soon as one begins moving to the next posture and should only be completed when one reaches that posture.[See 316]

2. Ensure that your back is kept in a straight line (completely level without bending it). Similarly, the shins (i.e. from the knee downwards) will be kept erect and the elbows will be kept straight.[317]

3. Keep your head straight and in line with your

---

316 (ثم) كما فرغ (يكبر) مع الإنحطاط (للركوع) للتمكن

قال العلامة ابن عابدين رحمه الله (قوله مع الإنحطاط) أفاد أن السنة كون إبتداء التكبير عن الخرور وانتهاءه عند استواء الظهر (رد المحتار ٤٩٣/١)

317 وينصب ساقيه (ويبسط ظهره) ويسوي ظهره بعجزه (غير رافع ولا منكس رأسه ويسبح فيه)

قال العلامة ابن عابدين رحمه الله قوله (وينصب ساقيه) فجعلهما شبه القوس كما يفعله كثير من العوام مكروه بحر (رد المحتار ٤٩٤/١)

حدثني عباس بن سهل قال اجتمع أبو حميد وأبو أسيد وسهل بن سعد ومحمد بن مسلمة فذكروا صلاة رسول الله صلى الله عليه وسلم فقال أبو حميد أنا أعلمكم بصلاة رسول الله صلى الله عليه وسلم فذكر بعض هذا قال ثم ركع فوضع يديه على ركبتيه كأنه قابض عليهما ووتر يديه فتجافى عن جنبيه قال ثم سجد فأمكن أنفه وجبهته ونحى يديه عن جنبيه ووضع كفيه حذو منكبيه ثم رفع رأسه حتى رجع كل عظم في موضعه حتى فرغ ثم جلس فافترش رجله اليسرى وأقبل بصدر اليمنى على قبلته ووضع كفه اليمنى على ركبته اليمنى وكفه اليسرى على ركبته اليسرى وأشار بأصبعه (سنن أبي داود، الرقم: ٧٣٤)

قال العلامة السندي: (قوله وتر يديه) هو بتشديد التاء في المجمع أي جعلهما كالوتر شبه به الراكع إذا مدهما قابضا على ركبتيه بالقوس إذا وترت انتهى (حاشية سنن أبي داود ١٠٧/١)

back. You should neither raise your head nor lower it.[See 317]

4. Grasp the knees firmly with the fingers spread apart.[318]

5. Fix the gaze on the feet in the posture of ruku.[319]

6. Ensure that the arms are kept away from the body.[320]

7. Recite the following tasbeeh thrice or any odd number of times:[321]

سُبْحَانَ رَبِّيَ الْعَظِيْم

Glorified is my Rabb, the most great.

8. Stand up from ruku while saying the tasmee:[322]

سَمِعَ اللّٰهُ لِمَنْ حَمِدَهْ

Allah تَبَارَكَ وَتَعَالَىٰ *hears the one who praises Him.*

---

[318] (و) يسن (تفريج أصابعه) لقوله صلى الله عليه وسلم لأنس رضي الله عنه إذا ركعت فضع كفيك على ركبتيك وفرج بين أصابعك وارفع يديك عن جنبيك ولا يطلب تفريج الأصابع إلا هنا ليتمكن من بسط الظهر

قال العلامة الطحاوي رحمه الله قوله (ولا يطلب تفريج الأصابع إلا هنا) أي التفريج التام كما أنه لا يطلب الضم التام إلا في السجود فيما عدا هذين يبقيها على خلقتها قوله (ليتمكن من بسط الظهر) الأولى أن يقول ليتمكن من الأخذ فإن التفريج لا دخل له في البسط بالتجربة (حاشية الطحطاوي على مراقي الفلاح ص.٢٦٦)

[319] (ولها آداب) ... (نظره إلى موضع سجوده حال قيامه وإلى ظهر قدميه حال ركوعه ...) (الدر المختار ٤٧٧/١)

[320] قال وينبغي أن يزاد مجافيا عضديه مستقبلا أصابعه فإنهما سنة كما في الزاهدي (رد المحتار ٤٩٤/١)

[321] ويقول في ركوعه سبحان ربي العظيم ثلاثا وذلك أدناه (الفتاوى الهندية ٧٤/١)

وصرحوا بأنه يكره أن ينقص عن الثلاث وأن الزيادة مستحبة بعد أن يختم على وتر خمس أو سبع ما لم يكن إماما فلا يطول (رد المحتار ٤٩٤/١)

[322] (ثم يرفع رأسه من ركوعه مسمعا ... ويكتفي به الإمام) وقالا يضم التحميد سرا (و) يكتفي (بالتحميد المؤتم) وأفضله اللهم ربنا ولك الحمد ثم حذف الواو ثم حذف اللهم فقط (ويجمع بينهما لو منفردا) على المعتمد يسمع رافعا ويحمد مستويا (الدر المختار ٤٩٦/١)

فإذا قال الإمام مقارنا للانتقال سمع الله لمن حمده يقول المقتدي مقارنا له ربنا لك الحمد (بدائع الصنائع ٥٦/٢)

followed by the tahmeed:

اَللّٰهُمَّ رَبَّنَا وَلَكَ الْحَمْد

O Allah تَبَارَكَ وَتَعَالَى, our Rabb, for You alone is all praise.

9. Stand up erect. After standing up from ruku, do not tie your hands. Instead, leave them at your sides. This posture is called qawmah. In qawmah, stand up erect with ta'deel-e-arkaan (the body should be completely at ease) before going into sajdah.[323]

---

[323] (ويقوم مستويا)

قال العلامة ابن عابدين رحمه الله (مستويا) هو للتأكيد فإن مطلق القيام إنما يكون باستواء الشقين وإنما أكد لغفلة الأكثرين عنه فليس بمستدرك

كما ظن قهستاني أو للتأسيس والمراد منه التعديل كما أفاده في العناية (رد المحتار ٤٩٧/١)

SAJDAH

1. Say the takbeer, and without raising your hands, proceed into sajdah.[324]

2. Ensure that your back is straight when going down into sajdah.[325]

3. Keep the hands on the knees while proceeding into sajdah.[326]

4. First place the knees on the ground, then the palms, then the nose and lastly the forehead.[327]

5. Place the palms parallel to the ears.[328]

6. Keep the fingers closed and facing towards the qiblah.[329]

7. Keep the elbows raised off the ground.[330]

8. Keep the hands away from the sides.[331]

---

[324] ثم إذا استوى قائما كبر وسجد (الفتاوى الهندية ٧٥/١)

[325] ويخر للسجود قائما مستويا لا منحنيا (رد المحتار ٤٩٧/١)

[326] عن أبي هريرة رضي الله عنه قال قال رسول الله صلى الله عليه وسلم إذا سجد أحدكم فلا يبرك كما يبرك الجمل وليضع يديه على ركبتيه (السنن الكبرى للبيهقي، الرقم: ٢٦٣٤)

[327] (ويسجد واضعا ركبتيه) أولا لقربهما من الأرض (ثم يديه) إلا لعذر (ثم وجهه) مقدما أنفه لما مر (الدر المختار ٤٩٧/١)

[328] ويضع يديه في السجود حذاء أذنيه ويوجه أصابعه نحو القبلة (الفتاوى الهندية ٧٥/١)

[329] ضاما أصابع يديه لتتوجه للقبلة (الدر المختار ٤٩٨/١)

[330] ولا يفترش ذراعيه (الفتاوى الهندية ٧٥/١)

[331] يبدي ضبعيه عن جنبيه (الفتاوى الهندية ٧٥/١)

9. Fix the gaze on the nose in sajdah.[332]

10. Keep a gap between the stomach and thighs.[333]

11. Keep the knees close to each other in sajdah so that they face towards the qiblah.[334]

12. Keep both the feet on the ground with the toes facing the qiblah.[335] One may join the heels of both

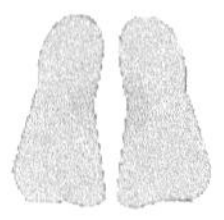

---

[332] ولها آداب نظره إلى ... أرنبة أنفه حال سجوده

قال العلامة ابن عابدين رحمه الله (قوله وإلى أرنبة أنفه) أي طرفه قاموس (رد المحتار ٤٧٨/١)

[333] ويباعد بطنه عن فخذيه ليظهر كل عضو بنفسه (الدر المختار ٥٠٣/١)

[334] عن أبي هريرة أن النبي صلى الله عليه وسلم قال إذا سجد أحدكم فلا يفترش يديه افتراش الكلب وليضم فخذيه (سنن أبي داود، الرقم: ٩٠١ ، صحيح ابن خزيمة، الرقم: ٦٥٣)

عن أبي حميد في صفة صلاة رسول الله صلى الله عليه وسلم قال وإذا سجد فرج بين فخذيه غير حامل بطنه على شيء من فخذيه (السنن الكبرى للبيهقي، الرقم: ٢٧١٢)

ووجه التوفيق بينهما ما قاله الشيخ التهانوي رحمه الله أن معنى قوله صلى الله عليه وسلم وليضم فخذيه أي ليقارب بينهما فالحاصل أنه لا يفرج بينهما كل التفريج ولا يباعد بينهما

قال مولانا ظفر أحمد التهانوي رحمه الله في إعلاء السنن بعد نقل كلام مولانا التهاوي رحمه الله السابق: ولم أر في ضم الفخذين وتفريجها تصريحا من الفقهاء إلا ما رد المحتار في بيان الركوع (قوله ويسن أن يلصق كعبيه) قال السيد أبو السعود وكذا في السجود أيضا وسبق في السنن أيضا اه والذي سبق هو قوله وإلصاق كعبيه في السجود سنة اه ولا يخفى أن إلصاق الكعبين يستدعي إلصاق الفخذين في الجملة أيضا فافهم والله أعلم وأما سنية إلصاق الكعبين في السجود فيدل عليه حديث عائشة وهو التاسع والعشرون من الباب وفيه فوجدته ساجدا راصا عقبيه أي ملصقا أحدهما بالآخر (إعلاء السنن ٣٢/٣)

[335] ويوجه أصابعه نحو القبلة وكذا أصابع رجليه (الفتاوى الهندية ٧٥/١)

ويسن أن يلصق كعبيه (الدر المختار ٤٩٣/١)

السؤال باسمه تعالى أيها العلماء العاملون والفضلاء الكاملون ما تقولون في إلصاق رجل كعبيه في الركوع والسجود أيعد هو من سنن الصلوة أم لا وبأي حديث صحيح ثابت هو ومن القائل به من الأئمة المعتبرين وكثير من علماء هذا الزمان ينكرون سنية ذلك ومنهم صاحب السعاية وغيره بينوا بالتحقيق وتوجروا على اليقين ونحن نريد أن نطبع فتواكم

الجواب لم نجد حديثا صريحا في سنية هذا الإلصاق في الركوع والسجود ولم يذكره من فقهائنا إلا صاحب الدر وشارح المنية ومن تبعهما وهم قليل ولم يتعرض له القدوري ولا صاحب الكنز والوقاية وغيرهم من أصحاب المتون المعتبرة الناقلين لظاهر الرواية وفي ترجيح الراجح لشيخنا (مولانا أشرف علي التهانوي) وقال العلامة عبد الحي اللكهنوي في السعاية إن قدوة القائلين بسنية الإلصاق من الحنفية هو الزاهدي وهو وإن كان إماما جليلا في الفقه لكنه مشهور بنقل الروايات الضعيفة صرح به ابن عابدين في تنقيح الفتاوى الحامدية وفي الفوائد البهية أنه كان معتزلي العقائد حنفي الفروع (النور صـ ١٦ ، متعلق شعبان سـ ٤٢ هـ) وكلام الطحاوي في معاني الآثار يفيد أن الإلصاق ليس مشروعا في شيئ من

the feet in sajdah or keep them apart. Both have been established in the Hadith.[336]

13. Recite the following tasbeeh thrice or any odd number of times:[337]

سُبْحَانَ رَبِّيَ الْأَعْلَى

Glorified is my Rabb, the most high.

14. Say the takbeer and sit up. This position is called jalsah.[338]

الأعضاء في الركوع ولا في السجود (للرجال) بل المشروع عكسه أي التجافي بينهما قال الطحاوي في بحث التطبيق ثم التمسنا حكم ذلك من طريق النظر كيف هو فرأينا التطبيق فيه التقاء اليدين ورأينا وضع اليدين على الركبتين فيه تفريقهما فأردنا أن ننظر في حكم أشكال ذلك في الصلاة كيف هو فرأينا السنة جاءت عن النبي صلى الله عليه وسلم بالتجافي في الركوع والسجود وأجمع المسلمون على ذلك فكان ذلك من تفريق الأعضاء وكمن قام في الصلاة أمر أن يراوح بين قدميه وقد روي ذلك عن ابن مسعود وهو الذي روى التطبيق فلما رأينا تفريق الأعضاء في هذا بعضها من بعض أولى من الإلصاق بعضها ببعض واختلفوا في إلصاقها وتفريقها في الركوع كان النظر على ذلك أن يكون ما اختلفوا فيه ذلك معطوفا على ما أجمعوا عليه منه فيكون التفريق فيما ذكرنا أفضل يكون في سائر الأعضاء كذلك (١/١٣٥–١٣٦) وبعد ذلك فلا حاجة إلى إقامة الدليل على سنية هذا الإلصاق إذا ثبت ضعف نقله في المذهب ونص الطحاوي على سنية التجافي بين الأعضاء في الركوع والسجود جميعا والله تعالى أعلم (إمداد الاحكام ١/٤٧٧–٤٧٨)

[336] قالت عائشة فقدت رسول الله صلى الله عليه وسلم وكان معي على فراشي فوجدته ساجدا راصا عقبيه مستقبلا بأطراف أصابعه للقبلة فسمعته يقول اللهم إني أعوذ برضاك من سخطك وبعفوك من عقوبتك وبك منك أني عليك لا أبلغ كل ما فيك فلما انصرف قال صلى الله عليه و سلم يا عائشة أحربك شيطانك فقلت ما لي من شيطان فقال ما من آدمي إلا له شيطان فقلت وأنت يا رسول الله قال وأنا ولكني دعوت الله عليه فأسلم (رواه ابن حبان ٥/٢٦٠ ، الرقم: ١٩٣٣) بإسناد صحيح كذا في التلخيص الحبير ١/٩٨ (إعلاء السنن ٣/٣٠) ، وكذا في صحيح ابن خزيمة (١/٣٢٨) وفي الحاشية: إسناده صحيح قال شعيب الأرنؤوط: إسناده صحيح على شرط مسلم حديث أبي حميد: كان إذا سجد أمكن أنفه وجبهته من الأرض ونحى يديه عن جنبيه ووضع كفيه حذو منكبيه ابن خزيمة في صحيحه بهذا ورواه أبو داود دون قوله من الأرض دون قوله في بعض الأخبار نقل أن النبي صلى الله عليه وسلم كان يفرق في السجود بين ركبتيه أبو داود في حديث أبي حميد وإذا سجد فرج بين فخذيه وفي البيهقي من حديث البراء كان إذا سجد وجه أصابعه قبل القبلة فتفاج يعني وسع بين رجليه (التلخيص الحبير، الرقم: ٣٨١)

[337] ويقول في سجوده سبحان ربي الأعلى ثلاثا وذلك أدناه كذا في المحيط ويستحب أن يزيد على الثلاث في الركوع والسجود بعد أن يختم بالوتر كذا في الهداية فالأدنى فيهما ثلاث مرات والأوسط خمس مرات وإلا كمل سبع مرات كذا في الزاد (الفتاوى الهندية ١/٧٥)

[338] (ثم يرفع رأسه مكبرا ...) ... (ويجلس بين السجدتين مطمئنا) (الدر المختار ١/٥٠٥)

JALSAH

1. In jalsah, place your palms on your thighs with your fingertips at the edge of your knees.[339]

2. Keep your fingers in their natural position (neither joined together nor far apart).[See 339]

3. Fix the gaze on the area between the lower chest and lap whilst in jalsah.[340]

4. Keep the right foot erect with its toes pressing against the ground and facing towards the qiblah.[341]

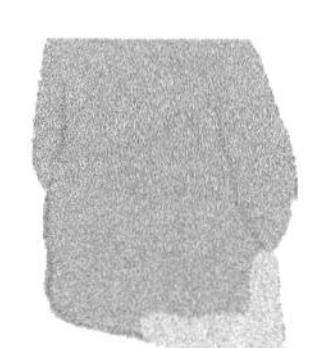

5. Place the left foot flat whilst sitting on it. Try to press its toes against the right foot thereby facing them towards the qiblah.[342]

---

[339] (ويضع يمناه على فخذه اليمنى ويسراه على اليسرى ويبسط أصابعه) مفرجة قليلا (جاعلا أطرافها عند ركبتيه) ولا يأخذ الركبة هو الأصح لتتوجه للقبلة (الدر المختار ٥٠٨/١)

[340] (ولها آداب) ... (نظره إلى ... حجره حال قعوده ...)
قال العلامة ابن عابدين رحمه الله (قوله وإلى حجره) بكسر الحاء والجيم والراء المهملة ما بين يديك من ثوبك قاموس وقال أيضا الحجر مثلثة المنع وحضن الإنسان والمناسب هنا الأول لأنه فسر الحضن بما دون الإبط إلى الكشح أو الصدر والعضدان وفسر الكشح بما بين الخاصرة إلى الضلع الجنب واستظهر في العزمية ضبطه بضم ففتح فزاي معجمة جمع حجزة وهي معقد الإزار ولا يخفى بعده (رد المحتار ٤٧٨/١)

[341] (... يفترش) الرجل (رجله اليسرى) فيجعلها بين أليتيه (ويجلس عليها وينصب رجله اليمنى) (الدر المختار ٥٠٨/١)

[342] (ويوجه أصابعه) في المنصوبة (نحو القبلة) هو السنة في الفرض والنفل
قال العلامة ابن عابدين رحمه الله (قوله في المنصوبة) أي الأصابع الكائنة في الرجل المنصوبة قال في السراج يعني رجله اليمنى لأن ما أمكنه أن يوجهه إلى القبلة فهو أولى اه وصرح بأن المراد اليمنى في المفتاح والخلاصة والخزانة فقوله في الدرر رجليه بالتثنية فيه إشكال لأن توجه أصابع اليسرى المفترشة نحو القبلة تكلف زائد كما في شرح الشيخ إسماعيل لكن نقل القهستاني مثل ما في الدرر عن الكافي والتحفة ثم قال فيوجه رجله اليسرى إلى اليمنى وأصابعها نحو القبلة بقدر الاستطاعة اه تأمل (رد المحتار ٥٠٨/١)

6. Remain in the position of jalsah with the body being completely at ease and calm before going into the second sajdah.[343]

7. Say the takbeer and proceed to the second sajdah as normal.[344]

---

[343] (ويجلس بين السجدتين مطمئنا) لما مر (الدر المختار ٥٠٥/١)

[344] (ويكبر ويسجد) ثانية (مطمئنا ويكبر للنهوض) على صدور قدميه (بلا اعتماد وقعود) استراحة ولو فعل لا بأس ويكره تقديم إحدى رجليه عند النهوض (الدر المختار ٥٠٦/١)

SECOND RAKAAT

1. After the second sajdah, say the takbeer and stand up for the second rakaat.[See 344]

2. When rising from sajdah, first raise the forehead, then the nose, then the hands and lastly the knees.[345]

3. When getting up, do not take support from the ground (unless there is a need to do so).[See 344]

4. Perform the second rakaat as normal (with the exception of thanaa and ta'awwuz).[346]

---

[345] قالوا إذا أراد السجود يضع أولا ما كان أقرب إلى الأرض فيضع ركبتيه أولا ثم يديه ثم أنفه ثم جبهته وإذا أراد الرفع يرفع أولا جبهته ثم أنفه ثم يديه ثم ركبتيه (الفتاوى الهندية ٧٥/١)

[346] (والركعة الثانية كالأولى) فيما مر (غير أنه لا يأتي بثناء ولا تعوذ فيها) إذ لم يشرعا إلا مرة (الدر المختار ٥٠٦/١)

QA'DAH AND SALAAM

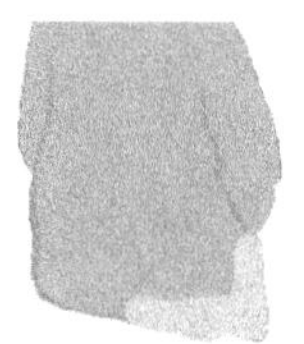

1. After the second sajdah of the second rakaat, sit in the position of qa'dah in the same manner as explained for jalsah.^{See 339, 340, 341 and 342}

2. Recite the tashahhud:[347]

اَلتَّحِيَّاتُ لِلّٰهِ وَالصَّلَوَاتُ وَالطَّيِّبَاتُ اَلسَّلَامُ عَلَيْكَ أَيُّهَا النَّبِيُّ وَرَحْمَةُ اللهِ وَبَرَكَاتُهُ اَلسَّلَامُ عَلَيْنَا وَعَلَى عِبَادِ اللهِ الصَّالِحِيْنَ أَشْهَدُ أَنْ لَّا إِلٰهَ إِلَّا اللهُ وَأَشْهَدُ أَنَّ مُحَمَّدًا عَبْدُهُ وَرَسُوْلُهُ

All verbal ibaadaat, physical ibaadaat and monetary ibaadaat be for Allah تَبَارَكَوَتَعَالَى. *May the special peace of Allah* تَبَارَكَوَتَعَالَى *descend upon you, O Nabi* صَلَّىٱللَّهُعَلَيْهِوَسَلَّمَ, *and Allah's* تَبَارَكَوَتَعَالَى *choicest mercies and blessings. May peace descend upon us and upon all the pious servants of Allah* تَبَارَكَوَتَعَالَى. *I bear witness that there is no deity except Allah* تَبَارَكَوَتَعَالَى *and I bear witness that Hazrat Muhammad* صَلَّىٱللَّهُعَلَيْهِوَسَلَّمَ *is His servant and messenger.*

3. When saying أَنْ لَّا إِلٰهَ, form a ring with the thumb and middle finger of the right hand, raise the index finger towards the qiblah and close the remaining two fingers (the small finger and finger next to it).

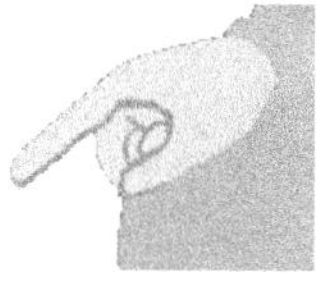

When saying الله إِلَّا, lower the index finger. The thumb and middle finger will remain joined like a ring until the end of the qa'dah. [348]

4. If you are performing a three or four rakaat salaah then you should not recite anything besides the above tashahhud. After reciting the tashahhud, stand up for the third rakaat. [349]

5. If it is the last qa'dah then recite Durood-e-Ebrahim after the tashahhud followed by a dua from the Quraan Majeed or Hadith. [350]

---

[348] (ولا يشير بسبابته عند الشهادة وعليه الفتوى) كما في الولوالجية والتجنيس والتجنيس وعمدة المفتي وعامة الفتاوى لكن المعتمد ما صححه الشراح ولا سيما المتأخرون كالكمال والحلبي والبهنسي والباقاني وشيخ الإسلام الجد وغيرهم أنه يشير لفعله عليه الصلاة والسلام ونسبوه لمحمد والإمام بل في متن درر البحار وشرحه غرر الأذكار المفتي به عندنا أنه يشير باسطا أصابعه كلها وفي الشرنبلالية عن البرهان الصحيح أنه يشير بمسبحته وحدها يرفعها عند النفي ويضعها عند الإثبات

قال العلامة ابن عابدين رحمه الله (ولا يشير بسبابته عند الشهادة وعليه الفتوى) ... ولهذا فسرت الإشارة بهذه الكيفية في عامة الكتب كالبدائع والنهاية ومعراج الدراية والذخيرة والظهيرية وفتح القدير وشرحي المنية والقهستاني والحلية والنهر وشرح الملتقى للبهنسي معزيا إلى شرح النقاية وشرحي درر البحار وغيرها كما ذكرت عباراتهم في رسالة سميتها (رفع التردد في عقد الأصابع عند التشهد) وحررت فيها أنه ليس لنا سوى قولين الأول وهو المشهور في المذهب بسط الأصابع بدون إشارة الثاني بسط الأصابع إلى حين الشهادة فيعقد عندها ويرفع السبابة عند النفي ويضعها عند الإثبات وهذا ما اعتمده المتأخرون لثبوته عن النبي بالأحاديث الصحيحة ولصحة نقله عن أئمتنا الثلاث فلذا قال في الفتح إن الأول خلاف الدراية والرواية (رد المحتار ٥٠٨/١ - ٥٠٩)

[349] (ولا يزيد) في الفرض (على التشهد في القعدة الأولى) إجماعا

قال العلامة ابن عابدين رحمه الله (قوله ولا يزيد في الفرض) أي وما ألحق به كالوتر والسنن الرواتب وإن نظر صاحب البحر فيها ولينظر حكم المنذور وقضاء النفل الذي أفسده والظاهر أنهما في حكم النفل لأن الوجوب فيها عارض ط (رد المحتار ٥١٠/١)

[350] (ويفعل في القعود الثاني) الافتراش (كالأول وتشهد) أيضا (وصلى على النبي صلى الله عليه وسلم) ... (ودعاء) ... (بالأدعية المذكورة في القرآن والسنة لا بما يشبه كلام الناس) (الدر المختار ٥١٢/١ - ٥٢٣)

The Durood-e-Ebrahim is as follows:

اَللّٰهُمَّ صَلِّ عَلٰى مُحَمَّدٍ وَّعَلٰى اٰلِ مُحَمَّدٍ كَمَا صَلَّيْتَ عَلٰى اِبْرَاهِيْمَ وَعَلٰى اٰلِ اِبْرَاهِيْمَ اِنَّكَ حَمِيْدٌ مَّجِيْدٌ

اَللّٰهُمَّ بَارِكْ عَلٰى مُحَمَّدٍ وَّعَلٰى اٰلِ مُحَمَّدٍ كَمَا بَارَكْتَ عَلٰى اِبْرَاهِيْمَ وَعَلٰى اٰلِ اِبْرَاهِيْمَ اِنَّكَ حَمِيْدٌ مَّجِيْدٌ

O Allah تَبَارَكَ وَتَعَالٰى *! Shower Your mercy on Hazrat Muhammad* صَلَّى اللهُ عَلَيْهِ وَسَلَّمَ *and his family as You showered Your mercy on Hazrat Ebrahim* عَلَيْهِ السَّلَامُ *and his family. Surely You are praiseworthy and most high.*

O Allah صَلَّى اللهُ عَلَيْهِ وَسَلَّمَ تَبَارَكَ وَتَعَالٰى *! Bless Hazrat Muhammad and his family as You have blessed Hazrat Ebrahim* عَلَيْهِ السَّلَامُ *and his family. Surely You are praiseworthy and most high.*

One may recite the following dua which is reported in the Hadith:[351]

اَللّٰهُمَّ اِنِّيْ ظَلَمْتُ نَفْسِيْ ظُلْمًا كَثِيْرًا وَّلَا يَغْفِرُ الذُّنُوْبَ اِلَّا اَنْتَ فَاغْفِرْ لِيْ مَغْفِرَةً مِّنْ عِنْدِكَ وَارْحَمْنِيْ اِنَّكَ اَنْتَ الْغَفُوْرُ الرَّحِيْمُ

---

351 ومن الأدعية المأثورة ما روي عن أبي بكر رضي الله عنه أنه قال لرسول الله صلى الله عليه وسلم علمني دعاء أدعو به في صلاتي فقال قل اللهم إني ظلمت نفسي ظلما كثيرا وإنه لا يغفر الذنوب إلا أنت فاغفر لي مغفرة من عندك وارحمني إنك أنت الغفور الرحيم... ويستحب أن يقول المصلي بعد ذكر الصلاة في آخر الصلاة رب اجعلني مقيم الصلاة ومن ذريتي ربنا وتقبل دعاء ربنا اغفر لي ولوالدي وللمؤمنين يوم يقوم الحساب كذا في التتارخانية ناقلا (الفتاوى الهندية ٧٦/١)

عن أبي بكر الصديق رضي الله عنه أنه قال لرسول الله صلى الله عليه وسلم علمني دعاء أدعو به في صلاتي قال قل اللهم إني ظلمت نفسي ظلما كثيرا ولا يغفر الذنوب إلا أنت فاغفر لي مغفرة من عندك وارحمني إنك أنت الغفور الرحيم (صحيح البخاري، الرقم: ٨٣٤)

O Allah اتَبَارَكَ وَتَعَالَى *! I have oppressed myself excessively (through committing sins), and no one can forgive sins besides You, so forgive me with special forgiveness from Your side and show mercy to me, for indeed You alone are all-forgiving and all-merciful.*

6. After completing your dua, make salaam by saying,

اَلسَّلَامُ عَلَيْكُمْ وَرَحْمَةُ اللّٰهِ

while turning your head to the right side, and then again while turning your head to the left side.[352 and 353]

7. Do not lower or jerk your head while making salaam.

8. When making salaam on either side, fix your gaze on your shoulders.[354]

9. Turn your face on both sides to the extent that the person behind will be able to see your cheek.[355]

10. After the salaam, recite أَسْتَغْفِرُ اللّٰه thrice.[356]

---

[352] ثم يسلم تسليمتين تسليمة عن يمينه وتسليمة عن يساره (الفتاوى الهندية ٧٦/١)

[353] قال الشيخ الكنكوهي في الكوكب ٢٨٩/١: (كان يسلم تسليمة واحدة) أي يأخذ فيها من تلقاء وجهه ويختمها إذا مال وجهه إلى اليمين وكذا الحكم في تسليم اليسار لكنها (أي عائشة رضي الله عنها) اكتفت بذكر تسليمة لما أن مقصودها بالذكر إنما هو بيان التسليمة من أين تبتدئ وبيان كيفيتها كيف هي قال الشيخ زكريا كاندهلوي رحمه الله في حاشية الكوكب وحاصل ما أفاده أن الحديث ليس بمسوق لبيان العدد بل لبيان ابتداء السلام بأن كان دأبه صلى الله عليه وسلم أن يبتدئ من تلقاء وجهه ويختمه إلى اليمين واليسار

[354] (ولها آداب) ... (نظره إلى ... وإلى منكبه الأيمن والأيسر عند التسليمة الأولى والثانية) (الدر المختار ٤٧٧/١)

[355] ويحول في التسليمة الأولى وجهه عن يمينه حتى يرى بياض خده الأيمن وفي التسليمة الثانية عن يساره حتى يرى بياض خده الأيسر (الفتاوى الهندية ٧٦/١)

11. Engage in dua as this is a time for the acceptance of duas.[357]

12. Recite Tasbeeh-e-Faatimi after every salaah.[358] Tasbeeh-e-Faatimi is for one to recite 33 times Subhaanallah, 33 times Alhamdulillah, 33 times Allahu Akbar, and complete the hundred by reciting:

لَا إِلٰهَ إِلَّا اللهُ وَحْدَهُ لَا شَرِيْكَ لَهُ لَهُ الْمُلْكُ وَلَهُ الْحَمْدُ وَهُوَ عَلَى كُلِّ شَيْءٍ قَدِيْر

There is no deity besides Allah تَبَارَكَ وَتَعَالَى *alone, who has no partner. To Him belongs the kingdom (of the entire universe), and only for Him belongs all praise and He alone has complete power over everything.*

---

356 (ويستغفرون الله) العظيم (ثلاثا) لقول ثوبان كان رسول الله صلى الله عليه وسلم إذا انصرف من صلاته استغفر الله تعالى ثلاثا وقال اللهم أنت السلام ومنك السلام تباركت يا ذا الجلال والإكرام رواه مسلم وقال صلى الله عليه وسلم من استغفر الله تعالى في دبر كل صلاة ثلاث مرات فقال أستغفر الله الذي لا إله إلا هو الحي القيوم وأتوب إليه غفرت له ذنوبه وإن كان فر من الزحف (حاشية الطحطاوي على مراقي الفلاح صـ ٣١٤)

357 (ثم يدعون لأنفسهم وللمسلمين) بالأدعية المأثورة الجامعة لقول أبي أمامة قيل يا رسول الله أي الدعاء أسمع قال جوف الليل الأخير ودبر الصلوات المكتوبات ولقوله صلى الله عليه وسلم إني لأحبك والله إني لأحبك يا معاذ لا تدعن دبر كل صلاة أن تقول اللهم أعني على ذكرك وشكرك وحسن عبادتك (حاشية الطحطاوي على مراقي الفلاح صـ ٣١٥)

358 ويسبحون الله ثلاثا وثلاثين ويحمدونه كذلك ويكبرونه كذلك (نور الإيضاح صـ ٨٠)

General Masaail Pertaining to Men's Salaah

1. **Q:** Should the muqtadi recite thanaa, ta'awwuz, tasmiyah and qiraat behind the imaam?

   A: The muqtadi will recite the thanaa and thereafter remain silent. He will not recite ta'awwuz, tasmiyah and qiraat behind the imaam.[See 311, 312 and 315]

2. **Q:** If the muqtadi joined the salaah at the time when the qiraat had commenced, then should he recite the thanaa?

   A: If the muqtadi joined the salaah at the time when the qiraat had commenced, he should not recite the thanaa. Instead, he should remain silent after saying the takbeer.[See 311]

3. **Q:** Will tasmiyah be recited after Surah Faatihah?

   A: The tasmiyah will only be recited after Surah Faatihah if one is going to commence a surah. If one is not going to commence any surah then tasmiyah should not be recited.[359]

4. **Q:** What are the sunnah qiraat for the different salaah, and is it sunnah to recite it in all the salaah (i.e. sunnah, witr and fardh) or only the fardh salaah?

---

[359] وقال في الإمداد وفي المحيط يقرأ في الخطبة سورة من القرآن أو آية فالأخبار قد تواترت أن النبي صلى الله عليه وسلم كان يقرأ القرآن في خطبته لا تخلو عن سورة أو آية ثم قال وإذا قرأ سورة تامة يتعوذ ثم يسمي قبلها وإن قرأ آية قيل يتعوذ ثم يسمي وأكثرهم قالوا يتعوذ ولا يسمي والاختلاف في القراءة في غير الخطبة كذلك اه ملخصا (رد المحتار ٢/١٤٨)

A: The sunnah qiraat for the five daily salaah is for one to recite from the mufassal surahs.

In Fajr and Zuhr, one should recite from the tiwaal-e-mufassal surahs i.e. from Surah Hujuraat till the end of Surah Inshiqaaq.

In Asr and Esha, one should recite from the awsaat-e-mufassal surahs i.e. from Surah Burooj till the end of Surah Qadr.

In Maghrib salaah, one should recite from the qisaar-e-mufassal surahs i.e. from Surah Bayyinah to Surah Naas.[360]

This is the sunnah qiraat to be recited for the various salaah, and hence one should endeavour to recite from these surahs in the various salaah. However, if one occasionally recites from any other part of the Quraan Majeed, it will not go against the sunnah, as it is reported in certain Ahaadith that at times, Hazrat Rasulullah ﷺ and the Sahaabah رَضِيَ ٱللَّهُ عَنْهُم also recited from other parts of the Quraan Majeed.[361]

---

[360] وأن تكون السورة المضمومة للفاتحة من طوال المفصل في الفجر والظهر ومن أوساطه في العصر والعشاء ومن قصاره في المغرب لو كان مقيمًا فالطوال من سورة الحجرات إلى البروج وأوساطه منها إلى لم يكن وقصاره منها إلى آخره (مراقي الفلاح مع حاشية الطحطاوي صـ ٢٦٢)

[361] عن ابن عباس عن أمه أم الفضل قالت خرج إلينا رسول الله صلى الله عليه وسلم وهو عاصب رأسه في مرضه فصلى المغرب فقرأ بالمرسلات (سنن الترمذي، الرقم: ٣٠٨)

As far as the length of the qiraat is concerned, the imaam should take into consideration the condition of the congregation that he is leading in salaah.[362]

As for witr salaah, sunnah salaah and nafl salaah, one may recite from any part of the Quraan Majeed one wishes. It should be borne in mind that there are several sunnah surahs which are reported in the Hadith to be recited in the witr salaah and certain sunnah salaah. One should endeavour to recite those surahs in the witr salaah and the various sunnah salaah.

5. **Q:** What is the sunnah qiraat or surahs to be recited in the witr salaah?

A: There are various masnoon surahs which may be recited in the witr salaah. Among the surahs that are reported in the Ahaadith to be recited in the witr salaah are the following:

---

[362] عن عثمان بن أبي العاص قال قلت وقال موسى في موضع آخر إن عثمان بن أبي العاص قال يا رسول الله اجعلني إمام قومي قال أنت إمامهم واقتد بأضعفهم واتخذ مؤذنا لا يأخذ على أذانه أجرا (سنن أبي داود، الرقم: ٥٣١)

ينبغي للإمام أن يقرأ مقدار ما يخف على القوم ولا يثقل عليهم بعد أن يكون على التمام لما روي عن عثمان بن أبي العاص الثقفي أنه قال آخر ما عهد إلي رسول الله صلى الله عليه وسلم أن أصلي بالقوم صلاة أضعفهم وروي عنه صلى الله عليه وسلم أنه قال من أم قوما فليصل بهم صلاة أضعفهم فإن فيهم الصغير والكبير وذا الحاجة وروي أن قوم معاذ لما شكوا إلى رسول الله صلى الله عليه وسلم تطويل القراءة دعاه فقال أفتان أنت يا معاذ قالها ثلاثا أين أنت من والسماء والطارق والشمس وضحاها قال الراوي فما رأيت رسول الله صلى الله عليه وسلم في موعظة أشد منه في تلك الموعظة وعن أنس رضي الله عنه أنه قال ما صليت خلف أحد أتم وأخف مما صليت خلف رسول الله صلى الله عليه وسلم وروي أنه صلى الله عليه وسلم قرأ بالمعوذتين في صلاة الفجر يوما فلما فرغ قالوا أوجزت فقال صلى الله عليه وسلم سمعت بكاء صبي فخشيت على أمه أن تفتن دل على أن الإمام ينبغي له أن يراعي حال قومه ولأن مراعاة حال القوم سبب لتكثير الجماعة فكان ذلك مندوبا إليه (بدائع الصنائع ٢٠٦/١)

a) Recite Surah Aa'laa in the first rakaat, Surah Kaafiroon in the second rakaat and Surah Ikhlaas in the third rakaat.[363]

b) Recite the end of Surah Baqarah (آمن الرسول) in the first rakaat, Surah Qadr in the second rakaat, and Surah Ikhlaas in the third rakaat.[364]

c) Recite the end of Surah Baqarah (آمن الرسول) in the first rakaat, Surah Kaafiroon in the second rakaat and Surah Ikhlaas in the third rakaat.[See 364]

d) Recite Surah Qadr in the first rakaat, Surah Kaafiroon in the second rakaat and Surah Ikhlaas in the third rakaat.[See 364]

e) Recite Surah Takaathur, Surah Qadr and Surah Zilzaal in the first rakaat, Surah Asr, Surah Nasr and Surah

---

[363] عن ابن عباس قال كان النبي صلى الله عليه وسلم يقرأ في الوتر ب سبح اسم ربك الأعلى وقل يا أيها الكافرون وقل هو الله أحد في ركعة ركعة (سنن الترمذي، الرقم: ٤٦٢)

[364] وعن سعيد بن جبير قال لما أمر عمر بن الخطاب أبي بن كعب أن يقوم بالناس في رمضان كان يوتر بهم فيقرأ في الركعة الأولى إنا أنزلناه في ليلة القدر وفي الثانية بقل يا أيها الكافرون وفي الثالثة قل هو الله أحد وعن سعيد بن جبير أنه كان يقرأ في الوتر في أول ركعة خاتمة البقرة وفي الثانية إنا أنزلناه في ليلة القدر وربما قرأ قل يا أيها الكافرون وفي الثالثة قل هو الله أحد (مختصر قيام الليل صـ ٣٠٤ ، ونقله العلامة السبكي رحمه الله عن محمد بن نصر رحمه الله صاحب قيام الليل في المنهل العذب المورود ٨/٥٥)

Kawthar in the second rakaat and Surah Kaafiroon, Surah Lahab and Surah Ikhlaas in the third rakaat.[365]

6. **Q:** If one raises his feet off the ground in the posture of sajdah, will his salaah be valid?

A: It is impermissible for one in the state of sajdah to raise his feet off the ground. If one raised both his feet for the duration of three subhanallah's, his salaah will break.[366]

7. **Q:** Is it permissible for a person who is able to perform the entire salaah standing, together with making the ruku normally and performing sajdah on the ground, to sit on a chair and perform Salaah?

A: It is not permissible for one who is able to perform salaah standing, together with making ruku and performing the sajdah on the ground, to sit on a chair. If the one who is able to perform the salaah in this manner sits on a chair and performs salaah, the salaah will not be valid. However, if a person cannot manage standing and is unable to perform

---

365 عن علي قال كان النبي صلى الله عليه وسلم يوتر بتسع سور من المفصل في الركعة الأولى ألهاكم التكاثر وإنا أنزلناه في ليلة القدر وإذا زلزلت وفي الثانية والعصر وإذا جاء نصر الله وإنا أعطيناك الكوثر وفي الثالثة قل يا أيها الكافرون وتبت وقل هو الله أحد (شرح معاني الآثار للطحاوي، الرقم: ١٧٢٤)

عن علي قال كان النبي صلى الله عليه وسلم يوتر بثلاث يقرأ فيهن بتسع سور من المفصل يقرأ في كل ركعة بثلاث سور آخرهن قل هو الله أحد (سنن الترمذي، الرقم: ٤٦٠)

366 فتاوى محمودية ٢٧٣/٩

sajdah on the ground, then it will be permissible for him to sit on a chair and perform the salaah.[367]

---

[367] (إذا تعذر على المريض كل القيام) وهو الحقيقي ومثله الحكمي ذكره فقال (أو تعسر) كل القيام (بوجود ألم شديد أو خاف) بأن غلب في ظنه بتجربة سابقة أو إخبار طبيب مسلم حاذق أو ظهور الحال (زيادة المرض أو) خاف (بطأه) أي طول المرض (به) أي بالقيام (صلى قاعدا بركوع وسجود) لما روي عن عمران بن الحصين قال كان بي بواسير فسألت النبي صلى الله عليه وسلم عن الصلاة فقال صل قائما فإن لم تستطع فقاعدا فإن لم تستطع فعلى جنب زاد النسائي فإن لم تستطع فمستلقيا لا يكلف الله نفسا إلا وسعها (ويقعد كيف شاء) أي كيف يتيسر له بغير ضرر من تربع أو غيره (في الأصح) من غير كراهة كذا روي عن الإمام للعذر (وإلا) بأن قدر على بعض القيام (قام بقدر ما يمكنه) بلا زيادة مشقة ولو بالتحريمة وقراءة آية وإن حصل به ألم شديد يقعد ابتداء كما لو عجز وقعد ابتداء هو المذهب الصحيح لأن الطاعة بحسب الطاقة (وإن تعذر الركوع والسجود) وقدر على القعود ولو مستندا (صلى قاعدا بالإيماء) للركوع والسجود برأسه ولا يجزيه مضجع (حاشية الطحطاوي على مراقي الفلاح ص ٤٣٠-٤٣١)

CHAPTER EIGHT

WOMEN'S SALAAH

Every aspect of the religion of Islam relating to women revolves around modesty and shame. It is in this regard that Islam commands women to remain within the confines of their homes, being totally concealed from the gazes of strange men, and not to leave their homes without a valid Shar'ee need.

The manner in which a woman is commanded to perform her Salaah — commencing from her attire for salaah to her postures during Salaah — all clearly point towards the aspect of concealment.

Hence, let alone the various other ibaadaat of Deen, the salaah of a woman alone illustrates the great degree of modesty and shame a woman is required to display. Hence, she is commanded to adopt the very same degree of modesty and shame which she displays in her salaah in other departments of her Deeni and worldly life.

CONCEALMENT

It is an undisputed fact that the physical composition of women is different to that of men. Shari'ah has taken this into consideration and thus ordained distinct rulings for men and women in many important aspects of Deen.

The underlying factor in the distinct rulings for women is that they have been commanded to do everything in a manner that is more concealing for them. This difference has also been considered in the various postures of salaah. A woman is commanded to carry out her postures in a way that is least revealing and most concealing.

Imaam Baihaqi رَحِمَهُٱللَّهُ has mentioned:

وجماع ما يفارق المرأة فيه الرجل من أحكام الصلاة راجع إلى الستر وهو أنها مأمورة بكل ما كان أستر لها (السنن الكبرى للبيهقي، الرقم: ٣١٩٦)

All the various aspects in a woman's salaah that differ from a man's salaah (i.e. the manner of fulfilling the various postures of salaah) are all based on satr (concealment). A female is commanded to carry out every posture of her salaah in a manner that conceals her body shape and limbs the most.

Hazrat Abdullah bin Umar رَضِيَٱللَّهُعَنْهُمَا says that during the era of Hazrat Rasulullah صَلَّىٱللَّهُعَلَيْهِوَسَلَّمَ, when performing salaah, the women were instructed to draw their limbs together as close as possible.[368]

---

368 عن نافع عن ابن عمر رضي الله عنهما أنه سئل كيف كن النساء يصلين على عهد رسول الله صلى الله عليه وسلم كن يتربعن ثم أمرن أن يحتفزن (مسند الإمام الأعظم للحصكفي على ترتيب السندي صـ ٧٣)

(عن نافع عن ابن عمر أنه سئل كيف كن النساء يصلين على عهد رسول الله صلى الله عليه وسلم) أي في زمانه صلى الله عليه وسلم (قال كن يتربعن) أي في حال قعودهن (ثم أمرن أن يحتفزن) بالحاء المهملة والفاء والزاء أي يضممن أعضاءهن بأن يتوركن في جلوسهن (شرح مسند الإمام أبي حنيفة للقاري صـ ١٩١)

صححه العلامة ظفر أحمد العثماني في إعلاء السنن (٢٧/٣)

THE FOUR MAZHABS

From the era of Hazrat Rasulullah ﷺ, the Sahaabah رضي الله عنهم, the Taabi'een رحمهم الله and the centuries that followed, women were commanded to perform salaah in a manner that varied from the salaah of men in certain aspects. The four mazhabs (viz. Hanafi, Maaliki, Shaafi'ee and Hambali mazhab) are all unanimous upon the fact that the salaah of women differs from the salaah of men in certain aspects.[369]

---

[369] المذهب الحنفي: ويجافي بطنه عن فخذيه كذا في الهداية والمرأة لا تجافي في ركوعها وسجودها وتقعد على رجليها وفي السجدة تفترش بطنها على فخذيها كذا في الخلاصة (الفتاوى الهندية ٧٥/١)

المذهب المالكي: المرأة يندب كونها منضمة في ركوعها وسجودها (حاشية الدسوقي ٢٤٩/١)

المذهب الشافعي: ولا فرق بين الرجال والنساء في عمل الصلاة إلا أن المرأة يستحب لها أن تضم بعضها إلى بعض وأن تلصق بطنها بفخذيها في السجود كأستر ما يكون وأحب ذلك لها في الركوع وفي جميع الصلاة وأن تكثف جلبابها وتجافيه راكعة وساجدة لئلا تصفها ثيابها وأن تخفض صوتها وان نابها شيئ في صلاتها صفقت (المجموع شرح المهذب ٣٤٦/٣)

المذهب الحنبلي: تجمع نفسها في الركوع والسجود وسائر صلاتها (المغني لابن قدامة ٣٣٩/١)

THE DESIRE OF HAZRAT RASULULLAH صَلَّى ٱللَّهُ عَلَيْهِ وَسَلَّمَ REGARDING WOMEN PERFORMING SALAAH IN THE CONFINES OF THEIR HOMES

While it was the burning desire of Hazrat Rasulullah صَلَّى ٱللَّهُ عَلَيْهِ وَسَلَّمَ that the men of his Ummah perform their salaah with jamaat in the musjid, it was his heart's desire that the women of his Ummah perform their salaah within the confines of their homes.

Hazrat Rasulullah صَلَّى ٱللَّهُ عَلَيْهِ وَسَلَّمَ encouraged women to perform their salaah within their homes and remain concealed from the eyes of men, to such an extent that he said, "The salaah of a woman in her bedroom is more rewarding than her salaah in the enclosed courtyard of her house, and her salaah in the innermost portion of the bedroom (a small room within the bedroom) is more rewarding than her salaah in her bedroom."[370]

Once, Hazrat Ummu Humaid رَضِيَ ٱللَّهُ عَنْهَا, the wife of Hazrat Abu Humaid As-Saa'idi رَضِيَ ٱللَّهُ عَنْهُ, came to Hazrat Rasulullah صَلَّى ٱللَّهُ عَلَيْهِ وَسَلَّمَ and said, "O Rasulullah صَلَّى ٱللَّهُ عَلَيْهِ وَسَلَّمَ, I long to perform salaah behind you." Hazrat Rasulullah صَلَّى ٱللَّهُ عَلَيْهِ وَسَلَّمَ replied, "I am aware that you long and desire to perform salaah behind me. However,

---

[370] عن عبد الله عن النبي صلى الله عليه وسلم قال صلاة المرأة في بيتها أفضل من صلاتها في حجرتها وصلاتها في مخدعها أفضل من صلاتها في بيتها (سنن أبي داود، الرقم: ٥٧٠)

your salaah in your bedroom is more rewarding than your salaah in any other part of your home. The salaah in any other part of your home is more rewarding than the salaah in your enclosed courtyard. The salaah in your enclosed courtyard is more rewarding than the salaah in the musjid of your locality. The salaah in the musjid of your locality is more rewarding than your salaah in my Musjid (Musjid-e-Nabawi)." Hazrat Ummu Humaid رَضِىَ اللهُ عَنْهَا (in compliance and obedience with the mubaarak desire of Hazrat Rasulullah صَلَّى اللهُ عَلَيْهِ وَسَلَّمَ,) instructed that a small place be reserved for her salaah in the innermost portion of her bedroom, and she would devotedly perform all her salaah at that place until the end of her life.[371]

<hr>

[371] عن عبد الله بن سويد الأنصاري عن عمته أم حميد امرأة أبي حميد الساعدي أنها جاءت النبي صلى الله عليه وسلم فقالت يا رسول الله إني أحب الصلاة معك قال قد علمت أنك تحبين الصلاة معي وصلاتك في بيتك خير من صلاتك في حجرتك وصلاتك في حجرتك خير من صلاتك في دارك وصلاتك في دارك خير من صلاتك في مسجد قومك وصلاتك في مسجد قومك خير من صلاتك في مسجدي قال فأمرت فبني لها مسجد في أقصى شيء من بيتها وأظلمه وكانت تصلي فيه حتى لقيت الله جل وعلا (صحيح ابن حبان، الرقم: ٢٢١٧)

STATEMENT OF HAZRAT IMAAM SHAAFI'EE رَحِمَهُ ٱللَّهُ

Hazrat Imaam Shaafi'ee رَحِمَهُ ٱللَّهُ has written in Ikhtilaaful Hadith:

We do not know of any of the respected wives of Hazrat Rasulullah صَلَّى ٱللَّهُ عَلَيْهِ وَسَلَّمَ leaving their homes to attend the Jumuah Salaah or any other salaah in the musjid, even though the respected wives of Hazrat Rasulullah صَلَّى ٱللَّهُ عَلَيْهِ وَسَلَّمَ, on account of their special position and relationship with Hazrat Rasulullah صَلَّى ٱللَّهُ عَلَيْهِ وَسَلَّمَ, would have been more rightful and worthy than any woman to fulfil the faraaidh in the musjid, yet they did not do this.

There were many women who were close to Hazrat Rasulullah صَلَّى ٱللَّهُ عَلَيْهِ وَسَلَّمَ, from the women of his household, his respected wives, his daughters, his slave women and the slave women that belonged to his household, yet I do not have knowledge of even a single woman from them who left the home to attend the Jumuah Salaah behind Hazrat Rasulullah صَلَّى ٱللَّهُ عَلَيْهِ وَسَلَّمَ, despite Jumuah Salaah being compulsory on the men to a greater degree than all the other salaah. Similarly, we do not have knowledge of any of them leaving the home to attend the congregational salaah, neither during the night nor during the day, nor did they even go to the musjid in Qubaa, although Hazrat Rasulullah صَلَّى ٱللَّهُ عَلَيْهِ وَسَلَّمَ would go to Qubaa, sometimes riding his conveyance and sometimes on foot, nor did they go to any of the other masaajid. I have no doubt that on account of their special relationship with Hazrat Rasulullah ﷺ, they were eager to acquire virtue and reward and they knew the avenues of earning reward better than other women, yet they did not go to the musjid for salaah.

I do not have knowledge of any of our pious predecessors instructing any one of their womenfolk to attend the Jumuah Salaah nor the congregational salaah, neither during the night nor during the day. If they knew that there was any virtue in the women leaving their homes and attending the congregational salaah, they would have definitely instructed them and permitted them to do so. Rather, it is related that Hazrat Rasulullah ﷺ said, "The salaah of a woman in her bedroom is better than her salaah in the communal room of her home, and her salaah in the communal room of her home is better than her salaah in the musjid."[372]

---

[372] ولم نعلم من أمهات المؤمنين امرأة خرجت إلى جمعة ولا جماعة في مسجد وأزواج رسول الله صلى الله عليه وسلم بمكانهن من رسول الله صلى الله عليه وسلم أولى بأداء الفرائض ... وقد كان مع رسول الله صلى الله عليه وسلم نساء من أهل بيته وبناته وأزواجه ومولياته وخدمه وخدم أهل بيته فما علمت منهن امرأة خرجت إلى شهود جمعة والجمعة واجبة على الرجال بأكثر من وجوب الجماعة في الصلوات غيرها ولا إلى جماعة غيرها في ليل أو نهار ولا إلى مسجد قباء فقد كان النبي صلى الله عليه وسلم يأتيه راكبا وماشيا ولا إلى غيره من المساجد وما أشك أنهن كن على الخير بمكانهن من رسول الله صلى الله عليه وسلم أحرص وبه أعلم من غيرهن ... وما علمت أحدا من سلف المسلمين أمر أحدا من نسائه بإتيان جمعة ولا جماعة من ليل ولا نهار ولو كان لهن في ذلك فضل أمروهن به وأذنوا لهن إليه بل قد روي والله أعلم عن النبي صلى الله عليه وسلم أنه قال صلاة المرأة في بيتها خير من صلاتها في حجرتها وصلاتها في حجرتها خير من صلاتها في المسجد أو المساجد (اختلاف الحديث ص ٦٢٥-٦٢٦)

BEFORE SALAAH

1. Particular care should be taken to dress appropriately for salaah. A woman should wear such clothing that will conceal her entire body and hair. It is disrespectful for her to wear tight-fitting clothing that reveals the shape of her body or to wear such thin, flimsy clothing through which the actual limbs can be seen. If the clothing is such that the limbs are visible through the clothing, the salaah will be invalid.[See 297]

2. Severe warnings have been sounded in the Hadith for those women who do not dress appropriately. Though the warning is general and does not specifically refer to dressing inappropriately during salaah, one would understand that when it is impermissible for a woman to dress in this manner out of salaah, then the impermissibility of her wearing such clothing when standing before Allah تَبَارَكَوَتَعَالَ in salaah will be even greater. Apart from this, the Fuqahaa have written that the salaah of a woman who is not clad properly during salaah and whose body limbs are visible through her clothing will not be valid.[373]

---

[373] عن أبي هريرة رضي الله عنه قال قال رسول الله صلى الله عليه وسلم صنفان من أهل النار لم أرهما قوم معهم سياط كأذناب البقر يضربون بها الناس ونساء كاسيات عاريات مميلات مائلات رؤوسهن كأسنمة البخت المائلة لا يدخلن الجنة ولا يجدن ريحها وإن ريحها ليوجد من مسيرة كذا وكذا (صحيح مسلم، الرقم: ٢١٢٨)

انظر أيضا 297

3. Cover the entire body including the hair. Only the face, palms and feet may be exposed.[374]

4. Prepare well in advance for salaah before the time of salaah enters.[See 292]

5. Apart from the physical preparation (wudhu, etc.), you should also prepare yourself mentally that you are going to present yourself in the court of your Rabb.[See 292]

6. Ensure that your body, clothes and the place on which the salaah is being performed are paak and clean.[See 296]

---

[374] (و) الرابع (ستر عورته) ... (وللحرة) ولو خنثى (جميع بدنها) حتى شعرها النازل في الأصح (خلا الوجه والكفين والقدمين) (الدر المختار ٤٠٥/١)

QIYAAM

1. Face the qiblah.[See 301]

2. Keep the feet together or as close as possible. Ensure that the feet face towards the qiblah.[375]

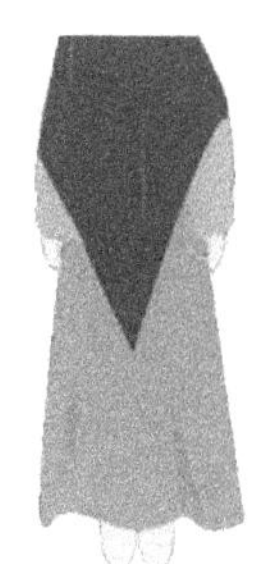

---

[375] أقول أما جزئيّة كيفية وضع النساء أقدامهن فلم نأل جهدا في البحث عنها في الكتب الفقهية الحنفية لكن لم نظفر بها ولأجل ذلك اختلف علماؤنا فيها إلى قولين القول الأول أن تفرج المرأة قدميها مثل الرجال ويحتج من ذهب إليه من العلماء بأن الكتب الفقهية لم تتعرض لهذه الجزئية فتشمل العبارة الفقهية (التي وردت مطلقة) الرجال والنساء جميعا وهي كما في الخلاصة وينبغي أن يكون بين القدمين أربع أصابع القول الثاني أن تضمّ قدميها ويقول من رآه من العلماء بأنه لا يلزم أن تشمل العبارة الفقهية المطلقة الرجال والنساء جميعا لأن كيفية الرجال تخالف كيفية النساء في مسائل كثيرة هذا إلى أن بعض عبارات الفقهاء المطلقة (التي وردت في كيفية وضع الأقدام في الركوع) أيضا تقتضي أن تكون الأقدام ملصقة ومنضمة وتعم الرجال والنساء كما في رد المحتار ويسن أن يلصق كعبيه مع أن الفقهاء يقصرون على النساء (كما قال الشيخ المفتي محمود الكنكوهي في حاشية بمشتي زيور) وذلك لأن القاعدة العامة في حق الرجال تخالفها ولما ثبت أن تلصق المرأة كعبيها في الركوع فالأحسن أن يكون قيامها كذلك أي بإلصاق القدمين وضمهما لئلا تكون الحالتان (القيام والركوع) مختلفتين فإن في ذلك تكلفا ظاهرا وإليك بعض الأحاديث التي تدل على الفرق بين الرجل والمرأة في بعض أركان الصلاة:

١) عن يزيد بن أبي حبيب أن رسول الله صلى الله عليه وسلم مر على امرأتين تصليان فقال إذا سجدتما فضما بعض اللحم إلى الأرض فإن المرأة ليست في ذلك كالرجل (السنن الكبرى للبيهقي، الرقم: ٣٣٢٥)

٢) عن علي رضي الله عنه قال إذا سجدت المرأة فلتحتفز ولتضم فخذيها (المصنف لابن أبي شيبة، الرقم: ٢٧٩٣)

٣) عن ابن عباس رضي الله عنهما أنه سئل عن صلاة المرأة فقال تجتمع وتحتفز (المصنف لابن أبي شيبة، الرقم: ٢٧٩٤)

٤) عن وائل بن حجر قال جئت إلى النبي صلى الله عليه وسلم فقال هذا وائل بن حجر جاءكم لم يجئكم رغبة ولا رهبة جاءكم حبا لله ولرسوله وبسط له رداءه وأجلسه إلى جنبه وضمه إليه وأصعده المنبر فخطب الناس فقال ارفقوا به فإنه حديث عهد بالملك فقال إن أهلي غلبوني على الذي لي قال أنا أعطيك وأعطيك ضعفه فقال لي رسول الله صلى الله عليه وسلم يا وائل بن حجر إذا صليت فاجعل يديك حذاء أذنيك والمرأة تجعل يديها حذاء ثدييها

قلت: له في الصحيحين في رفع اليدين غير هذا الحديث رواه الطبراني من طريق ميمونة بنت حجر بن عبد الجبار عن عمتها أم يحيى بنت عبد الجبار ولم أعرفها وبقية رجاله ثقات (مجمع الزوائد، الرقم: ١٦٠٠٥ ، المعجم الكبير للطبراني، الرقم: ٢٨)

٥) عن عبد الله بن عمر قال قال رسول الله صلى الله عليه وسلم إذا جلست المرأة في الصلاة وضعت فخذها على فخذها الأخرى وإذا سجدت ألصقت بطنها في فخذيها كأستر ما يكون لها وإن الله تعالى ينظر إليها ويقول يا ملائكتي أشهدكم أني قد غفرت لها (السنن الكبرى للبيهقي، الرقم: ٣٣٢٤)

3. Raise both the hands up to the chest (i.e. the fingers will be in line with the shoulders) without removing the hands from beneath the burqa.[376]

4. When raising the hands, ensure that the palms are facing the qiblah and the fingers are kept in their natural position, neither spread apart nor tightly closed.[See 304]

5. Once the hands are raised parallel to the shoulders, recite the takbeer (Allahu Akbar).[See 306]

6. The head should be kept straight without tilting it forward or bending it back when reciting the takbeer.[See 305]

7. Lower the hands while saying the takbeer and fold them on the chest.[377]

فهذه الأحاديث بمجموعها تدل على شيئين الأول الفرق بين الرجال والنساء في بعض أحوال الصلاة والثاني كيفية ضمّ القدمين ووصلها للنساء في كل ركن وذلك أستر لهن كما ثبت في حديث عبد الله بن عمر الذي مرّ ذكره وجاء في حديث عبد الله ابن عبّاس أيضا أنه لما سئل عن صلاة المرأة قال تجتمع فمن ذلك نعلم أن ضمّ المرأة قدميها في القيام والركوع أستر وأجمع من تفريجها قدميها وذلك أقرب إلى السنة

وفي المغني: فصل (أي في رفع الأيدي عند التحريمة في الصلاة) والإمام والمأموم والمنفرد في هذا سواء وكذلك الفريضة والنافلة لأن الأخبار لا تفريق فيها فأما المرأة فذكر القاضي فيها روايتين عن أحمد إحداهما ترفع لما روى الخلال بإسناده عن أم الدرداء وحفصة بنت سيرين أنهما كانتا ترفعان أيديهما وهو قول طاوس ولأن من شرع في حقه التكبير شرع في حقه الرفع كالرجل فعلى هذا ترفع قليلا قال أحمد رفع دون الرفع والثانية لا يشرع لأنه في معنى التجافي ولا يشرع ذلك لها بل تجمع نفسها في الركوع والسجود وسائر صلاتها (المغني ١/١٩٦)

انظر أيضا 303

[376] المرأة تخالف الرجل في مسائل ... ومنها أنها لا تخرج كفيها من كميها عند التكبير وترفع يديها حذاء منكبيها (حاشية الطحطاوي على مراقي الفلاح صـ ٥٩) (رد المحتار ١/٥٠٤)

والمرأة تستر كفيها حذرا من كشف ذراعيها (حاشية الطحطاوي على مراقي الفلاح صـ ٢٧٦)

فصل (أي في رفع الأيدي عند التحريمة في الصلاة) والإمام والمأموم والمنفرد في هذا سواء وكذلك الفريضة والنافلة لأن الأخبار لا تفريق فيها فأما المرأة فذكر القاضي فيها روايتين عن أحمد إحداهما ترفع لما روى الخلال بإسناده عن أم الدرداء وحفصة بنت سيرين أنهما كانتا ترفعان أيديهما وهو قول طاوس ولأن من شرع في حقه التكبير شرع في حقه الرفع كالرجل فعلى هذا ترفع قليلا قال أحمد رفع دون الرفع والثانية لا يشرع لأنه في معنى التجافي ولا يشرع ذلك لها بل تجمع نفسها في الركوع والسجود وسائر صلاتها (المغني ١/١٩٦)

8. Place the right palm on the back of the left hand with the fingers joined together, without any gap in-between. Do not form a circle with the thumb and small finger of the right hand, nor grasp the left hand (as done by males). See 368 and 377

9. Fix the gaze on the place of sajdah during the standing posture. See 309

10. Recite the thanaa. See 310 and 311

سُبْحَانَكَ اللّٰهُمَّ وَبِحَمْدِكَ وَتَبَارَكَ اسْمُكَ وَتَعَالٰى جَدُّكَ وَلَا اِلٰهَ غَيْرُكَ

Glory be to You O Allah تَبَارَكَوَتَعَالٰى! *Praise be to You, blessed is Your name, very lofty is Your majesty, and there is no deity besides You.*

11. Recite ta'awwuz and tasmiyah silently. See 312

Ta'awwuz is to recite:

أَعُوْذُ بِاللهِ مِنَ الشَّيْطَانِ الرَّجِيْمِ

I seek protection in Allah تَبَارَكَوَتَعَالٰى *from the accursed Shaitaan.*

---

³⁷⁷ وتضع المرأة والخنثى الكف على الكف تحت ثديها

قال العلامة ابن عابدين رحمه الله (قوله تحت ثديها) كذا في بعض نسخ المنية وفي بعضها على ثديها قال في الحلية وكان الأولى أن يقول على صدرها كما قاله الجم الغفير لا على ثديها وإن كان الوضع على الصدر قد يستلزم ذلك بأن يقع بعض ساعد كل يد على الثدي لكن هذا ليس هو المقصود بالإفادة (رد المحتار ١ / ٤٨٦– ٤٨٧)

والمرأة تضعهما على ثديها كذا في المنية (الفتاوى الهندية ٧٣/١)

(و) يسن (وضع المرأة يديها على صدرها من غير تحليق) لأنه أستر لها (حاشية الطحطاوي على مراقي الفلاح ص ٢٥٩)

انظر أيضا 306

Tasmiyah is to recite:

بِسْمِ اللهِ الرَّحْمٰنِ الرَّحِيْم

In the name of Allah تَبَارَكَ وَتَعَالَى, *the most kind, the most merciful.*

12. Recite Surah Faatihah followed by qiraat.[See 313]

    Note: Women should not perform their salaah aloud. They should perform every salaah silently.[378]

13. Recite "aameen" after surah Faatihah.[See 313]

14. Recite tasmiyah before the surah.[See 314]

    Note: The tasmiyah will only be recited (after Surah Faatihah) if one is going to recite a surah. If one is not going to commence any surah then tasmiyah should not be recited.[See 359]

15. If you are performing a three or four rakaat fardh salaah, then in the third and fourth rakaat you will only recite Surah Faatihah. You should not recite any surah after reciting Surah Faatihah.

    In the third and fourth rakaat of the fardh salaah, Surah Faatihah will be recited by the imaam and munfarid (the one performing salaah alone). The muqtadi who is performing salaah behind the imaam will remain silent and not recite anything in all the rakaats.

---

[378] المرأة تخالف الرجل في مسائل ... ولا تجهر في موضع الجهر (حاشية الطحطاوي على مراقي الفلاح صـ ٢٥٩)

16. If you are performing sunnah or nafl salaah, you will recite qiraat in all the rakaats, regardless of whether you are performing two rakaats or four rakaats.

RUKU AND QAWMAH

1. Say the takbeer and go into ruku.[See 316]

    Note: The takbeeraat-e-intiqaaliyyah (takbeer which is recited when moving from one posture to another) should be commenced as soon as one begins moving to the next posture and should only be completed when one reaches that posture.[See 316]

2. Bend slightly to the extent that the fingers are able to touch the knees.[379]

3. Keep the fingers together.[380]

    Note: One will not grasp the knees fully nor spread out the fingers. Similarly, the head and back will not be kept in a straight line (as done by men when making ruku).[See 380]

4. Keep the arms close to the sides.[381]

5. The ankles of both the feet should be kept together.[See 381]

---

[379] وتنحني في الركوع قليلا ولا تعقد ولا تفرج فيه أصابعها بل تضمها وتضع يديها على ركبتيها ولا تحني ركبتيها وتنضم في ركوعها وسجودها (رد المحتار ١ / ٥٠٤)

[380] ولا تفرج أصابعها في الركوع وتنحني في الركوع قليلا بحيث تبلغ حد الركوع فلا تزيد على ذلك لأنه أستر لها (حاشية الطحطاوي على مراقي الفلاح ص ٢٥٩)

[381] وتلزم مرفقيها بجنبيها فيه (حاشية الطحطاوي على مراقي الفلاح ص ٢٥٩)

عن ابن عباس رضي الله عنهما أنه سئل عن صلاة المرأة فقال تجتمع وتحتفز (المصنف لابن أبي شيبة، الرقم: ٢٧٩٤)

6. Fix the gaze on the feet in the posture of ruku.[See 319]

7. Recite the following tasbeeh thrice or any odd number of times:

سُبْحَانَ رَبِّيَ الْعَظِيْم

Glorified is my Rabb, the most great. [See 321]

8. Stand up from ruku while saying the tasmee:

سَمِعَ اللّٰهُ لِمَنْ حَمِدَهْ

Allah تَبَارَكَ وَتَعَالَى *hears the one who praises Him.*

followed by the tahmeed:

اَللّٰهُمَّ رَبَّنَا وَلَكَ الْحَمْد

O Allah تَبَارَكَ وَتَعَالَى, *our Rabb, for You alone is all praise.*[See 322]

9. Stand up erect. After standing up from ruku, do not tie your hands. Instead, leave them at your sides. This posture is called qawmah. In qawmah, stand up erect with ta'deel-e-arkaan (the body should be completely at ease) before going into sajdah.[See 323]

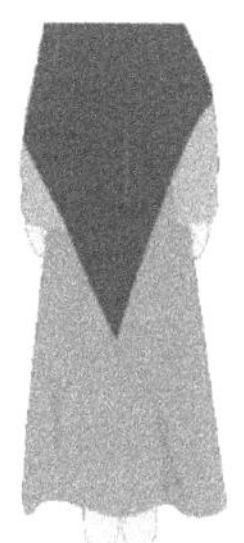

SAJDAH

1. Say the takbeer and proceed into sajdah.[See 324]

2. First place the knees on the ground, then the palms, then the nose and lastly the forehead.[See 327]

3. Keep the fingers closed, facing towards the qiblah.[See 329]

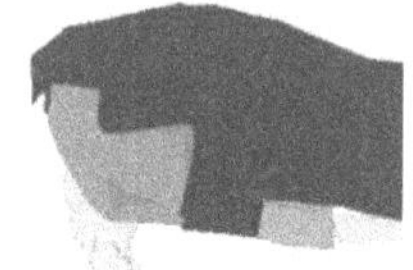

4. Place the palms parallel to the ears.[See 328]

5. Draw the limbs of the body close together and press them firmly without allowing any gap in between.[382]

6. Keep the stomach joined to both the thighs and the arms to the sides.[383]

7. Keep both the forearms/elbows on the ground.[384]

8. The feet should not be upright. Instead, they should be placed flat on the ground on the right-hand side.[385]

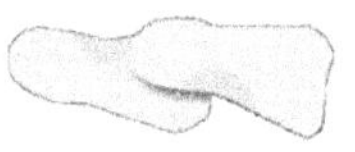

---

[382] وتنضم في ركوعها وسجودها (رد المحتار ٥٠٤/١)

عن يزيد بن أبي حبيب أن رسول الله صلى الله عليه وسلم مر على امرأتين تصليان فقال إذا سجدتما فضما بعض اللحم إلى الأرض فإن المرأة ليست في ذلك كالرجل (السنن الكبرى للبيهقي، الرقم: ٣٢٠١)

[383] (والمرأة تنخفض) فلا تبدي عضديها (وتلصق بطنها بفخذيها) لأنه أستر (الدر المختار ٥٠٤/١)

[384] وتفترش ذراعيها (رد المحتار ٥٠٤/١)

[385] لا تنصب أصابع القدمين (البحر الرائق ٣٣٩/١)

عن ابن عباس رضي الله عنهما أنه سئل عن صلاة المرأة فقال تجتمع وتحتفز (المصنف لابن أبي شيبة، الرقم: ٢٧٩٤)

9. Fix the gaze on the nose in sajdah.[See 332]

10. Recite the following tasbeeh thrice or any odd number of times:

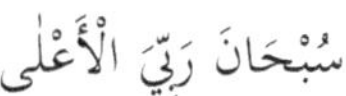

Glorified is my Rabb, the most high.[See 337]

11. Say the takbeer and sit up in the position of jalsah.[See 338]

عن علي رضي الله عنه قال إذا سجدت المرأة فلتحتفز ولتضم فخذيها (المصنف لابن أبي شيبة، الرقم: ٢٧٩٣)

JALSAH

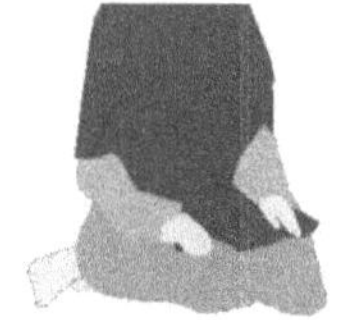

1. Sit on the left buttock and place both the feet on the right side.[386]

2. The thighs should be joined together.[See 386]

3. Place the hands on the thighs with the fingers together and the fingertips at the edge of the knees.[387]

4. Fix the gaze on the area between the lower chest and lap whilst in jalsah.[See 340]

5. Remain in the position of jalsah with the body being completely at ease and calm before going into the second sajdah.[See 343]

6. Say the takbeer and proceed to the second sajdah as normal.[See 344]

---

[386] وتجلس متوركة في كل قعود بأن تجلس على أليتها اليسرى وتخرج كلتا رجليها من الجانب الأيمن وتضع فخذيها على بعضها وتجعل الساق الأيمن على الساق الأيسر كما في مجمع الأنهر (حاشية الطحطاوي على مراقي الفلاح ص ٢٥٩)

وذكر في البحر أنها لا تنصب أصابع القدمين (رد المحتار ١/٥٠٤)

أبو حنيفة عن نافع عن ابن عمر رضي الله عنهما أنه سئل كيف كان النساء يصلين على عهد رسول الله صلى الله عليه وسلم قال كن يتربعن ثم أمرن أن يحتفزن (جامع المسانيد ١/٤٠٠)

قلت (الشيخ ظفر أحمد التهانوي): هذا إسناد صحيح أخرجه القاضي عمر بن الحسن الأشناني عن علي بن محمد البزار عن أحمد بن محمد بن خالد عن زر بن نجيح عن إبراهيم ابن المهدي عن أبي جواب الأحوص بن جواب عن سفيان الثوري عن أبي حنيفة بسنده اه (إعلاء السنن ٢٧/٣)

[387] وتتورك في التشهد وتضع فيه يديها تبلغ أصابعها ركبتيها وتضم فيه أصابعها (رد المحتار ١/٥٠٤)

SECOND RAKAAT

1. After the second sajdah say the takbeer and stand up for the second rakaat.[See 344]

2. When rising from sajdah, first raise the forehead, then the nose, then the hands and lastly the knees.[See 345]

3. When getting up, do not take support from the ground (unless there is a need to do so).[See 344]

4. Perform the second rakaat as normal except that thanaa and ta'awwuz will not be recited at the beginning.[See 346]

QA'DAH AND SALAAM

1. After the second sajdah of the second rakaat, sit in the position of qa'dah in the same manner as explained for jalsah.[See 386 and 387]

2. Recite the tashahhud:[See 347]

اَلتَّحِيَّاتُ لِلّٰهِ وَالصَّلَوَاتُ وَالطَّيِّبَاتُ اَلسَّلَامُ عَلَيْكَ أَيُّهَا النَّبِيُّ وَرَحْمَةُ اللّٰهِ وَبَرَكَاتُهُ اَلسَّلَامُ عَلَيْنَا وَعَلٰى عِبَادِ اللّٰهِ الصَّالِحِيْنَ أَشْهَدُ أَنْ لَّا إِلٰهَ إِلَّا اللّٰهُ وَأَشْهَدُ أَنَّ مُحَمَّدًا عَبْدُهُ وَرَسُوْلُهُ

All verbal ibaadaat, physical ibaadaat and monetary ibaadaat be for Allah تَبَارَكَ وَتَعَالَى. May the special peace of Allah تَبَارَكَ وَتَعَالَى descend upon you, O Nabi صَلَّى اللّٰهُ عَلَيْهِ وَسَلَّمَ, and Allah's تَبَارَكَ وَتَعَالَى choicest mercies and blessings. May peace descend upon us and upon all the pious servants of Allah تَبَارَكَ وَتَعَالَى. I bear witness that there is no deity except Allah تَبَارَكَ وَتَعَالَى and I bear witness that Hazrat Muhammad صَلَّى اللّٰهُ عَلَيْهِ وَسَلَّمَ is His servant and messenger.

3. When saying أَنْ لَّا إِلٰهَ, form a ring with the thumb and middle finger of the right hand, raise the index finger towards the qiblah and close the remaining two fingers (the small finger and finger next to it). When saying إِلَّا اللّٰه, lower the index finger. The thumb and middle finger will remain joined like a ring until the end of the qa'dah. [See 348]

4. If you are performing a three or four rakaat salaah then you should not recite anything besides the above tashahhud.

After reciting the tashahhud, stand up for the third rakaat.[See 349]

5. If it is the last qa'dah then recite Durood-e-Ebrahim after the tashahhud followed by a dua from the Quraan Majeed or Hadith.[See 350]

The Durood-e-Ebrahim is as follows:

اَللّٰهُمَّ صَلِّ عَلٰى مُحَمَّدٍ وَّعَلٰى اٰلِ مُحَمَّدٍ كَمَا صَلَّيْتَ عَلٰى اِبْرَاهِيْمَ وَعَلٰى اٰلِ اِبْرَاهِيْمَ اِنَّكَ حَمِيْدٌ مَّجِيْدٌ

اَللّٰهُمَّ بَارِكْ عَلٰى مُحَمَّدٍ وَّعَلٰى اٰلِ مُحَمَّدٍ كَمَا بَارَكْتَ عَلٰى اِبْرَاهِيْمَ وَعَلٰى اٰلِ اِبْرَاهِيْمَ اِنَّكَ حَمِيْدٌ مَّجِيْدٌ

O Allah تَبَارَكَ وَتَعَالَى *! Shower Your mercy on Hazrat Muhammad* صَلَّى ٱللّٰهُ عَلَيْهِ وَسَلَّمَ *and his family as You showered Your mercy on Hazrat Ebrahim* عَلَيْهِ ٱلسَّلَامُ *and his family. Surely You are praiseworthy and most high.*

O Allah تَبَارَكَ وَتَعَالَى *! Bless Hazrat Muhammad* صَلَّى ٱللّٰهُ عَلَيْهِ وَسَلَّمَ *and his family as You have blessed Hazrat Ebrahim* عَلَيْهِ ٱلسَّلَامُ *and his family. Surely You are praiseworthy and most high.*

One may recite the following dua which is reported in the Hadith:[See 351]

اَللّٰهُمَّ اِنِّيْ ظَلَمْتُ نَفْسِيْ ظُلْمًا كَثِيْرًا وَّلَا يَغْفِرُ الذُّنُوْبَ اِلَّا أَنْتَ فَاغْفِرْ لِيْ مَغْفِرَةً مِّنْ عِنْدِكَ وَارْحَمْنِيْ اِنَّكَ أَنْتَ الْغَفُوْرُ الرَّحِيْمُ

O Allah ﺗَﺒَﺎﺭَﻙَﻭَﺗَﻌَﺎﻟَﻰ! I have oppressed myself excessively (through committing sins), and no one can forgive sins besides You, so forgive me with special forgiveness from Your side and show mercy to me, for indeed You alone are all-forgiving and all-merciful.

6. After completing your dua, make salaam by saying,

اَلسَّلَامُ عَلَيْكُمْ وَرَحْمَةُ اللّٰه

while turning your head to the right side, and then again while turning your head to the left side.[See 352 and 353]

7. Do not lower or jerk your head while making salaam.

8. When making salaam on either side, fix your gaze on your shoulders.[See 354]

9. Turn your face on both sides to the extent that the cheek can be seen from behind.[See 355]

10. After the salaam, recite أَسْتَغْفِرُ الله thrice.[See 356]

11. Engage in dua (as this is a time for the acceptance of duas).[See 357]

12. Recite Tasbeeh-e-Faatimi after every salaah.[See 358] Tasbeeh-e-Faatimi is for one to recite 33 times Subhaanallah, 33 times Alhamdulillah, 33 times Allahu Akbar, and complete the hundred by reciting:

لَا إِلٰهَ إِلَّا اللّٰهُ وَحْدَهُ لَا شَرِيْكَ لَهُ لَهُ الْمُلْكُ وَلَهُ الْحَمْدُ وَهُوَ عَلٰى كُلِّ شَيْءٍ قَدِيْر

There is no deity besides Allah تَبَارَكَ وَتَعَالَ *alone, who has no partner. To Him belongs the kingdom (of the entire universe), and only for Him belongs all praise and He alone has complete power over everything.*

www.ingramcontent.com/pod-product-compliance
Lightning Source LLC
LaVergne TN
LVHW020729200726
843506LV00009B/685